NO MORE WAR MEMES

A REALISTIC PRACTICAL PROGRAM OF CULTURAL ENGINEERING TO ELIMINATE WAR FROM HUMAN SOCIETY FOREVER

JOE REBHOLZ

ISBN 1442179732

EAN-13 9781442179738

Src: NO MORE WAR MEMES 25MAY09

For all those who
Would have been killed
In the wars that won't happen.

Table of Contents.

6

PORTRAIT: Rest in Peace 20.3R.

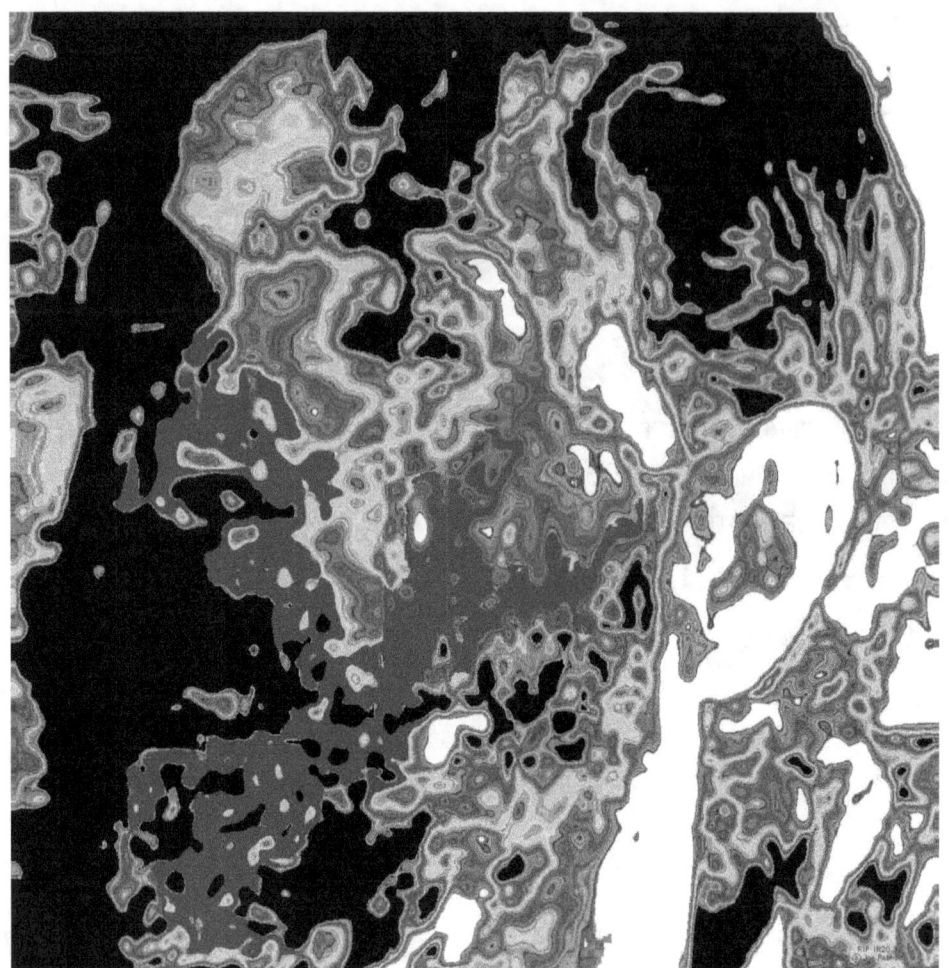

Preface.

This book comes from my peripheral involvement with the anti-war movement. As an artist I have made several hundred portraits of people killed in wars. The portraits are my memorials. But rather than glorifying those killed, I wanted to emphasize their human beauty, and the horror, tragedy and pain of their loss. The portraits are based on photographs from the Internet of actual people killed in recent wars. I wanted to start with real images of real people killed in wars to keep connected with the terrible reality of their real loss. I wanted some of the reality of these now dead people to live on, even if only as a fragment of an image, as a relic of their lives. The few portraits I have made represent for me all those killed. Some were included in the book *"Cost of Freedom"* by [Annis, Palacek, and Trettien, 2007]. Some were shown in local galleries. For this I was denounced by proponents of the current war. This caused me to wonder why we keep having wars, and how people become so fanatical in their support of wars. This book is the result.

I have included a few of these portraits in this book for the same reason I made them. I want us, the living, to think long and hard, about what we do, and imagine some of the suffering we cause, when we go to war. I see people who were once alive, beautiful, happy, and whole, now dead, returned to dust and atoms. I wonder if they were afraid before they died. I think about the sadness, anger, pain, and suffering, of their parents, their brothers and sisters, their wives or husbands, their children, and their friends. I think about the fun and pleasures, and joy and love, and happiness, all the good times with family and friends, those killed will never again experience. I think about my own children. It makes me angry when I realize that we don't have to continue this cycle of war after war after war. We now have the knowledge, and power, to eliminate war from human society forever. It will take time and work. But we can do this. That is what this book is about.

This book is not intended to be a science exposition. Rather, it is intended to spur action, based on recent science as described in the references. I want you, the reader, to do everything you can, to eliminate war from our societies, forever.

PORTRAIT: Rest in Peace 67.

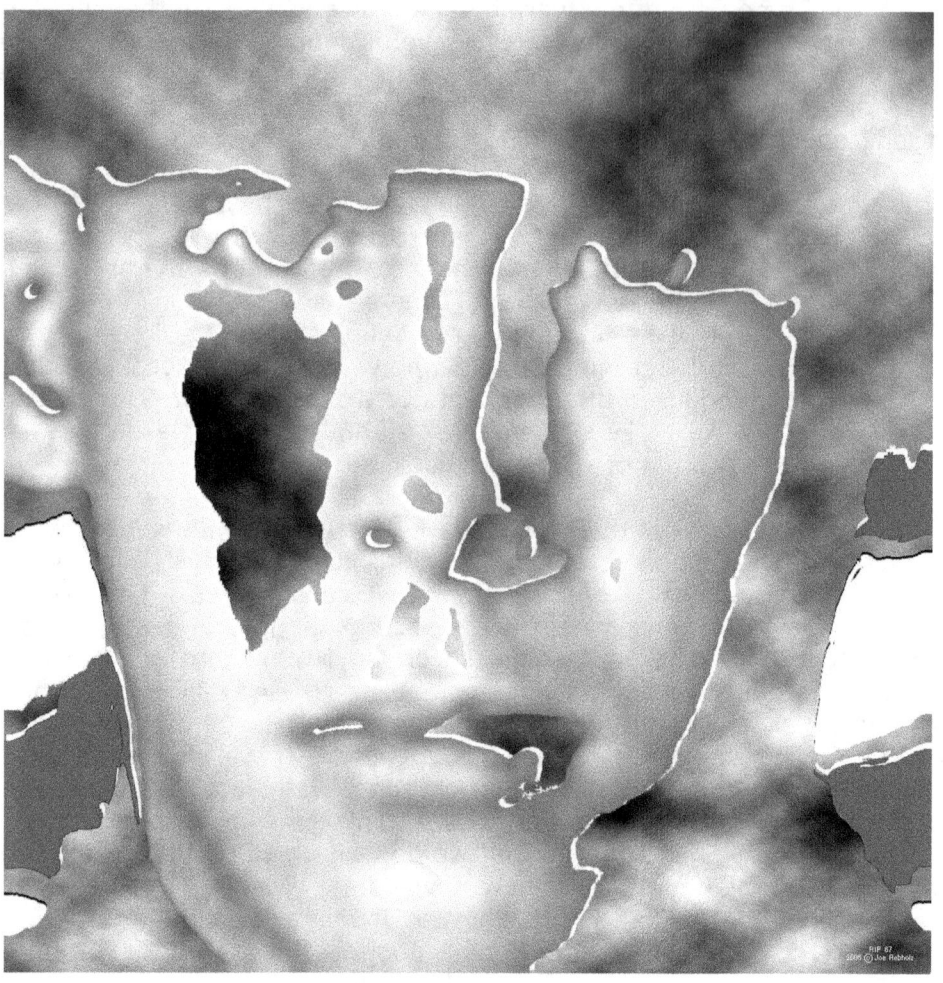

Chapter 1: An Anti-War Program.

This first chapter previews ideas that will be developed further in the rest of the book.

Disgust and anger.

Imagine today that you are going somewhere with some of your friends, in a car. You are drinking a soft drink. When you are finished with it, you open the window and throw the container out of the car. What would your friends think or say to you? It probably wouldn't be nice. There would be words like: "What are you, crazy? stupid? ignorant? uncool? uncouth? gross? disgusting?". Your friends might never again invite you to go anywhere with them. I know people who would stop the car, make you get out, go back and pick up the container; and if you refused, they would drive off and leave you standing in the road. Today, this negative reaction to trashing the environment would occur in maybe 90% of the population in the United States and Europe. Yet 50 years ago, there probably would have been no reaction. Just so, the day will come, when 90% of the world's population will react with similar disgust and anger, when some foolish political leader tries to stir up a war.

Environmentalism has changed the world.

A vast proportion of the population in many countries has completely reversed fundamental thoughts and behaviors in 50 years. And these thoughts and behaviors will spread to the whole world before too long. These new thoughts have led to laws that have changed and molded our world. Environmental ideas have changed our automobiles, our factories, our power generation methods, our houses, our travel, our work, our leisure activities, what we eat, our research, and knowledge. The environmental ideas have brought about huge cultural and economic changes in just 50 years.

Similar cultural changes can eliminate war.

The fact of the environmental movement proves that similar cultural changes can eliminate war. Not only the environmental movement but also the women's liberation movement, the near elimination of slavery, the rise of representative government, and all the other vast cultural changes of the past few hundred years, prove that we can make the significant cultural changes we need.

Wars are a system problem.

Wars are always a net loss to humanity. And every living person on the planet is a potential victim of war. Wars violate our transcendent ideals of Goodness, Beauty, Justice, and Truth. Wars are a sickness, a disease of our societies, and our cultures. Wars are pathologies, malfunctions, absurdities, insanities of our societies and cultures. Wars are a system problem. The system is not working well. The system has run amok. The system is killing people, injuring people, destroying civility, destroying property, and weakening our spirits. System problems require system solutions. That is why it is ineffective to just keep opposing the current war or wars, whatever they may be. This is not a system solution. The systems are our cultures which determine our societies. So, a system solution requires changing our cultures.

Prevention is better than cure.

To oppose the current war, to stand on the sidewalk with an anti-war sign, while the vast majority of your fellow citizens drive by with hardly a notice, to witness against the war by your lonely actions, to be ridiculed, to be called traitor, to endure this separation, demonstrates a truly independent, strong, courageous, noble, and moral person. Sadly, often, it's too late. The war is already underway, or the momentum for war is so great, the leaders have secretly been preparing for months or years, they have positioned soldiers and equipment, they have fine tuned their propaganda, so that any protests are overwhelmed. By the time enough public sentiment has grown to possibly make a difference, the war has mostly run its course, is maybe half way over. And who knows whether the anti-war protests hasten the end, or whether the war participants have so exhausted themselves, that they are hardly able to continue. So, just as it is better to prevent disease instead of trying to cure it after it has taken hold, it is better to create a healthy organism, a healthy culture, in which the disease of war will not occur.

A practical, realistic program.

This book outlines a practical, realistic program that over time will bring about the elimination of war from this planet. We can bring about a non-violent, evolutionary change, in all the world's war promoting cultures, through conscious thought and direction. The program works through conscious thought and direction by individuals who themselves decide to work to eliminate war from this planet. Everyone who adopts these or similar ideas, and spreads them to others, can do this consciously, and thoughtfully in their own way. No leaders are needed. We don't have to fool anyone or force anyone. There are no tricks. There are no techniques people can't understand.

A simple evolutionary idea.

The simple idea is that war will no longer occur, when enough people all over the planet, have changed their mistaken attitudes, and beliefs, about war. If the minds of enough people are changed in a culture, then the culture changes. This book shows step by step how we can get enough of the planet's population to change enough of their ideas and beliefs about war. Of course this will take time and effort. We change our own ideas, and then spread the idea of change, and the specific methods, and tools of change, to others, by means of an ever expanding anti-war movement. There is no need for any force or violence. There is no need for enemies to be overcome, and no need for hostility or confrontation. No governments need be overthrown Thus this program is evolutionary.

Comprehensive research.

A necessary part of the program is a comprehensive research program for the social sciences. This includes more research on the costs and benefits of war, such as the book "*The Three Trillion Dollar War*", [Stiglitz & Bilmes, 2008], research on the causes of war such as the book "*An Introduction to the Causes of War*" [Cashman & Robinson, 2007], how wars get started and how they end as in the book "*Why War?*", [Smith, 2005]. [See the References section.] Much valuable and important work has been done. But more research is needed to look at wars from every possible point of view. The research needs to include detailed historical analysis of additional previous wars as in [Cashman & Robinson, 2007]. We also need research on how to best bring about change in individual psychology as well as group behavior. We need research by historians, economists, political scientists, psychologists, anthropologists, sociologists, linguists, neuroscientists, and any other scientists, scholars, writers, poets, and artists, whose work can show how and why wars occur, and how to develop improved methods of change.

Forget the battles.

The orientation of some research will need to be changed. We need more detailed historical research on the social and cultural processes that have led to each of the wars of the twentieth century. We need to know more about why and how the wars got started, and less about how they were fought battle by battle. Battles matter only to those who want to know how to fight better battles in the future. Battles matter only if wars can bring some net benefit. But humanity always loses. The battles are irrelevant. The strategy and tactics employed by the various combatants are meaningless. The outcome is always the same: a more or less net loss to humanity. So forget the battles. We want to know, in every detail, how and why these wars got started. We need to separate the propaganda put out by the leaders from what they actually believed, if this is at all possible. It may not always be possible, because it's hard to know when a leader believes his own propaganda. But we must try. And we need to analyze the propaganda campaigns in every detail, so everybody can know what works well and what does not, and how it can be unmasked, when it is tried again in the future.

World wide anti-war movement.

So the core of this program is to develop and promote a comprehensive mass anti-war movement based on individual personal direct action, with a clear mission: to help people all over the world, to change their minds about war. This movement will spread the ideas and promote the research needed. The anti-war movement will energize individual action, develop organizations to continue the process, to press for the relevant research, summarize and interpret the research, monitor progress, and continue to promote the program.

Ideas, culture, memes, behavior.

Culture is a complex system of interactions among people, ideas, the things people create, and the rest of the world. If we change our ideas we will change our cultures. Since this program is about us changing our cultures, this means we must change some of our ideas. We change our ideas all the time. We get new ideas. We change old ones. All our ideas are connected to other ideas. So, often when one idea changes, others must change also. The science of memetics looks at how we get ideas, how we pass them on to others, how the ideas in our minds are connected. We might say memetics is the study of the lives of ideas, how they spread, or don't spread, from person to person in a culture, how ideas change, and how they associate with other ideas. Memetics asks questions like: Why do some ideas spread more easily than others? Why do some ideas stay the same for long periods of time whereas others change? Memetics is the ecology of ideas.

Memes. (pronounced MEEMS.)

When ideas are looked at from this point of view, they are called memes. There are several definitions more or less similar. Here are some definitions of the word meme from dictionary.reference.com.

A unit of cultural information, such as a cultural practice or idea, that is transmitted verbally or by repeated action from one mind to another.

A cultural item that is transmitted by repetition in a manner analogous to the biological transmission of genes.

A cultural unit (an idea or value or pattern of behavior) that is passed from one person to another by non-genetic means (as by imitation); "memes are the cultural counterpart of genes"

[By analogy with "gene"] Richard Dawkins's term for an idea considered as a replicator, especially with the connotation that memes parasitize people into propagating them much as viruses do.

The references section contains several books about memes or memetics: [Dawkins, 1976, *The Selfish Gene*], [Lynch, 1996, *Thought Contagion*], [Brodie 1996, *Virus of the Mind*], [Blackmore 1999, *The Meme Machine*]. [Dennett 1991, *Consciousness Explained*], and [Dennett, 1995, *Darwin's Dangerous Idea*] also have discussions of memetics. More recent research has been done in this area although the results are not always expressed in terms of memes. Here are some recent books: [Lakoff, 2008, *The Political Mind*], [Westen, 2007, *The Political Brain*], and [Damasio, 2003, *Looking for Spinoza*].

Meme dynamics.

To say *meme* instead of *idea* is, in a way, just another point of view. But the emphasis is different. When we say *meme* instead of *idea*, we are emphasizing the spreadability, changeability, persistence, and evanescence of ideas. We are examining the dynamics of ideas, their life histories through time, and space, and people, and how they are associated with other ideas. The everyday point of view is that ideas spread from person to person in our cultures because of their truth or usefulness. Memetics emphasizes that these are only part of the explanation. Often the reasons ideas spread have very little to do with their truth or usefulness. Through memetics we hope to understand all the factors involved in spreading ideas.

Memes can be true, false, good, bad, and everything in between.

Our minds are filled with ideas, memes. Some may be true, some may be useful, some may be false, some useless, some make us feel good, some sad, and on and on and on. All our memes are intertwined with our emotions and our behavior. Some memes are dangerous in that they can lead to harmful results. We have wars because enough people have enough memes that lead them to war. It's as simple as that. And as complex.

Evaluate our memes.

Our memes do not totally control our behavior, but they surely influence behavior. We have physical bodies. We have instincts. Most people, most of the time, control their instincts. We are severely socialized. We usually behave as we have been taught to behave in our culture. We have the ability to examine at least some of our memes, and change them if we choose. The purpose of this program is to get all of us to examine our own memes, to see which ones lead to wars, and how that happens. Then we can eliminate those memes, or change them, or limit where and how they are used, so they no longer lead to war. We can choose to do this thoughtfully and deliberately. We do change our ideas all the time by thinking, reading, talking, by all our interactions with other people and the world. So we can change our war ideas. We can do this. One person at a time. And we can spread the idea to more and more people.

We will identify and examine war memes.

In Chapter 6, we will identify and examine war memes that we may have. We will look at ways memes may be changed or limited. The list in chapter 6 is just the start. We can expect to find many more memes that on the whole, or in some part, lead to war.

Clean our mental environments like we clean our physical environment.

Essential to this program is to continue the identification and analysis of war memes wherever it leads in the future. Thoughtful people everywhere can contribute. Psychologists and other scientists of the mind and culture can do research on the ecology of war memes, and the results may be used by individuals in cleaning up their own minds. Just as in the environmental movement, we clean pollutants from our physical space, in this anti-war movement we can clean up dangerous and harmful war memes from our mental and cultural environments. So this program can be seen as an extension of the environmental movement.

Not only memetics.

Although this program uses the science of memetics, we should also use whatever other sciences may be able to contribute to the program of cleaning our minds of war ideas. And of course, if you should feel that saying *meme* doesn't add much beyond just saying *idea*, feel free to make the substitution as you read on. But it will be easier to think in terms of memes. The meme point of view is useful. And by whatever name, the science of the ecology of ideas will flourish.

Meme fights not effective.

One reason this program is needed is because the current anti-war movement attempts to battle war memes directly, as a meme fight, to counteract war memes with anti-war memes. People protest against the current war, whatever it may be, by attempting to apply logic, or anti-war memes, to dislodge the war memes from those in favor of the current war. Although this is a most noble effort, it is not often effective because by the time the current war is underway, it's too late. There are way too many people already infected with the war memes, that the few opponents of the war, in wielding their anti-war memes, have no chance of winning that meme battle. So the cycle of wars continues.

A higher strategy.

We need a different strategy. We can be effective if we take a different view. We can look at the problem from a higher level. We back away from the noise, confusion, and limited effectiveness, of the current war meme fight. We take a systems approach. As Archimedes said, "*Give me a place to stand on, and I will move the Earth*." So in this program, we do not just oppose the current war, but rather we will deflect, interrupt, and stop the processes that lead to war. These processes are psychological, sociological, political, and cultural. We will go to the root of the problem of war, to the war memes that are circulating through our minds, and throughout our cultural systems.

Disinfect and inoculate culture.

In Chapter 7, we will show how the war memes always have an inherent advantage over peace memes. So we have to go to a higher level strategy, a strategy beyond a direct contest between war and peace memes, a strategy that works at the cultural level. The solution is to methodically disinfect our culture of our war memes, and then inoculate our culture against future infections, as if memes were viruses. We can do this by first disinfecting ourselves of war memes, and then inoculating ourselves against accepting any war memes in the future. We do this independently of any particular war, and without getting bogged down in the minutiae of arguments for the current war, in the current war meme fight. We then spread this process far and wide. The disinfection process is to identify war memes, deconstruct them, and modify, eliminate, or replace them in ourselves, and show others how to do the same. We will be inoculated when we are aware of the existence and effects of war memes, when we are able to identify them, when we are aware of how they may be pushed on us, and when we refuse them entry into our minds. When enough people all over the planet do this our cultures will be disinfected from, and inoculated against, war memes, and wars will no longer occur.

Anti-virus memes.

Another way of viewing this program is to make an analogy with computer viruses and anti-virus software. This program will help people construct the equivalent of anti-virus programs in their minds that will detect war memes that are currently resident there and neutralize them.

Then the anti-virus programs in people's minds will join their meme filters to prevent the entrance of new war memes into their minds in the future. [Aunger, 2002].

Clear and simple program.

The logic of this program is simple:

1) Wars are always a net loss to humanity.
2) Every human being is a potential victim of war.
3) Wars violate our ideals.
4) Therefore we should work to eliminate wars.

Wars occur because many people have war memes which, contrary to their best interests, repeatedly lead them to war. Therefore if we can change or eliminate these war memes, in enough people, in enough countries of the planet, then wars will not occur. We can do this. The proof that we can do this is that other vast cultural changes have occurred in the past. With our current understanding of human psychology, and human cultures, we have the tools needed to do this. We have the knowledge and tools to consciously change our war cultures by identifying, and eliminating, our war memes. Just as the environmental movement removes harmful substances from our physical planetary environments, the anti-war movement can remove the harmful war memes from our mental and spiritual environments. We can take the environmental movement as a shining example and use it as our model. The knowledge and tools we now have will allow this change to occur faster and more completely than the vast cultural changes of the past. More research will make this process even more efficient over time.

Preview.

In Chapter 2, we will examine the costs and benefits of wars in the past one hundred years or so. We will show that although a few individuals, corporations, and on very rare occasions, individual countries, may benefit from war, in all cases, wars are a net cost to humanity. Every living person is a potential victim of war. And wars violate our ideals. We will also examine some of the processes that lead to war, and show how the limited powers of some of our memes necessarily prevent us from correctly evaluating proposed wars.

In Chapter 3, we will review previous significant cultural changes, as proofs of principle, that the cultural changes proposed here are indeed possible. We can change the world through cultural engineering.

In Chapter 4, we will look at the environmental movement as a model and guide for the anti-war movement.

In Chapter 5 we will look at memetic engineering, and how memes work in detail. We will examine how people change their memes, eliminate ones they don't want, and add new ones. We will examine meme defenses: what makes people more susceptible to absorbing memes they may not want, and what people can do to avoid absorbing memes they don't want. We look at forceful, as well as subtle, methods of meme implantation. We look at myths, stories, and metaphors as memes.

In Chapter 6, we look at a sample list of war memes, and deconstruct them in detail. Why do they lead to war? How do they work? How effective are they? Are there any good parts to any of them? How can they be changed or eliminated? We will find that war memes are sneaky. They often occur where you wouldn't expect them to be. They can be entwined with memes which are beneficial to people. Our investigations in Chapter 6 will lead to many surprises and unexpected conclusions. We will look at the population dynamics of a number of memes. We will show how leaders can become trapped by their ideologies, come to have interests harmful to their populations, and deliberately or not, spread war memes to their populations.

In Chapter 7, we discuss the population dynamics of war memes and show how this gives war memes an inherent memetic advantage over peace memes. We look at cycles of war and peace memes, why war memes are self spreading, while peace memes are self extinguishing, and how this leads to a serious danger to this program.

In Chapter 8, we discuss the critical influence of the mass media in spreading war memes, how the media, by their nature, push war memes, bypass meme filters, define reality, diminish people, and allow the few to control the many.

In Chapters 9, we discuss memes and meme evolution in more detail. We define memes and information. We show how the same meme can be in many brains at the same time. We discuss how memes enter our brains, and the relations between words and memes. We look at the connections between memes and feelings, and how these may be damaged in some people. We consider two impediments to our understanding of war: Stalin's Law, and the belief in universal reason. We look at meme evolution, meme acquisition, meme filtering, and how memes are stored in our brains.

In Chapter 10, we discuss meme organisms, and memes that promote memetic evolution. We look at human, as well as non human, meme organisms, how meme organisms develop and protect their memes. We look at meme organism goals, the self development meme, the meme to lose oneself in a cause greater than oneself, meme takeover, the love meme, the free speech, liberty, and democracy memes. We discuss some memes that inhibit meme evolution. We consider cooperation among meme organisms, and look at sports to show that competition is cooperation. We note that modularity in meme organisms requires cooperation. Finally we discuss the unity of individual and community, and the future of meme evolution.

In Chapter 11, we look at how this program might work out.

In Chapter 12, we transition from thought to action, from memes to behavior.

PORTRAIT: Rest in Peace 19.1 M.

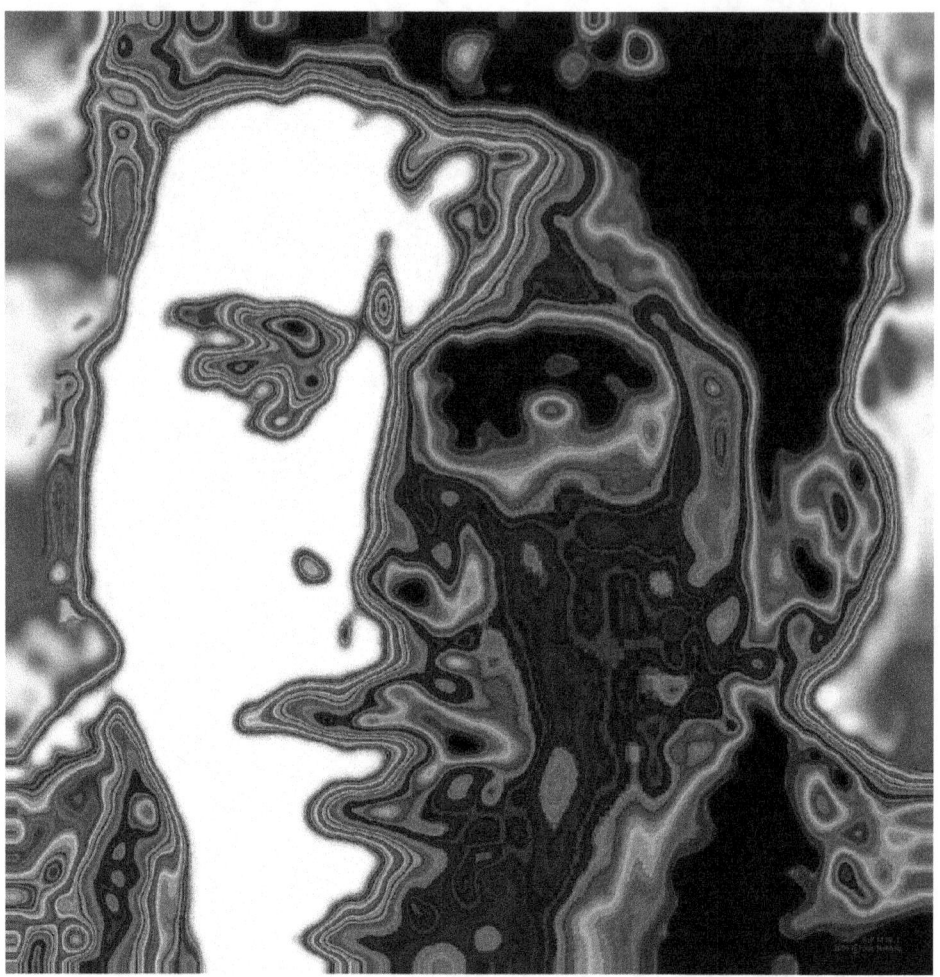

Chapter 2: War is Always a Net Loss to Humanity.

This chapter lays out why we need to change our war cultures.

A change of administration.

"On the battlefield of Okinawa 107,500 Japanese soldiers had been killed in just under four weeks' fighting, their bodies counted on the battlefield. A further 20,000 were believed to have died in the caves into which they fled, against which the Americans used flame-throwers and explosives. Many local Okinawans were also killed in the fighting, at least 80,000. The American losses were lower but formidable: 7,613 on land and 4,907 at sea, many as a result of kamikaze attacks. A small island had changed hands in battle, and more than 200,000 human beings were dead." [Gilbert, 2001, page 313].

The political administration of one small island changed from Japan to the United States. What the United States gained, Japan lost. Whenever territory or property is taken by one side in a war, exactly the same things are lost by the other side. The value gained by one exactly equals the value lost by the other. The net value for humanity from this transaction is zero. On Okinawa, humanity lost more than 200,000 people killed, many injured, and great destruction of property. Can anyone name a benefit to offset this loss?

List the costs of war.

Most people know in their hearts that wars are senseless. Many books have been written about the costs and horrors of war. [Stiglitz & Bilmes, 2008], How many books have been written about the benefits of war? To see the absurdity of war, all you have to do is step back, away from the current war, whatever it may be. Consider the wars of the last one hundred years or so. The farther back in time you go, the more absurd they seem. What was World War I all about? Most people have no idea. What did the winners get? Did the losers lose more than the winners lost, in people killed, people wounded, material things destroyed? Every country involved had large numbers of its soldiers killed, many wounded, and much destruction of material things: ships, vehicles, guns, bombs, explosives, buildings. In many of the warring countries, millions of civilians were killed. So add it all up. Add up all the soldiers killed in all the countries involved. Add up all civilians killed. Add up all the numbers of people wounded. Add up the numbers of ships sunk. Add up all the bombs, all the artillery shells fired, all the bullets, all the poison gas, all the tanks built and destroyed, all the horses killed, all the farm animals, all the wildlife, all the vehicles destroyed, all the buildings blown up or burnt down, all the bridges knocked down. Also add the cost of the damage or destruction of all the intangible cultural institutions such as civility, respect for laws, rules of commerce, art, science, the beauty and pleasures of life.

List the benefits of war.

Now for each category above, add up the benefits of this war. How many new adult soldiers did this war create from nothing? Zero. How many new non combatants? Zero. How many wounds did not occur on account of this war? Zero. How many ships that were built for the war were left at the end? Some number greater than or equal to zero. The Germans blew up and sank 75 of their large warships in one afternoon at the end of the war rather than turn them over to the French. How many bombs and other munitions were left? What's the value of these munitions absent a war? How many buildings did the war build? How many bridges did the war construct? What else did the war produce in material things? What else did the war do for human welfare? Did it make people happier? Were people's lives better in any way as a result of World War I? Add up the costs. Add up the benefits. There can be no doubt the costs for humanity are much, much greater than any benefits.

Intangible benefits.

Please don't try to assert intangible benefits like "*making the world safe for democracy.*" That's bullshit propaganda, and we all know it. That's an example of an essentially meaningless, *yet effective*, bit of propaganda that mixes fear, and glorious sounding, far off, undiscounted hypotheticals. What does this mean? What's an undiscounted hypothetical? It means the future is uncertain, and when there is a long chain of speculative events or actions, that must occur before actual harm or benefit, our brains just glom onto the horrific or glorious final event, as if it were inevitable, and just about to happen. But in reality, each independent event in the chain of hypotheticals has a less than certain probability of happening, and the correct way to consider the end event is to multiply all the probabilities of the independent events in the chain. If we do this, we are correctly discounting the future hypothetical event. If we are including money values in our expectation of gain or loss we must also take account of the future value of money. But this is not the way our ordinary undisciplined brains work. The brain feels and acts as if the horrific or wonderful last event in the chain is virtually certain when in reality, it's likelihood of happening is very, very low. This is one example of the sort of defective thinking that leads to war.

Example of a future undiscounted hypothetical.

Consider the domino theory that was used to justify the United States intervention in Vietnam. It was said that if South Vietnam fell to the communists, that would be the first domino of countries that would fall to communism. The whole world would become communist if this first domino in the chain, Vietnam, fell. There is your future undiscounted hypothetical: the whole world becoming communist. The United States and Vietnam fought a long and bloody war, and more than 50,000 United States soldiers died, and more than 5 million Vietnamese died, and millions of Cambodians and Laotians died. But the United States lost the war and had to leave quickly. South Vietnam was totally taken over by the evil communists. So the domino fell and then what? Nothing! Nothing else happened. Not a thing happened. No other country fell to communism. Fifteen years later, communism collapsed from its own internal deficiencies. Communism is over. So much for future, undiscounted, hypotheticals.

Wars create nothing.

The book "*The Three Trillion Dollar War*", [Stiglitz & Bilmes, 2008], gives a through economic analysis of the cost of the Iraq war. The 3 trillion dollars was only for costs to the United States. A complete economic analysis is needed for Iraq. Similar economic analyses need to be done for all participating countries for WW I, WW II, for Korea, for Vietnam, for the Gulf War, and for any other recent wars. The gross results will always be the same. The costs for humanity always are way greater than any benefits. This isn't surprising. It's really very simple. Wars destroy things and people. When the administration of some territory changes hands, nothing is created. Wars create nothing. Except pain and suffering and maybe hostility and hatreds which can lead to more wars. Any presumed gains by one nation are outweighed by all the death and destruction caused by the war as a whole.

100 million people killed.

Below is a table of some of the numbers of people killed in wars of the 20th century. Different sources give different numbers. Perhaps one hundred million people were killed in all wars of the 20th century.

NUMBER OF PEOPLE KILLED DUE TO FOUR WARS OF THE TWENTIETH CENTURY. [White, 2003].

World War I:	21.5 Million.
World War II:	55 Million.
Korean War:	More than 400,000 soldiers, Unknown numbers of civilians.
Vietnam War:	5.1 Million.

Final nails in the coffins of wars.

Now, just in case there are any doubts, to put the final nails in the coffins of wars, we need economists, to work with historians, to examine each of the wars of the 20th century in detail, using the most objective scientific historical methods, and economic tools, to prove, once and for all, rigorously and scientifically, the assertions made above. They can calculate, in complete detail, the actual costs, in current dollars, of each war of the 20th century. Maybe some of the smaller wars would make good PhD theses, or maybe even Masters' theses, for economics and history graduate students.

Does anyone benefit from wars?

Notice that the above was framed in terms of costs and benefits for humanity as a whole. This leaves open the possibility that some individual countries or groups, might have a net benefit from engaging in war. For example, it has been said that American farmers benefited from WW I. This is possible. However rigorous historical and economic analysis will show that in almost all cases whole countries also suffer net losses from wars. But there is no doubt, that particular groups, and particular individuals, within warring countries, can and do have net economic benefits from wars. Particular industries may benefit, particular corporations may have large profits, and of course some individuals make a lot of money from war. When groups or individuals within a country benefit from a war, it is generally at the expense of other groups and individuals in the same country. That is, some groups' benefits result from the losses of other groups, industries, corporations, or individuals, in the same country. Profits made from making bombs and airplanes, could have been made by the housing industry, if the labor and material that went into building bombs and airplanes, had gone into building houses instead. The bombs and airplanes are destroyed, (or if any are left at the end of the war, they are generally useless, since they are superseded by newer and better versions for the next war), whereas the houses might have been of benefit to many families for many years to come, if they had been built, instead of the bombs and airplanes. So the net for a country is still a loss even though some groups and individuals within the country may benefit. The benefits for some groups and individuals in a country are offset by losses for other groups and individuals, usually in the same country. The profits made by making war material could have been made by the housing industry, but were not. And after the war, the war material is gone, but the houses that could have been built, would have still existed. We need economists and historians to research and document these cases as well.

European free lunch from United States taxpayers.

The American farmers made a lot of money in WW I at the expense of all the American taxpayers because the Europeans bought the farm products with money lent to them by the United States government. They never paid back the loans. The same holds for the weapons the United States made and sent to them.

Everyone richer without war.

Even though some corporations and individuals may make money from wars, if a large enough number of people are enlightened as to the net losses to all of humanity, the majority will be able to prevent war processes from starting, or cut them off before it's too late. Sooner or later, people will see that using all the labor and resources that are now wasted in wars, for beneficial purposes instead of war, can make everyone richer. Most people, who now make money from wars, will be happy to make even a little less, as long as they have enough to live comfortably, if they could use their energy and abilities for non-war purposes.

Countries almost always have net losses.

Even if it should be shown that some war or wars are a net benefit to one or more countries, these would surely be rare exceptions. Such a result would not invalidate the fundamental conclusion that wars are always a net loss to humanity as a whole.

Wars are a potential danger to everyone.

Once a war gets started, no one knows how long it will last, or how many countries will get sucked in. As long as nuclear weapons exist, they could be used. Soldiers are clearly at risk of death and physical and mental injury. Civilians can be at risk of death and injury also. People are victims of war whenever someone they love is killed or injured. Technology advances will allow more and more poor countries and groups to make cheap intelligent efficient weapons that will not easily be countered by rich nations. Guided missiles and drones could easily be designed and built by high school students today, using microchips, global positioning system receivers, and cell phones. Aside from the physical dangers from wars, there are secondary effects of wars. Today, all societies and nations are interconnected economically through globalization much more than in the past. A foolish war in one part of the planet could well bring about economic disaster and collapse to the whole planetary trading and economic system affecting everybody. So wars are a potential danger to everyone.

Our interconnectedness.

There is a more profound way in which all people of this planet are interconnected. We each exist within everyone else. Each person I know and love exists in a real way within me. And vice versa: In each person who knows me I exist in a real way. I really mean real, not just as a way of speaking. [Hofstadter, 2006]. The more two people know and love one another, the more memes they have in common. And the more memes they share, the more each one exists, lives within the other. When we imagine the pain, suffering, anger, grief, joy, happiness, good times with family and friends, of any person, that person exists, lives, within us. We have mechanisms in our brains that allow us to actually feel the same things other people feel when we imagine their suffering or joy [Damasio, 2003]. So if we work to eliminate war, if we dedicate some of our time and energy to this goal, we are not being selfless. The idea that to do good we must somehow or somewhat sacrifice something of our selves is a mistake. There is no tradeoff here. There is no dichotomy. If we work to help other human beings, if we work to make the world a better place, we are not diminishing ourselves. Rather we are growing, expanding our individual selves. We are making our own selves better, greater, more beautiful, more just, more truly human. But when war occurs anywhere in the world, it hurts all of us, it diminishes all of us, and it's bad for our souls. This is one more reason we all should work to eliminate war forever.

Old and new.

In an important sense this is a very new idea as the reference to Douglass Hofstadter's and Antonio Damasio's books above indicates. Hofstadter shows in a real scientific way, in terms of memes, that we each exist in everybody else. I exist in a bigger way in those people closest to me, the people I know well and love dearly. In people I know and love less well, and who correspondingly know and love me less well, I exist in a smaller version. For someone I have never heard of and who has never heard of me, we exist in each other in an even smaller, yet essential, way. I emphasize that this is real, not just a way of speaking. On the other hand this truth is very old, thousands of years old. The scriptures say we are all children of God. We are all sisters and brothers. Sadly this has become a platitude. That is we hear it so often we have lost its meaning. To say we are all sisters and brothers means we really know, in an essentially human way, every other human being on the planet as well as we know a biological sister or brother. Every other human being is, in a fundamental real way, like us and when we harm any one of them we harm ourselves. We feel what they feel. They feel what we feel. Jesus, in speaking about poor people, said: *"What you do to the least of these, you do to me."* So the truth --- that we each exist in everyone else --- gives a modern explanation, in terms of memetics, for the ancient recognition that we are all sisters and brothers.

War is bad, ugly, unjust, and based on lies.

Wars violate our transcendent values. Transcendent values are the values that are behind all our other discussions and values. [Balkin, 1998]. They are such things as: Goodness, Beauty, Justice, and Truth.

Why every leader should always work to avoid war.

Since: 1) Wars are always a net loss to humanity, i.e., are always dysfunctional for humanity, and 2) Wars are almost always dysfunctional for any individual country engaging in a war, and 3) Given the very small probability, that a war could be beneficial to an individual country, and the fact that no leader can possibly know for certain, or with any high probability at all, that his war would be beneficial for his country, then 4) Every leader, of every country, should always work to avoid war.

Why almost every person on the planet should work to eliminate war.

Since: 1) Wars are always a net loss to humanity, i.e., are always dysfunctional for humanity, and 2) Wars are potentially harmful for almost all people, whether they participate in a particular war or not, no matter where on the planet they may live, and 3) Given the very small number of people on the planet who might have a positive probability that a war could be beneficial to them, and the fact that no individual can possibly know for certain, or with any high probability at all, that a war would be beneficial to them, then 4) Almost all people of every country of the planet should work to eliminate war.

Those who think they might benefit from a war can never be sure.

Even Daddy Warbucks will have to hope that his children or grandchildren don't get sucked into a war and be injured or killed, and he must also hope that the war doesn't get so out of control, that it kills himself or anyone he loves. Besides, Daddy is probably smart enough to make money in other ways than through war.

War will be no more.

Since wars are a net cost to humanity, sooner or later, with a vigorous and ever expanding anti-war movement, a large enough number of people will realize this so that war will be no more. The purpose of this book is to describe a program which will speed up this process so that we will reach the goal of no more war sooner rather than later.

How and why do wars get started?

If wars are always a net cost to humanity, and also almost always a net cost to each country participating in the war, how and why do wars get started? Wars can start by a mutual escalation process between two or more countries based on mutual fear and mistrust. WW I is an example. Wars can be started by a leader or leaders in a country who decide to conquer some other country. WW II and the Iraq war are examples. These leaders propagandize their own population to support their war. Wars can be started by ethnic or nationalistic conflicts in some obscure country which then sucks in larger countries. The large countries do not recognize, or give sufficient weight to, the nationalistic or ethnic factors, but rather see the factions as contestants in a broader ideological contest. The process by which large countries get sucked into small wars is often an escalation process. In the twentieth century this process involved many mistakes by naive or conniving leaders on all sides. The Korean and Vietnam wars are examples.

In the Causes of War literature what I have called a "*mutual escalation process*" is called a "*conflict spiral*".

"*In conflict spirals, the prevailing dynamic is that conflictual actions by one side increase the perception of threat and hostility in the other, which lead to responses that are equally conflictual or even more conflictual. These reciprocal hostilities are further propelled by blowback onto domestic politics in both states; hostile acts by the rival state create domestic political support for even tougher measures and decrease the political influence of accomodationists who seek to diffuse the crisis. At some point neither side may be capable, politically, of avoiding war.*" [Cashman & Robinson, 2007, page 288].

Fertile narratives.

Ethnic and nationalistic wars often germinate from minds well fertilized with national and ethnic narratives, stories, passed down through succeeding generations. The people of each side remember stories of massacres, atrocities, and other injustices, and actively pass on these stories to their children. In some cases, people are still retelling narratives of injustices committed against their ethnic group, hundreds, and even thousands, of years ago! Conniving political leaders use these stories to gain power by stirring up fear, hatred, and anger in their populations, and thereby lead their people to wars.

Causes of War.

There are many other scenarios that modern political scientists have discovered that lead to wars. See for example, "*An Introduction to the Causes of War*", [Cashman & Robinson, 2007]. They analyze the causes of war on multiple levels. They look at factors relating to individual people. They call that The Individual Level. They also consider: The Substate Level; The Nation-State Level; The Dyadic Level (interactions between two countries); The International System Level; and Multilevel Analysis. We will look at war memes related to all of these in more detail in Chapter 6.

Evaluating priceless intangible memes.

We have examined the costs of war by totaling the value of all the material goods destroyed, and totaling all the people killed and wounded. We looked for benefits of wars, and found no material benefits, to offset the great costs. Any benefits, in terms of what motivates most people to support war, seem to be contained in glorious sounding, far off, hypothetical benefits, such as preserving our way of life, our religion, liberty, democracy, socialism, or whatever, against some enemy. We might call these priceless intangibles. Some examples expressed as slogans are: *"Give me liberty or give me death", "Making the world safe for democracy"*, and *"We must defeat evil, godless communism."* In historical perspective, in hindsight, we have dismissed these as propaganda. The ideals expressed in these propagandistic slogans were either not attained at all, or not attained as the result of war, or were not worth the cost of the wars, or could have been attained at much less cost than through war. So how is it that these ideals were valued above all the death and destruction of war? When we consider material things we can put a monetary value on each house, building, vehicle, weapon, destroyed in a war. There are problems in assigning monetary values to human lives and human ideals, especially far off hypothetical ideals. It's not that it cannot be done. There are insurance company, and state worker's compensation tables, which include nominal valuations for loss of life, and injuries suffered. After the World Trade Center destruction, the life of each person killed was assigned a monetary value, which was paid to their relatives. But there is no consensus on how to value human life. And I doubt if a monetary value has ever been placed on, for example, liberty. So what do humans do then, when faced with a decision they must make, between, say, the destruction and death represented by a war, and fear of some possible distant future loss of liberty? It is hard to do any computations no matter how approximate. It doesn't do any good to value a human life as infinite since then the loss of even one life would out weigh everything else. Unless maybe the ideal, say liberty, were also given a value of infinity. In this case we would have a cost of infinity, for lives lost, versus a benefit of infinity, for liberty preserved, and no way to choose one over the other. If the ideal is given infinite value, and human life a finite value, then the answer would always come out in favor of the ideal. The ideal would be worth more than all human life on earth. That's absurd. So neither valuing human life, nor human ideals, as infinite helps to make a decision.

Memes rule!

But people do choose. They go to war or they refuse to go. So how do they decide? Their memes decide. There is a contest, or war, of memes in each mind. This contest does not resemble a computation, like calculating the plusses and minuses. The result will depend on the strengths of the contesting memes. And the strengths of the memes depend on our feelings, and unknown other factors, having little or nothing to do with the welfare of humanity. This is one reason why we continue to have wars. The pro-war and anti-war memes fight it out in our minds. It's a contest where the rules are mostly unknown to us. It all somehow depends on the strengths and interconnections of the competing memes and the unknown mechanisms in the human brain behind the contest. These mechanisms, whatever they are, are the result of genetic and memetic evolution. The collective benefit to humanity is unlikely to have been a factor in either of these evolutions. [Dennett, 1995]. The memes don't care about us. The universe of replicating entities called memes, exists in us and in our artifacts, and is mostly independent of our conscious thoughts. They copy themselves and spread to vast numbers of people through the mass media. Their purposes are not our purposes. They evolve mostly independent of our biological, genetic evolution. We are only vehicles for them. Our lives and deaths mean nothing to them except, at present, they need us as hosts. In the future we may not be needed. So for the war memes, wars are good. In wars they get to spread to huge numbers of people. This is one reason why wars don't make sense to our rational minds, and yet, we keep repeating war after war after war. We, our rational minds, are not in control. The memes are.

Memes don't do arithmetic.

The memes for the value of a human life, and the memes for the value of our ideals, for example, liberty, do not operate in a mind according to the laws of arithmetic. This is because these memes, as all memes, are intertwined with our emotions and feelings. The amount of emotion or feeling associated with, or attached to, a meme is a measure of that meme's importance to us [Damasio, 2003]. The mechanisms by which the memes struggle for existence or supremacy in our minds necessarily involve our feelings and the changing of the emotional values attached to the memes. But our feelings and emotions do not work by the rules of arithmetic. *The meme for the deaths of one million people does not have one million times the feeling and emotion as the meme for the death of one person.* So the memes can't get it right. They can't get the value of liberty for one person or the value of liberty for one million people right either. Josef Stalin, cold and cruel as he was, may have understood this. He supposedly said it this way: *"The death of one person is a tragedy, but the death of one million is only a statistic."*

Steely cold rationality versus one picture of a dead baby?

On the other hand, visual images whether art or simple photographs, of those killed in a war, are very powerful. They are so powerful that one such image can completely turn a person against a war. One visual image of death can *scare the hell out of us*. What's going on here? The phrase *1 million killed* hardly moves us. Yet one picture of a dead child can knock us over. And people think we can handle war rationally! Why do you think our media scrupulously avoid any pictures of the dead? War memes cannot stand any pictures of what they do. One picture of a dead child is worth more than *1 million killed* in emotional response any time! Are we rational? We don't have the rationality to handle war. Those who think they are hard headed realists will say that the emotional response to a picture of a dead child is not realistic. They may be right. That's my point: our memes, we, can't get it right. Which is the correct response: 1) the ho-hum response to *1 million killed*, or 2) the emotional response to a picture of a dead child? All we have to evaluate war is our brains and our memes. Both of the above are normal responses by the human system. Both provide us with information about war. Which is correct? Which better corresponds to reality? Which one is the human response? Which response is the higher response? Which brings us closer to to our great transcendent values of Goodness, Beauty, Justice, and Truth?

Which do you choose to represent for you the reality of war? So look at that picture, or try to comprehend 1 million deaths. Cry your heart out or try to be steely cold rational. Which is the truth? What should we do?

<u>Images and words.</u>

Words enter our minds in linear sequences. Our logic is based on analyzing these words as they come in. Most of our meme filters are logic or word based. A visual image comes in all at once, not bit by sequential bit. All the bits, all the data, come in at once, in parallel. This allows visual images to sometimes bypass our meme filters. Our minds are able to think in terms of visual images. The thinking is different from our logical, linear, word sequence kind of thinking. Who is to say which kind of thinking is best? Both are ways the outside world affects us, presents itself to us. Both represent channels by which the world causes a response from us. We may consider the linear, logical, word way to be preferable for decision making. But how do we know that the visual way does not produce a more valid response in us to the world? Maybe the emotional response to the image of a dead child is a better response in us in terms of our continued well being, our success in the world, our continued existence in the world. Our aprehension of the world through images came long before we had any words or logic. It is a much older and direct aprehension of reality. The truth I see in an image of a dead child surpasses logic at least with respect to war. In any case, regarding war, we know meme logic is insufficient.

<u>We get it wrong.</u>

What all this means is that, when we make decisions about war versus no war, on the basis of nice sounding slogans, or far off hypothetical ideals, versus unknown numbers of deaths and injuries, and unknown destruction of material things, on the basis of gut feelings, on the basis of our emotions and totally inadequate rationality, via our memes, our decisions are not likely to have any connection to the welfare of humanity. Often our decisions have no connection to our own personal welfare either, or that of our family, friends, or country. We are unable to intuitively correctly evaluate wars. We get it wrong.

<u>Rationally remove irrational memes that lead to war.</u>

Just as we cannot do complex arithmetic in our minds, but rather must step out of our minds and use artifacts, like calculators or pencils and paper, in order to make correct decisions about wars, we also must step out of our intuitive minds, and go to another external level, and think culturally, and think about and deconstruct our war memes. We must think about our thought processes, and consciously modify or remove, the memetic components that lead us astray to war. We must rationally remove the irrational memes that lead us to war. Instead of making intuitive judgments, that are only partly based on reason, but mostly based on the unknown and unconscious activities of memes in our minds, we must go to an external view of our mental activity, and correct the decision making process, by identifying and modifying, or removing, the harmful non rational war memes, which corrupt our decision making processes.

Mental artifacts, computers, might evaluate proposed wars.

Suppose we, or our leaders, despite knowing that wars are a net cost to humanity, don't care about that, but think somehow we can beat the odds and get some benefit for our country by fighting a war, or get some financial benefit to ourselves. If we wish to do the exercise of actually evaluating a proposed war, in some monetary sense, assigning cash values to lives lost, body parts blown away and so on, we would need some external methodology such as a computer, because a proposed war has way too many possibilities, too many ways it might unfold, for any strictly intuitive evaluation. Wars are way too uncertain. There are too many unknowns that can only be guessed at. We can evaluate past wars as outlined above. Add up all the losses. Add up all the benefits. Compare the two. For past wars we can get actual data on material goods destroyed, we can count the bodies; we can determine whether the winners received any benefits. If actual numbers are not available we can use estimates. For future proposed wars, the monetary values of all the death and destruction and the ideals supposedly attained or lost will have to be estimated. Ranges of values and probabilities of various contingencies can be used. Although there is presently no consensus on how to value a life lost or an injury, and few ideas how to value liberty or a person's way of life, we could research and develop such methodologies. Economics can be extended to include valuations of death and valuations of ideals. We can assign monetary values to each life lost and each injury. With respect to ideals, psychologists can investigate the relative valuations people put on various ideals. People do trade off ideals against one another. In times of fear people willingly trade liberty for promised security. People will give inconsistent answers, but we can pick a number. We can properly take into account future uncertain events such as the attainment of any ideals. We would need a computer, to simulate the proposed war. Any such simulation would require huge amounts of data collection and multiple scenario construction. It would require probably many hundreds or thousands of person-years of work. Any such methodology would have uneasy acceptance at first. Over time we might converge to consensus. This would not be perfect. But, perfect is the enemy of the good. This might seem to be better than what we do now. Now all we are able to do is wing it, go with our gut feelings, repeat simple-minded slogans, wave our arms, shout and scream at those who disagree with us.

In great gory detail.

Note that any simulations like the above, even if they were possible, would only be able to give probabilities of advantage or disadvantage to one side or another. They would not be able to predict winners and losers. They would only give probabilities. So anyone so demented as to seek personal advantage by starting a war still could not get a definitive answer. The net cost to humanity would still always be negative. The simulations would only spell this out, through multiple diverse iterations, in great gory detail.

Are wars totally unpredictable?

Some will say the preceding is ridiculous. They will say wars are absolutely too uncertain ever to be amenable to such a methodology. Unforeseen consequences always happen. Military planners have a saying to the effect that after the first battle, all plans have to be thrown out. This can be empirically tested. For past wars historians can list what was predicted to occur and compare that to what actually happened. And it will almost surely turn out that indeed wars are totally unpredictable. Then this will, in and of itself, be a powerful reason never to start a war in the first place. If wars are totally unpredictable, then this contradicts any propaganda promising future benefits or avoidance of harm by going to war. Actually it's not quite right to say that wars are totally unpredictable. We can predict with the greatest confidence that all wars cause death and destruction and that all wars are a net loss to humanity. What is unpredictable is how any particular war will unfold, just who and how many of us will be killed or injured, who's and how much property will be destroyed, how long the war will last, or how much it will cost in money.

Meme wars cause human wars.

Human wars in another sense are also meme wars. In the sense that modern wars are ideologically marketed, these human wars are direct results of the wars between or among memes. Consider capitalism, communism, fascism, socialism, democracy, free markets, totalitarianism, nationalism, ethnocentrism, religions. The wars among these memes are total. One tactic many of these memes can use is to cause their hosts to kill the hosts of the enemy memes. A human war is a handy way to do this. The memes don't care about human life. The memes for some religions will cause their hosts to kill or threaten to kill any person who criticizes the religion. These are very good memes. These are among the best memes ever evolved. Human wars are only one way memes fight it out. The wars among these memes continue in the absence of human wars.

Leaders use fear.

If a conniving leader, or an escalation process (conflict spiral), or some other process, can cause the replication of enough fear laden war memes in the minds of enough of the population then we will have war. Otherwise we will not. The war memes are always fear laden because the leader or escalation process build up fears of loss of our lives or loss of our liberties or suppression of our religion or other ideals by the enemy. Even if a leader thinks he can gain some material resources or wealth from the countries he proposes to conquer, rarely will he include these among the war memes he pushes. Fear is always a factor. It is most effective. The nearest thing to exceptions might be wars of national liberation or colonial wars to grab the resources of less developed countries in which some positive benefit to the population is promised by the leader.

<u>Clear and simple.</u>

The program of this book is not based on any methodology like the computer methodology outlined above. So it does not depend on the success of any such methodology. It is much simpler than that. It is to go to the root causes of war: the war memes in peoples' minds. The core of this program is simply to identify war memes, deconstruct them, and then change or remove them from ourselves, and via a world wide anti-war movement, convince enough other people in each country of the world to do the same. If a large enough number of people in each country, probably a majority, are immune to war memes, they will not be seduced into wars whether by foolish or conniving leaders or via mutual escalation or any other process by which wars start. The preconditions for war will no longer exist in people's minds. The causes of wars will not be there. And even tyrants need some sort of consent from enough people in their country to start a war. At some point this program may make sense even to leaders and tyrants, but this is not required.

<u>The last war.</u>

It will probably be many years until this program is successful and the last war has occurred. At that time nobody will know that that war was the last war. So, most countries will keep their armies until some time, probably long after, the last war has been fought. It may be fifty, or one hundred, or maybe two hundred years, before enough people realize, and accept with confidence, that the era of war on planet earth is over. Then they will realize that armies are unnecessary, and they will disband them. Many people will live who would have died in the wars that won't happen.

PORTRAIT: Rest in Peace 103.3.

Chapter 3: Cultural Engineering: We Can Change the World.

This program may seem grandiose. It requires changing cultures world wide. This is surely a huge task. How can we be confident that this is possible? And if it is possible, how can we make it happen?

Controlled evolution.

Throughout history people have been taught, or trained, to be humble, to consider themselves as second class, compared to the leaders. This of course makes it easier for leaders. We've been taught to *"respect authority"*. This is surely a powerful meme, which we will discuss further in Chapter 6. We've been trained that we don't have power, that only the leaders have power, that we don't know, that only the leaders know. We're helpless. We don't know what to do. Only the leaders know what we should do. And of course they will tell us. See the book *"The Powers That Be"*, by Walter Wink. [Wink, 1998]. We've been trained not to trust our own feelings and thinking, but instead to look to other people for guidance. The leaders tell us that the status quo is pretty good or maybe the best that could possibly be. So they say don't try to change it. There might be good reason for this meme, if the only alternative to the status quo was revolution, because revolutions, like wars, can be very bloody and destructive, and go way beyond where people thought they would, and do way more harm than good. But we don't have to have a violent revolution. We know revolutions are dangerous. We can have evolution. Controlled evolution. We now understand some of the principles of cultural and social evolution through the work of social scientists. People throughout the world are becoming more educated. More people than ever before in history can think for themselves. Many of us don't need leaders to tell us what to do anymore. So it is now possible, maybe for the first time in history, for us, all the people of the earth, to change ourselves, without having to rely on leaders for guidance. We can do this calmly, rationally, methodically, peacefully, from our own choice. We can easily communicate via the Internet, with anyone else in the world. We can start now. Our science is good enough now, our understanding is good enough now, that people everywhere can adopt this program easily, by understanding how it will work, and they can understand through their emotions and feelings, as well as with their reason and logic, that this program will work. They must understand it for it to work. This program must spread to some kind of majority in most countries of the world for it to work. We, all of us together, can make this happen.

Cultural reversals.

History shows that ideas can spread anywhere and everywhere. And this whole program is about ideas in people's minds. In the past, there have been great reversals in the prevailing ideas in a society, a country, or a culture, and even in all of humanity. All of humanity once lived by gathering fruits and vegetables, or hunting animals for food. Most of humanity used to believe in multiple gods. Today, most of humanity believes in one God. Slavery was widespread in the world, and it was fundamental to economic progress, from ancient times until very recently in the 1800's. Now, it's essentially, but not completely, gone. What happened? Ideas changed. The meme which says **it's wrong for one person to own another,** spread to enough people, that governments, prodded by their people, finally made it illegal. This meme had to displace other memes. Did anyone design a program to get rid of slavery? Probably not, at least not in the sense of the program proposed here. Of course individual people and groups worked for this meme. That is, they spread it into other minds. But the process was not coordinated on a global scale. It just evolved. Nonetheless slavery has been largely ended.

Slavery was fundamental.

Slavery has existed from ancient times until very recently. In ancient Greece, at the birth of democracy, slavery continued to exist along with democracy. In the late seventeen hundreds, at the birth of the United States of America, slavery existed and continued to exist. Somehow people could believe, at the same time, that *"All men are created equal, and are endowed by their creator with certain unalienable rights, and among these are life, liberty, and the pursuit of happiness...",* and that it was OK to own slaves. Slavery was justified by holy scriptures. Slavery was supported and defended by most religions. Slave labor was fundamental to the economies of North, Central, and South America as well as Europe through the Eighteenth and most of the Nineteenth centuries. Without slavery, the development of America, Europe, and much of the rest of the world, would have been very much slower. Slavery was totally intertwined with the existing cultures. Yet in 1838 all the slaves in England's American colonies, 800,000 human beings, were peacefully freed. And in the United States, a terrible and bloody civil war, was fought over whether slavery should be contained, or be allowed to expand, and as a result of that war, 4,000,000 human beings were freed. [Davis, 2006].

Anti-slavery activism.

How did this happen? How could an institution, that had been for more than 2000 years, such a valuable and important part of world culture, so fundamental to the economic systems, of most of the world, come to an end? Ideas did it! Memes did it! Certain people did it! Certain people let certain memes take hold of them, possess them. Memes like: **all humans are children of God**; **all people are created equal**; and **all people have certain basic rights, including the rights to life and liberty**. Or simply memes like: **slavery is unjust;** and **slavery is wrong**. These people made it their mission, most often based on their religious faiths, to spread these memes, as far and wide as they could. Some devoted their lives to this process. They gave speeches. They traveled from towns, to cities, and to the countryside. They wrote newspaper articles, pamphlets, and books. They convinced other people to join them. They created anti slavery societies. They got huge numbers of people to sign anti slavery petitions, and they presented these petitions to their governments. In England, they questioned candidates for parliament about their positions on slavery. They thereby got enough members of parliament elected to pass laws to abolish slavery. In the United States, they spread the memes to enough people, to cause them to oppose the extension of slavery to new states. This led to the civil war. And Abraham Lincoln freed the slaves in the United States.

Altruistic memes.

Most of this discussion of slavery is based on my reading of the book, "*Inhuman Bondage*", by David Brion Davis. [Davis, 2006]. I respect him and other historians, and all scholars greatly, for their dedication and hard work, so that we may understand the past, and thus the present, and maybe the future. But as I read his chapters on Abolitionism, the idea of *Memes!* kept coming to mind, as he discussed historians' perplexity, at why England passed the law abolishing slavery in 1833, when it was so clearly against their very valuable economic self interest. Davis discusses how various historians struggled to find seemingly contorted economic explanations, anything besides the simple power of an idea. It's as if some scholars are uncomfortable unless they can find an explanation in terms of some grand concept like economic self interest. For example, Davis says:

"In his earlier work, having shattered the Williams tradition that antislavery succeeded because it advanced Britan's economic self interest, Drescher addressed the quite different issue of explaining the power and immense public support of abolitionism. After rejecting economic interest as a motive, he emphasized the distinctive 'political culture' that led a significant proportion of the British population to oppose slavery. By making informal comparisons with other countries, especially France, Drescher dramatized the remarkable uniqueness of the active British opposition to slavery, which cut across lines of class, party, and religion. This support, especially from the unenfranchised masses, cannot be explained by economic interest, at least in any conventional sense. Drescher argued that it depended on widespread literacy and a tradition of political consciousness and activism." --- [Davis, 2006, pages 245, 246].

There seems to be a general tendency among scholars, to seek and accept only grand explanations for human events, in terms of, for example, economics, class struggle, biology, and genetics. The socio-biologists struggled to find evolutionary explanations for altruistic behavior in some animals and humans. They have given valid genetic evolutionary explanations for some animals such as bees and ants. But there is no genetic, biological, explanation needed for altruism in humans, since all that's needed are some altruistic memes. All that's needed is that people believe in some altruistic meme. It doesn't have to be true or connected to their welfare, economics, or anything else. Of course, all memes are connected to other memes, but the connections do not have to be to any of these traditional grand concepts. In seeking only grand explanations, we can miss the truth. Small explanations, like changing memes, are not considered valid. So the historians continue to scratch their heads, about how it could possibly be, that England ended slavery in 1838, when it was so obviously against individuals', and the country's, economic interests. The simple explanation is that the abolition memes, pushed by activists to a receptive population, had a population explosion in England, but not in France.

<u>Anti-slavery meme population explosion.</u>

So the abolition of slavery was the result of a vast cultural change, in most of human cultures, that came about, by changing the memes about slavery, in enough people in England, for them to abolish slavery peacefully, and by legislation, and in the United States, to change the slavery memes, in enough people in the North, to cause the Civil War. The memes against slavery were circulating around in human cultures, at low population levels, for hundreds, or thousands, of years, until around 1800. The United States Revolutionary War, and the French Revolution, brought about a population explosion of the **liberty** meme. And then a few abolitionists, extending the application of the **liberty** meme, started a population explosion of anti-slavery memes. The process is somewhat like viruses that circulate at low levels for many years, and then mutate, have a population explosion, and cause a world wide epidemic. The anti-slavery memes didn't necessarily mutate for their population explosion, but rather they were more actively, and deliberately, spread by the abolitionists, whose anti-slavery memes were fortified by other ideas, memes, circulating in their heads, about the nobility, and perfectibility, of people. David Brion Davis says it this way:

"The abolitionists' position conveyed three fundamental convictions: (1) that since all men and women have the ability to do that which is right and just, they are therefore morally accountable for their actions; (2) that the intolerable evils of society are those that degrade the image of God in man, stunting or corrupting the individual's capacity for dignity, self control, and self respect; (3) that the goal of all reform is to free individuals from being manipulated like animals, or, as one Garrisonian put it, that the goal of abolitionism was '<u>the redemption of man from the dominion of man</u>.'" --- [Davis, 2006, page 253, emphasis in original].

Early abolitionists, like anti-war activists today, were condemned and persecuted. But they were very determined, even fanatical, for their cause, and worked tirelessly for years to spread anti-slavery memes. David Brion Davis continues:

"Like the early Protestant reformers of the sixteenth century, abolitionists were confident they had discovered and uncovered the fatal flaws of the entire social system; they were determined to clarify and reanimate an altogether different approach to self-fulfillment. It is significant that the main targets of radical reformers were precisely those forces that stunted or impeded the full development of an individual's moral capacities, as defined by the religious revivals: the violence and aggression of dueling and war; capital punishment and retributive punishment in general, which brings out the lowest, most un-Christian and bestial impulses of human nature; alcohol which dulls or extinguishes a sense of social responsibility while stimulating aggression, self-assertion, and 'animal passions'; laws and institutions that discriminate against women, depriving them of self respect and subjecting them to male violence and

sexual exploitation and degradation; above all, black slavery, the very epitome of institutionalized violence and debasement of the human spirit, treating humans as objects or animals, subject to unlimited coercion and manipulation." --- [Davis, 2006, page 255].

Women were property.

Not long ago, women were considered to be the property of their fathers, or after they were traded, or sold, to another man, to be his bride, they were considered to be his property. Women could not own property. Any money they might earn belonged to their husband. Husbands could freely beat their wives. Husbands controlled their wives lives as they could a slave. Women could not refuse sex with their husband no matter how much a drunken creep he might be. Wives needed their husband's permission to do anything in public, or even be in public. Women were essentially slaves of men. These behaviors, these memes, were firmly believed, backed up by laws and customs, by almost all governments and religions. This was the culture in the United States and in most countries as recently as 1800. Sadly, this treatment of women as objects, or property, still occurs today, in some parts of the world.

Women's struggle for freedom.

Around 1800, a very few exceptional women rebelled, at least in spirit. They worked for women's rights. They were often inspired by their religious faiths. They often worked alongside the abolitionists. They slowly brought about changes in laws and customs. But women still didn't obtain the right to vote, as a fundamental right, in the United States, until 1919, after more than 100 years of struggle. See the book *"Century of Struggle"*, by Eleanor Flexner & Ellen Fitzpatrick. [Flexner & Fitzpatrick, 1959].

Feminine subjugation memes.

In the 1950's in the United States, memes described in the book *"The Feminine Mystique"*, by Betty Friedan, [Friedan, 1963], confined women to their homes, almost as if they were prisoners, prevented most women from getting advanced degrees, or entering the professions, made them subservient to men almost as if they had been slaves. These memes were so widespread in American culture that they even severely distorted the social sciences. They prevented the development of economically valuable talents and skills in women, damaged their mental health, and that of their husbands and children. They wasted lives. But things have changed, somewhat. Betty Friedan's book examined these memes, and proposed their modification or replacement, by memes for human freedom, growth, and development.

Consciousness raising: a meme explosion.

Later in the late 60's and early 70's the memes for feminism, the memes for women's liberation, the memes for freedom for women, had a population explosion. Feminists organized themselves into activist groups. These groups successively looked at the numerous specific ways and means by which women were subjugated. The women formed consciousness raising groups. This was an amazing and powerful idea.

The women would meet many times, and for many hours, and in an egalitarian and democratic way, they would discuss, analyze, and deconstruct, the memes which were holding them down. Of course there were disagreements and conflicts, but they kept the goal of freedom and equality in mind. By this process, they decided on new memes they wanted to replace the oppressive memes. They then spread these to other women's organizations, and to the wider public, by demonstrations, marches, articles in newspapers, magazines, through their art, and of course, by the examples of their own changed behaviors. The consciousness raising sessions women activists engaged in after 1960 were their methods, their processes, for identifying the anti-woman memes, eliminating them, or changing them, identifying the new freedom memes they wanted, and implanting them firmly, deeply into their minds. Their speeches, conventions, and political actions, were their methods of spreading the process, and the memes, to the rest of the world. Of course they didn't use the word *meme* since it hadn't been invented yet, but they were doing exactly what I propose we do in the anti-war movement: identify the memes causing the harm, change or eliminate them in ourselves, and then spread the word, spread the memes, to the rest of the world. As a result, American women, and many other women around the world, are considerably more free than they were in the 1950's. Our whole culture has been changed significantly and fundamentally.

Legislation is not enough: memes must be changed in people's minds.

Both the abolition of slavery, and the women's liberation movement, had the apparent advantage, compared to our anti-war movement, of being able to focus on specific legislation as their goals. But this was also a disadvantage, because when these specific legislative goals were attained, the reformers thought the struggle was over. They were sadly mistaken. This led to the doldrums of continued practical oppression of blacks in the South, and much less than complete freedom throughout the whole United States, and for the women's liberation movement between 1920 and 1960, a backsliding into the feminine mystique. [Friedan, 1963]. Women and blacks were not truly free. The laws had been changed, but most of the anti-woman, and anti-black memes in most people's minds had not been changed at all. **There is no effective change until there is meme change in a large enough number of minds.**

Anti-war consciousness raising.

Consciousness raising for the anti-war movement might start with veterans, especially wounded veterans. These people have directly suffered the most from wars. They have been most abused. Those who have suffered the most, by being injured themselves, or by having seen the horrors of war close up, already know the injustice, and the ugliness. Veterans who have seen death, lived with death up close, smelled, and tasted death, don't need any pictures or art to convince them of the horrors of war. The families and friends of those killed or injured probably don't need much convincing either. Then all the others who may not have seen death and destruction up close, but who have nevertheless suffered and been oppressed in whatever ways: women, blacks, gays, and other minorities, are probably ready for consciousness raising about war. Actually I believe almost everybody is ready to say no to war. We all know in our hearts that there is something seriously, seriously wrong with war. After all, there is a common thread in all of these movements. It is freedom from exploitation, freedom from being used, and abused, and pushed around, by memes that are not good for people. Notice here I am not blaming the people who have the war memes. That's because these people, and most all of us, are doing the best we can with the knowledge and information we have at any point in time. People are mostly not conscious of the memes they have, and how these memes influence their behavior. So it is better to focus on the war memes, rather than the people who have them.

Other cultural revolutions.

Monarchy has been ended. Almost all present day monarchs are for decoration only. The ones that are not for decoration are tyrannies in disguise, benevolent or bloody. Some monarchies were overthrown by revolutions. Others just evolved into irrelevance. The process took several hundred to a thousand years depending on when you want to consider the start to be. If you start with the American and French Revolutions, then the process to the present took a little more than 200 years. If you want to look at the reforms in the Magna Charta as the start, then the process took 1000 years. The process is essentially complete, but not exactly. For example kings in some countries rule as tyrants. And there are still some dictators who try to pass on their authority to their sons. Representative government spread as monarchy declined. So the memes for representative governments gradually replaced the memes for authoritarian rule to the extant that, through revolution or evolution, monarchies have faded away.

Communism vanished in an historical instant.

Communism seems to have just melted away in 1989 alone. It was a complete surprise. Nobody expected it. Just a few years before, everybody in the non-communist world believed it was a serious threat that would continue indefinitely. A huge movement, a great empire, a vast culture of hundreds of millions of people changed, vanished in an historical instant. Communism, which many people once thought was inevitably the wave of the future, came and went in less than 150 years. The memes supporting communism gradually changed, weakened, and were replaced by other memes until the whole structure was unsustainable.

Current cultural revolutions or evolutions.

The feminist movement will soon assure, for the first time in human history, equal rights for half the human race, which up until very recently, has been dominated by the other half. The memes for fundamental human rights are spreading to many parts of the world. Even in existing dictatorships, at least in some cases, these memes restrain the dictators. The Internet, and cell phones, in 15 or 20 years have gone from nothing, to changing the whole world, in many, many ways, and are now changing the world in ways we will understand only at some future time. And the Internet is all about memes going round and round the world, at near the speed of light, and storing, and making available to every human, all of human knowledge. It's happening so quickly, there is no way we can appreciate what it's doing to our cultures. Cell phones, email, and the internet, are providing vast unappreciated improvements in economic productivity. There are great reductions in energy consumption because people can conduct business, research things, order things, pay for things over the Internet and have them delivered to their homes or offices in a few days. Some physical things, like paper books, magazines, and newspapers, no longer need to exist. People do not have to physically travel to buy almost anything. The information and knowledge that you can obtain in a few minutes on the Internet is much, much greater than if you had lived inside the finest library in the world twenty years ago. This is even greater productivity improvement. There are significant cultural changes due to Internet social networking, ready availability of books, music, movies, video games, and pornography. These all represent tremendous social and cultural changes, in a very short period of time. Indeed an extreme meme's eye point of view sees the Internet as having been created by memes so that they can spread themselves farther and faster. [Blackmore, 1999].

Environmental movement changed the world.

The environmental movement went from essentially nothing, to almost worldwide acceptance in 50 years. This movement was not pre-planned. The memes appeared in a few people, and spread to others, generated new memes, mutated, and brought about environmental organizations, which accelerated their spread. The environmental movement has significantly changed human behavior world wide in 50 years. The memes for the environmental movement came from the bottom up. The world leaders have been the last to get it. And many of them still don't. This proves we can make similar significant changes in the world wide attitudes toward war, in most of the world's population, without waiting for the leaders. The environmental movement spread memes world wide that significantly changed human behavior, without any conscious planning, at least in the beginning. Similarly, with conscious planning, and with much better tools, we, the anti-war movement can eliminate war.

This program goes to the source of the problem of war.

We might ask how this anti-war movement, and program, are different from other movements and programs, which propose simply to educate people, around the world, about the negative aspects of something, and which ask them to change their behaviors relating to it. Such strategies can work. But these strategies are not focused enough. The essential difference, in this program, is that we zero in on the fundamental preconditions for wars in people's minds. We go right to the fundamental, the most basic causes of war, and eliminate them. We do not just ask people to change their behavior. We show them how to do this. We show them how to identify memes that lead to war, and show them how to change these memes, using the latest knowledge from the sciences. Behavior and memes are intertwined. Change one and the other changes. The focus is on people changing their memes, since even one changed meme can have far reaching effects on many behaviors. Focusing on memes is more powerful than focusing on behaviors. A person's behavior is controlled and directed by the memes in that person's mind.

Conscious spreading of these ideas.

And this is a planned program, involving spreading these ideas, out from the existing anti-war movement, to the rest of the world. Integral to this program is enlisting social scientists, writers, scholars, teachers and anyone else to work and do research, that will support and spread this program. Essential to this program is the conscious spreading of these ideas, and the further ideas that will be developed by the social sciences, to the whole human population, just as the environmental movement's ideas are spreading to the whole human population. The program will be successful when these ideas are spread to enough people. People will come to see that these ideas can work, and then they will be willing to adopt them, and work to promote these ideas, wherever and however they can. The anti-war movement will build upon itself, as any successful movement does. Its successes will bring greater successes. The research will lead to more research. The ideas will spread to more and more people.

Program evolution.

This program will evolve and change in the future. This is to be expected. The specific methods people use to change themselves do not matter, as long as they are effective in attaining a war free world through peaceful evolution. Many thinking, feeling, sensible, people will guide this anti-war movement as it grows and evolves into the future, just as the environmental movement is now guided.

Conscious plan.

Most movements historically have not developed from much of a conscious plan. This program will be guided by conscious thought because it is all about consciously understanding our thought processes and our memes. Using the latest science, we can consciously examine our memes, and analyze how our memes and behavior interact, to produce desirable, or undesirable, results. As a movement, we can do this methodically, through application of existing social sciences, and use the results from future social science, as they are discovered and published.

Cultural engineering.

Our cultures will scientifically examine themselves, and change themselves, in order to eliminate war. We can say this is cultural engineering. This idea may be scary for some people. Culture examining itself and changing itself sounds spooky. There seems to be some sort of loop here. If our culture needs fixing, how can it fix itself? Douglas Hofstadter [1979, 2006] calls such things strange loops. But there is no need to fear. There is no paradox here. It's just that, in the past, people avoided studying some strange loops because they didn't know how to deal with them, and they sometimes did lead to paradoxes. But Kurt Godel, [Godel, 1931, 1962], and [Hofstadter, 1979, 2006], showed how useful and powerful such ideas can be. See also [Balkin, 1998]. Some may fear we shouldn't consciously mess with something as complex as our cultures, because we might mess things up. There is a fear, in some people, of applying human knowledge to new areas. It is as if it were somehow forbidden, to apply our new understandings, to explore, to go where no one has gone before. But, is it better to let our cultures drift randomly, without any thought? Our cultures change whether we like it or not. Individuals and groups, try to, and do change our cultures, for their own purposes, all the time. They probably do not think of themselves as consciously changing culture, but nevertheless people are always doing it. The idea of changing our cultures is nothing new at all. Whenever legislators make up new laws they are trying to change our cultures. Books, movies, wars, ideas, and technological advances, are always at work changing our cultures, more or less randomly, but according to their own inner memetic logics. So it does make sense to apply our thought, knowledge, and science, to this process of cultural change.

Cultural drift.

We especially should not just let our cultures drift, when we can see them heading toward catastrophes. We've let our cultures drift into war too many times. We now have the knowledge, and power, for the first time, to steer our cultures away from the whirlpools and rocks of war. The environmental movement is now consciously steering our cultures away from devastating our only home, our planet earth. It is engineering our physical environment. This anti-war movement and program can steer us away from war. We need to take the helm now.

Memes or behavior?

Most previous movements have focused on direct changes to human behavior. The anti-war movement also wants to change human behavior, the behavior that leads to war. Behavior and memes are intertwined. Previous movements have focused on changing the behavior and only incidentally on the intertwined memes. For example, when people realized that the major cause of polluted rivers was the dumping of industrial chemical waste into our rivers and streams, they immediately, sensibly, pressed for laws, to stop these practices. But the memes in the minds of the polluters were not changed. Of course, over time, these forced changes in behavior brought about some changes in the memes too. But the environmental movement, at least in the early years, did not exploit the changed memes. Some environmentalists continued to see corporations as implacable enemies even after many corporate leaders had accepted the new memes. The environmental movement focused on direct action to change behavior, and with good reason, because that was effective. The corresponding memes were only dug out later, kicking and screaming all the way. The environmental movement was able to commandeer the power of the state to force changes in the behavior of individuals. They perhaps only realized later that they were changing memes too.

The environmental movement could focus on tangible things.

The environmental movement had another advantage. They could focus on physical things rather than memes. And of course the meme concept did not exist when the environmental movement started. The environmentalists could focus on visible, or measurable, or other material, or otherwise commonly known, things, like DDT, chemicals and sewage in lakes and rivers, chemicals in the air, animals and plants becoming extinct. These are all things people could see or measure in their everyday lives, in their familiar surroundings. In the case of wars, by the time we see the tangible results, the physical destruction of buildings and infrastructure, the dead bodies, the physically and mentally wounded, coming home, it's too late. The war is well underway. The social and cultural processes, the memes, are all wound up, moving ahead, mostly unstoppable, until the warring factions have exhausted themselves. So the anti war movement must go directly to the memes, the precursors, the preconditions, in the minds of people, because there are no tangible, material, harmful things we can point people to, until it is too late. You might think people would remember past wars, but people tend to forget bad things, and who pays attention to history anymore? Wars are more or less episodic, while environmental degradation is cumulative. So the anti war movement must focus on the memes, so that the war processes can be stopped before it is too late.

Memes lead, behavior follows.

The environmental movement can clean up the world one river at a time, one country at a time, and the people living near the newly cleaned rivers and in the cleaned up countries can see and enjoy the benefits as they are brought about. But the-anti war movement cannot eliminate war piecemeal. We may not see success until we have succeeded everywhere. And for the anti-war movement, there doesn't seem to be any way to directly use laws to change the behaviors we want to change. We can't outlaw war. Who would enforce the law? Use force to eliminate the use of force? That's a contradiction. So the anti-war movement must work indirectly. It must help people change their own minds, one at a time. Help them identify war memes infecting them, and show them how to eliminate them, or change them. When the memes have been changed, the behaviors are changed also. These people will no longer support war. They will not be conned by leaders using fear laden, undiscounted, future hypotheticals. When there are enough such people throughout the world, there will be no more war.

Political leaders irrelevant.

The anti-war movement, at least in the beginning, need have nothing to do with governments. It need not involve political leaders. Of course we should hope and expect that political leaders at some point get the message too. But in the beginning they are irrelevant. Like in the environmental movement, the leaders may be the last to get the message. They will probably not try to suppress these ideas, because at first, they will see them as foolish, misguided, pie-in-the-sky. They may see them as far off in the future, possibly affecting only future wars. They will not oppose a program they see as well meaning, but utopian. Later, when the memetic logic of this program is more accepted, the leaders may come around too.

Some wars may be prevented soon.

Although I implied above that this program will have no benefits until it succeeds completely, that may not be so. As people clean up their war memes, they will become more aware of the dangers and irrationality of the war memes. They will be more aware of the tricks foolish or conniving leaders try to play on their populations, when they try to whip up war memes. This may be enough to prevent that leader, in that one country, from starting his war, even though these memes have not significantly spread outside that one country. Also if a large enough number of people in one country has cleaned out their war memes, this might be enough to prevent an escalation of hostilities with another country, even with a country where none of the people have yet cleaned out their war memes. So a war may be avoided, that otherwise would have occurred, if only one of two countries, in a possible hostile escalation, chooses not to escalate. It takes two to tangle.

A war that doesn't happen is invisible.

But a war that doesn't happen is invisible. So we probably won't see our successes, until some glorious day in the future, when we realize that, for a long time now, there have been no more wars!

Does it seem too easy?

Some of you must have some doubts. You might be thinking: How can something so small as changing a handful of memes, maybe 50, or 100, or how many? do something so big as eliminating war from human society forever? Memes may individually be small. But we are talking about changing an organized powerful set of them in most of the human population. That's not small. That's big. It's going to take a lot of work and time. It's going to take work by a large number of individual people, and organizations, around the world. But this can be done. As to the bigness of eliminating war from human society forever, yes, that's big, that's really big! And that's all the more reason to inspire everyone to work for it. And as we discussed above, similar big changes in our cultures have been brought about in the past: abolition of slavery, women's liberation, and the environmental revolution. And why wouldn't eliminating war memes work? What else is there that determines human behavior? There's the socio-biological idea that we are just animals unable to control our aggressive instincts. But that's wrong. Human history shows progressive control of our instincts by our memes. We may or may not have aggressive instincts. Even if we do have aggressive instincts, where's the proof that we can't control them? The socio-biologists take it as an article of faith, or by their implicit definition of instinct, that instincts cannot be controlled. Show me the proof that instincts cannot be controlled. Human history shows otherwise. It shows that more and more our memes are controlling our behavior. That's what memes are for!

PORTRAIT: Rest in Peace 124.2.

Chapter 4: The Environmental Movement as Model.

Cultural reversals.

As we discussed in the previous chapter, throughout history, from time to time, revolutionary or evolutionary cultural changes have occurred. Examples are some of the well known political revolutions such as the American and French Revolutions. Over a period of time the idea of rule by kings was displaced by the ideas of democracy. Slavery was largely eliminated. In many parts of the world, women are gaining equal rights with men. More recently there have been the Internet and the environmental movement.

Learn from other movements.

The anti-war movement should analyze these and other movements in detail, to see what were the driving forces, and to see how those cultural changes came about. In this way we can find lessons that can be applied to make the anti-war movement more effective.

Our shining example.

In particular we should look at the environmental movement, and take lessons from it. In 1950 there wasn't much of an environmental movement. People threw trash from car windows. Sewage and chemical by-products from manufacturing were dumped into rivers and lakes. Most everybody did not see a problem. But then a few people noticed problems. Fish were disappearing from rivers and lakes. Rachael Carson wrote the book *Silent Spring* which connected DDT to decreasing bird populations. [Carson, 1962]. Scientists began to measure the pollutants, identify sources, and propose ways to change. Harmful consequences of air and water pollution to human health were researched and publicized. A movement was begun. Ideas spread. People who loved the outdoors, wilderness, and all of nature, and others began to pay attention and urge action to reverse the damage that was now becoming obvious. Individuals were urged to take personal steps in their own lives to preserve the environment. Individuals changed their behaviors. No more throwing trash from car windows. Fewer people bought fur coats. Fewer people bought ivory. Then communities took actions. Laws were passed controlling what could be dumped into rivers and lakes. Factory smokestack emissions were controlled by law. Automobile emissions were controlled by law.

The environmental movement is a cultural revolution.

The environmental movement continues. It is by no means complete. But in large parts of the world, it has amounted to a cultural revolution. People's minds have been changed. Old ways of thinking have been eliminated. Totally new ideas have been absorbed into the minds of the vast majority of the population in industrialized countries. The meme that says our planet can be used as a trash dump by humanity is fading fast. The meme that says we can burn up all the gas, oil, and coal in the earth is following right behind. These new ideas correspond to the new actions, new behaviors that make up the environmental movement. In 1950 no one could have predicted this. The movement seems to have sprung up from nowhere, with no warning. Of course there were a few lonely voices like John Muir who got the United States national park system started in the early 1900's. But sometime after 1950 or 1960, a true mass movement began, and it has been and still is gaining momentum.

The environmental movement is community.

The environmental movement can only succeed if almost everybody participates. A single person can't do it. The ideas had to spread to most of the population. The ideas had to spread so that they became pervasive in our culture. Environmental ideas are now taught in our schools. Environmental memes will soon be in everyone. Those few people who still don't get it, those I am leaving out when I am almost always saying *"almost all"*, can't help but to go along because of all the negative vibes they get from their peers if they don't live by environmental memes. So some of them go along even if they don't agree or don't understand. The last holdouts will die out. This same pattern seems to apply to all great cultural change movements. The last holdouts die out because the new memes are absorbed by children more easily than by some older adults.

The anti-war movement like the environmental movement is based on science.

The anti-war movement can be like the environmental movement in many ways. We need people to understand the net negative costs of war. We need historians and social scientists to analyze and measure these costs and publicize them until the last skeptic is satisfied or dies of old age. Whereas the environmental movement relied mostly on physical scientists, chemists, physicists, geologists, biologists, and so on, the anti-war movement needs help from the social scientists, historians, economists, psychologists, sociologists, political scientists, anthropologists, linguists, neuroscientists. This will be the great historical opportunity for social scientists. They have always been considered second class to the physical scientists. The anti-war movement is clearly of utmost importance for the future of humanity, and if the social sciences can apply themselves, and help eliminate war as a human social cultural activity, then they will have shown, for all time, that they are relevant, have real world consequences, and are indeed indispensable for the future of humanity.

Not just science but the humanities too.

This anti-war movement is not only based on science. It also needs to appeal to our complete human nature. So we need help from the humanities. And who but the writers, poets, artists of all kinds, painters, playwrights, movie makers, video game creators, are the most expert memetic engineers? By the way, there is no divide between science and the humanities. They both serve our transcendent values: Goodness, Beauty, Justice, and Truth.

Individual actions.

Just as there were individual actions, that people could take in the environmental movement, in the anti-war movement, there are also things individual people can do, in their own lives, independent of government actions, or the actions of others, that will make a difference. People can educate themselves as to the costs of wars, in terms of material things, and lives, wasted. They can educate themselves as to how to change their own minds, and the minds of others. They can change their own behavior, removing the analogs of war, aggression and conflict, from their own lives, by adhering to the practices of non violent communication, as presented in the books by Marshall Rosenberg listed in the references section. [Rosenberg, 2005a, 2005b], or similar personal philosophies. And of course they can carry out the suggestions in this book. They can found or join anti-war organizations. And they can spread the word.

Individuals clean up local war memes.

Individuals in each country or ethnic group can join together to investigate, analyze, and publicize, the historical and cultural narratives of their nation or group. They can publicize the absurdity of present day hatreds because of something their great, great, great grandparents may or may not have done to their enemies' great, great, great grandparents. They can form movements to promote reconciliation. Maybe they can work to get each side in old disputes to bury their past hurts with all the long buried dead bodies, and get each to forgive, to apologize, to the other, on behalf of their ancestors. It may seem that an apology for the actions of long dead ancestors can have little effect on the living, but it can be a powerful way to bury old counterproductive memes.

No laws needed.

In the environmental movement there came a time for community action in the form of laws. What's the analogy for the anti-war movement as envisioned here? If we're going to have individuals identify war memes and mimetically engineer them into benign, neutral, or anti-war memes, where is there a place for laws? We do not want to, and we could not, outlaw certain speech or ideas. The meme for **free speech** is just too beautiful, and powerful, to be constrained, except in those very rare cases where some speech might be immediately harmful, as in shouting *fire* in a crowded building. Also the **free speech** meme is a powerful force for positive memetic evolution. So we do not want laws being passed to constrain speech or memes. However just as today environmentalism is taught in most schools in western countries, even elementary schools, we must teach the ideas of the anti-war movement, changing them as appropriate to each culture, and as the anti-war movement evolves, and our knowledge improves. Also at some point, the governments could be involved in sponsoring research.

No need to oppose economic interests.

The fact that governmental action is not required, in terms of laws enacted or treaties signed, provides an advantage to the anti-war movement compared to the environmental movement. The anti-war movement does not have large economic interests that must be reversed, like the economic changes required to reverse global warming. The weapons industries will fade away only after war has been eliminated for a long time. Countries will not get rid of their armies until long after the last war has been fought. All that's required, is that large enough numbers of people, realize that while a few may profit from wars, all the rest of humanity loses, suffers loss, either directly in lives and property destroyed, or indirectly in terms of taxes, and resources wasted in wars, resources that might have been used beneficially. When enough people realize this, they will no longer allow the few to benefit at the expense of everyone else. When enough people in each country realize, that only a few individuals or corporations in that country benefit from wars, at the expense of the rest of the population and corporations of that country, the majorities in that country will be much less likely to tolerate wars. All of humanity will pay the cost of reversing global warming, but only a very small number of the already wealthy will have lower profits, or have to find their profits elsewhere, when war is eliminated. And the rest of humanity, by far the vast majority, will greatly benefit, materially and spiritually, from the absence of wars.

Environmental organizations.

The environmental movement has many organizations that promote various aspects of environmentalism. As of Jan. 6, 2008, Wikipedia listed 51 international environmental organizations, 84 United States environmental organizations, 6 international anti-war organizations, and 37 United States Anti-war organizations.

Future anti-war organizations.

Many of the anti-war organizations concentrate on opposing the current war, or whatever happens to be the current war, and they do not focus on the systemic elimination of war. We need the focus on the current war, whatever it may be, not only for the hope of constraining it from growing or lasting longer, but also to draw public attention to the dangers of war in general. But we also need some long view anti-war organizations. To focus only on the current war, whatever it may be, is not enough. It is as if the anti-war movement, in focusing on the current war, is like environmentalists focusing on cleaning up a single river. This work is necessary, but much more is needed to clean up all the war memes, in all the minds in the world. These long view organizations will surely evolve from the current anti-war organizations in due time. When a large enough number of people, in any country, become aware of the costs of war, the dangers of war, and the fact that we don't have to keep having wars, the politicians will gradually come around, as they did come around to environmentalism. And in due time, it may be appropriate, to have some laws restricting some personal, and corporate behaviors, that have been proven to lead to war. But laws are not necessary. This program will work without restrictive laws. Since this program cannot depend on the use of force or laws, it is of the utmost importance that there be a well organized anti-war movement, with many diverse anti-war organizations, large and small, all intent on peacefully spreading these or similar ideas to the whole planet.

Alliance with the environmental movement.

The environmental movement and the anti-war movement should see themselves as allies and support one another. Clearly wars are severely environmentally destructive. Wars waste vast amounts of energy, of fossil fuels, both directly through use by military vehicles, trucks, tanks, airplanes, missiles, and ships, as well as indirectly through all the wasted production of bombs, missiles, vehicles, and also the waste of all the infrastructure, houses, and buildings destroyed. Wars release vast amounts of poisons and toxins into the air, water, and land. Don't forget the massive defoliation of tropical Vietnam. The Vietnamese and some United States veterans of that war are still suffering the effects of that attempted environmental destruction. A World War Three would devastate the planet and reverse all the progress the environmental movement has accomplished. Large scale use of Nuclear weapons would devastate the environment of the whole planet for thousands of years, with radioactive isotopes at levels that the animals and plants of the earth have never dealt with before. There could be a nuclear winter, and another mass extinction of life on earth, even greater than the current mass extinction caused by exploitation of the environment by expanding human populations. It would be as if the environmental movement had never happened. It all would have been for nothing. But sadly any remnants of humanity would not even be able to appreciate the loss. On the other hand, if the environmental movement does not succeed in reversing global warming, the social unrest due to the unequal abilities of rich and poor countries to cope with the effects of global warming would likely seriously increase the memes for war. Each movement needs the other. Each movement must support the other.

Many synergistic movements, all necessary.

Do we need another big movement? Don't we already have enough to do? Who has time to participate in, or money to contribute to, another movement? We have human rights movements, women's liberation movements, classic environmentalism, and now global warming. All these are important. They all need to succeed or the future of humanity is bleak. We must not think *either/or*; we must think *and*. The anti-war movement and the above movements are parts of one whole project: maintaining and improving human existence and all life on earth as an integrated whole interacting community. None can be left out. All are synergistic. They must work together and support one another. What kind of humanity will we have if one half, one gender, continues to be held back by the other? What kind of humanity will we be if humans continue to be treated unfairly, unjustly, on account of their race, ethnicity, or religion? What is our future if the natural world is exploited without limit, or if global warming so seriously messes up the world that it will look like nothing we have seen before? What if we have a World War III in this century that produces a nuclear winter? The more interdependent our social, political, economic, natural, and cultural worlds becomes, the easier it is for the whole thing to crash like a house of cards. There is no reason to believe that the vast system of interacting, evolving memes is stable. Like other complex chaotic systems, it is subject to catastrophic crashes without much notice. We need to solve all these problems.

Chapter 5: Memetic Engineering.

A futile attempt to keep memes out.

"[In 1980] Not wanting to expose its citizens to Western ideas, the Soviet authorities tried to exercise stringent control over those who would have access to fax machines. At the end of each Moscow University day, the office fax machines would be dismantled, to prevent students from using them after hours. But control of communications, an essential adjunct to control of thought, was becoming harder and harder to maintain in the face of increasingly rapid technological developments." [Gilbert, 2001, page 549].

Memes.

The idea of meme is relatively new. It was introduced by Richard Dawkins in his book *The Selfish Gene,* [Dawkins, 1976]. There are various definitions of meme. Here is a simple one:

Meme: A unit of cultural information, such as a cultural practice or idea, that is transmitted verbally or by repeated action from one mind to another.

A powerful idea.

Why are there several slightly different definitions of meme? Because it is a very powerful concept. It covers vast territories. A powerful idea can be used in many ways. Depending on our purpose, we refine the definition to suit our intentions. This is not a defect. It's an advantage. Don't be surprised that meme has different meanings in different places. Many words are like that. That's part of their power. Over time humanity will settle on various specific definitions of different types of memes.

A meme is an idea.

The definition above refers to *a unit of cultural information*. For our purposes now we can say that a meme is an idea. Consider for example sunglasses. We can say that wearing sunglasses is a unit of cultural information. Is that an idea? If it's not an idea, then there is an idea associated with it, namely the idea of wearing sunglasses. So for our purposes here and now, to keep it simple, you can think of a meme as an idea. Later we will go back to the original definition of meme in terms of information.

Memes travel and change.

When we speak of ideas as memes, we are emphasizing how they spread from person to person. Some spread easily, others not. Some change over time in a single person's mind. Sometimes a meme changes as it goes out of one person's mind and into the mind of another. Clearly sometimes the words we use do not express an idea the way we want. If the meme is traveling by being expressed in spoken words, the words may not be heard exactly correctly by the receiving person. The receiving person may have heard the words correctly but she may have different meanings for one or more of the words than the speaker had. So we see there are many ways a meme can change in going from one person to another. These examples might suggest that memes must always change in transmission. But we all know from our everyday experience, that many memes change little enough, that it makes sense to say that many people can have the same idea. And just as with electronic data communication, the reliability of data transmission can be increased arbitrarily by various redundancies. The important memes will have evolved analogous redundancies, to give the reliability necessary for their purposes.

A sea of memes.

We are awash in a vast sea of memes, most very mundane, but some with far reaching consequences. The mundane memes don't go very far. They go from one person, to one or a few other people, and no farther. The interesting memes, the big memes for our purposes, are the ones that affect large numbers of people. They provide some stability to our societies and define our cultures. For example all kinds of memes having to do with: person, property, work, money, liberty, government, law, taxes, duty, civility, games, entertainment, leisure time, health, age, self, family, friend, spouse, justice, morality, and on and on. All the important things affecting our lives have bundles of important, widespread memes associated with them.

Memes travel together.

Sometimes people speak of meme complexes. That's a group of memes that tend to go around together. The memes in a meme complex are connected to one another in some way. They might have a logical connection, or an emotional connection, or some other connection. A sentence is a collection of memes in a specific order. A sentence is also a meme. Also, a story is a collection of memes, sentences, in a specific order, and like a sentence, a story is also a meme. We can also call a meme complex an association of memes. Or we can call them a bundle of memes, or a pack of memes. Most big memes are probably actually meme complexes. Whether we speak of meme or meme complex will depend on our purpose at the time.

We can group memes to suit our purposes.

Where does one meme stop and another start? What are the boundaries of a meme? When we imagine a brick, for example, it's usually quite clear where the brick ends and other stuff starts. Is the idea of a sexy woman leaning against a shiny brand new truck one meme or two? Or is it a meme complex consisting of two memes: **sexy woman** and **shiny brand new truck**? Or maybe it's eight memes: **sexy**, **woman**, **leaning**, **against**, **shiny**, **brand**, **new**, and **truck**. Or maybe it's more than eight. It depends on our particular purpose in a particular situation how we might analyze a meme or meme complex. It's of course the same as with ideas. We are free to divide up and associate ideas as we see fit. We can call any group of ideas a single idea if we want. And we do this all the time depending on our purposes. It's the same with memes since memes are ideas. And often we can analyze what at first looks like a single meme into many memes. Don't be put off by this. It's not a defect. A mathematician, or another rigorous thinker, might say that that meme is not well defined. It's too fuzzy. All this means is that meme is not the kind of idea that those mathematicians and others are commonly used to using. But mathematicians and others have used fuzzy ideas in the past. Indeed they have invented specific methods for dealing with such ideas. They and we can learn to deal with memes also.

Memes, instincts and emotions.

Why do some memes spread far and wide and others not? Memes mostly dwell in our minds. They are intertwined with our emotions and behaviors. Humans, like other animals, have instincts. We have instincts for dealing with danger, food, sex, and other things. Our instincts are important for our survival. So, our instincts have strong emotions associated with them. Memes that can manage to get entangled with instincts have an advantage over those memes that don't because we pay a lot of attention to our instincts. We must or we wouldn't survive. The amounts of the various emotions associated with an instinct or a meme are measures of how important the instinct or meme is to us [Damasio, 2003]. So we pay a lot of attention to such memes associated with instincts or to strong emotions. We are more likely to absorb them.

Meme mobility.

How does a meme get from one person to another? For a meme to go from one person to another it must first leave the first person, travel to the second person, and then get into the mind of the second person. These are the three necessary steps in this process.

Step 1: How to leave a mind.

How and why do memes leave one person's mind in the first step? They leave the minds of advertisers because the advertisers want us to buy their products or services. Memes leave the mouths of politicians mostly because the politicians want to convince us that they, the politicians, want the same things we want, and so they thereby hope to get our support in terms of money and votes. In our everyday lives when we talk to other people, we usually want something from them. For example: *Let's have lunch*. There has to be a reason for a meme to leave a person's mind. The person has to have some reason to speak or act. That reason is a special type of meme called a **spread me** meme. A meme bundle which includes a strong **spread me** meme has an advantage over a meme bundle with a weaker **spread me** meme. A **spread me** meme in a meme bundle makes the person housing that meme bundle want to spread it to others. Without it the meme bundle goes nowhere. Many important meme bundles have strong **spread me** memes. The strength of the **spread me** meme affects how effectively a meme bundle spreads. We humans like to talk. We brag. We care about others. We like to help. We like to give advice. We're social creatures. We don't like to be alone. Some people can't resist telling others what to do. All these memes help other memes get out of our minds and on their way to the minds of others. They all may be seen as various kinds of **spread me** memes.

Meme replication.

When we speak of a meme leaving one mind, what leaves is a copy of the meme in mind 1. Usually the original meme stays in mind 1. When mind 1 makes a copy of a meme and sends the copy on its way, we say the meme was replicated. That's just a fancy word for copy. So we speak of the same meme being in multiple places just as we can say two people have the same idea.

Token memes.

Many times the meme that leaves a mind is a token or name for a larger meme that remains in the mind. If I say the word *automobile* and you hear it, the whole **automobile** meme does not move from my mind to your mind. Only the word *automobile* travels from my mind to yours. You already have a version of the **automobile** meme in your mind.

Step 2: Travel outside of minds.

The traveling from one person to a second person is the second step in the three step process of meme transmission. The number of ways this can happen has been growing exponentially through history. In the ancient past, the only way for a meme to get from person 1 to person 2 directly, was for the two people to be close enough that person 2 could hear, and understand, person 1's speech. Or person 2 could observe person 1's behavior, and get the meme that way. Person 2 might see person 1 wearing a necklace and decide he wants one too. So in this case the meme went from person 1 to person 2 without any words involved. Of course a meme could travel through intermediaries. It could have gone from person 1 to person 3 and then from person 3 to person 2. But to go a great distance this way it might take years. After writing was invented, a king could send a messenger with a letter on a horse. So the king of England could get memes to his subsidiary nobles in the farthest places in the country in some number of days. In those days it took some time to organize a war. Books, and later newspapers and magazines, provided other ways for memes to travel. These were the first mass media. Railroads were faster than horses. The telegraph was even faster. The telephone allowed conversations between two people separated by great distances. Radio could cross oceans. Now we have mass media: movies, radio, and television. These allow mass transmission of memes from the elites to the masses. The cell phone and the Internet allow essentially free communication between any two individuals on the planet. So now there are many more ways, and they are very accurate, for memes to travel the space between people.

Writing allows memes to travel through time accurately. The sad state of the few remaining cultures that are transmitted orally says a lot about the effectiveness and accuracy of technological meme time travel.

Most speech, most letters, the telegraph, and the telephone transmit memes from one person to one other person. Books, especially after the invention of printing presses, newspapers, magazines, radio, movies, television transmit memes from one person to many other people. Many,

many copies of one person's memes can be made. Some speech and some letters could transmit memes from one person to a small number of other people. The Internet is both one to many and one to one. With movies, television, and videos on the Internet memes can easily be transmitted through observed behavior, that is, visually, as well as by spoken or written words. So with modern mass media, one person's memes can be simultaneously transmitted to millions of other people, and the modes of transmission are both via words and images. And sounds, for example, music and actual speech.

<u>Step 3: Getting into another mind.</u>

How about the third step in meme travel? What are the circumstances by which memes enter minds and are accepted and incorporated or are refused entry? The receiving mind already has many memes in it. The memes residing in a mind are already more or less compatible in one or more senses. They are not necessarily logically compatible. It is a very rare person who does not harbor contradictory memes. Physicists who simultaneously host the meme complex for General Relativity and the meme complex for Quantum Mechanics are harboring logically contradictory memes. Mathematicians, before calculus was cleaned up in the 19th century, hosted logically contradictory memes, because calculus, as they understood it at the time, led to many obvious contradictions. Yet they continued to believe in and use calculus. Often emotional compatibility is important for sets of memes in a single mind, but not a requirement. So for a mind to accept a new meme, it must somehow fit in with the memes already there. We are only recently beginning to understand what *fit in* means. So minds have some kind of filtering processes, compatibility checking, involving thinking and emotions, and other factors that determine whether a new meme is accepted or not. [Lakoff, 2008], [Feldman, 2006].

<u>Memes can slip in unnoticed.</u>

Sometimes meme 1 may enter a mind easily because it readily fits in with the memes already there. If meme 2 is somehow associated with meme 1, meme 2 can slip in maybe unnoticed, even though meme 2 does not fit well. The association can be logical. If meme 2 is a logical consequence of meme 1, since most humans are often rational, meme 2 can often enter since it is a logical consequence of meme 1. If meme 2 is an immediate logical consequence of meme 1, it is more likely to gain entry than if it is a distant logical consequence of meme 1. Any other association besides logical can also work. For example if the words expressing meme 1 and meme 2 are similar in spelling, or sound similar, even if the meanings are quite different, meme 2 may slip in along with meme 1. It has even been shown that when people are presented with memes of the form "not X" and later asked to remember, as time passes, they are more and more likely to remember the meme "X" instead of the meme "not X" which was presented to them. So a meme can bring along its negation! All the association mechanisms of poetry, literature, and other art, can and do work to slip in memes! Psychologists have discovered many methods to increase the chances that memes can get in. Subliminal images bias people toward the memes in the subliminal image. [Westen, 2007].

<u>Trojan horse memes.</u>

> *Once upon a time some Greeks were attacking the city of Troy, and were not having much success. They could not get through the walls protecting the city. So, the story goes, they built a huge wooden horse that was hollow inside. They hid a number of their armed soldiers inside the hollow horse. They pulled the wooden horse up close to the city gates. Then they got into their boats and sailed off. The Trojans, seeing the wooden horse and that the Greeks had sailed off, were naturally curious, and maybe thought the horse was a gift. So they brought it inside their city. That night the Greek soldiers came out of the horse and fought the Trojans, and opened the gates for the rest of the Greeks who had returned. In this way, the Greeks defeated Troy.*

The Trojan horse story is a good metaphor for how unwanted memes can be slipped into your mind unnoticed by you.

Sometimes a meme complex, or bundle, spreads more easily, if the bundle contains one or more memes associated with an instinct. Consider a television commercial spreading the meme **a sexy woman leaning against a shiny brand new truck**. A person seeing this commercial, is likely to pay more attention to this commercial, than to one containing only **a shiny brand new truck**. So he's more likely to let the whole bundle into his mind. Several days later, long after the commercial is gone from his conscious mind, he is wondering why he is thinking about buying a new truck, when he has a fine two year old truck in his driveway, still being paid for. Maybe the commercial barely went into his conscious mind. Maybe it bypassed his consciousness completely. It doesn't matter whether it went through his consciousness or not. What matters is that, although the attractiveness of the woman, leaning on the truck, is what caught his interest, the whole bundle got in, and it made him want a new truck. And he has no idea why he wants a new truck. Our interest in sex is used over and over in commercials. The most important point of this simple example is that memes can get into our minds totally independent of their truth or usefulness to us. They are almost always complex memes, bundles of memes. When a bundle of memes comes into our minds, only some of the individual memes may be of interest to us, and we often are unaware of many of the others in the bundle. But the whole bundle gets through. In this, and other ways, the ability of memes to spread widely, can have little or nothing to do with their truth or usefulness.

<u>Fear, anger, and excitement can help memes slip in.</u>

Just as sex sells trucks, soft drinks, clothes, and cigarettes, fear, anger, and excitement, sell wars. Like all animals, we have an instinct for self preservation when faced with an immediate danger. Most animals either fight or run away when another animal threatens them. This is a very primitive and obviously very important instinct. Animals that happened to have a weak version of this instinct were less likely to survive than others. So it's not at all surprising that we have this very strong instinct. It's important, not only because it was necessary for our ancestors' survival, but also because we need it in our daily lives today. We need to pay attention when we are driving for hazardous road conditions as well as unexpected actions by other drivers. We need to avoid other dangers in our physical environments. There are dangers in our social environments also. Sometimes our interests conflict with other people's interests. Some people are sometimes hostile, deceitful, or criminal. So we are very sensitive to dangers and threats. We pay special attention to anything that looks like it might be dangerous or threatening. So just as sex got the man's attention to sneak in the meme for buying a truck, so fear, anger, excitement, and other strong emotions associated with dangers and threats, can get our attention and help other memes get into our minds. Some commercials and products and whole institutions are based directly on fear. For example: insurance, savings, locks, gated communities, more police, armies, tougher laws, news.

Fear sells war.

How do fear and other emotions sell war? Alarmist, paranoid, or just conniving political leaders, assert that some thing or some action, by another country, is a danger or threat to us. The threat is some action that will cause harm, that will supposedly happen to us, and is almost always far off in the future, and dependent on quite a number of other things happening first. So these make the actual occurrence of the harm very uncertain. So this threat is in a bundle of memes. One of the memes in the bundle is the **danger** meme. That gets our attention. Another is a meme for the actual harm that supposedly will happen to us. Other memes in the package are memes for all the other things that must happen, before the harm to us actually occurs. These memes usually come in the form of a story. What the **fear** or **danger** memes in the story do, is to get us so agitated, that we gloss over all the other, uncertain things that must happen, before the supposed harm actually befalls us. The **fear** or **danger** memes let the whole bundle, the whole story, into our minds, without any critical examination, which might have revealed its implausibility, or absurdity, or alternative possibilities, or alternative actions that we might take, besides the war that our leader is proposing. The **fear** or **danger** memes can distract our meme filters. Of course a similar scenario may be playing out in the other country, directed by its alarmist, paranoid, or simply conniving, leader.

Education plants memes in minds.

There are many other ways to get memes into people's minds. The informal, and formal, education of our children, from birth through adulthood, is a deliberate spreading of memes, from us into our children. Aaron Lynch discusses this particular mode of meme transmission and how it affects the relative frequency of memes from one human generation to another in his book, "*Thought Contagion*". [Lynch, 1996].

Ideal meme bundle.

An ideal meme bundle would include one or more memes to help it get out of a mind, and one or more memes to help it get into other minds. It might also have some memes that help in the transmission from person 1 to person 2. For example the bundle might contain the meme **talk loud**. Or a book, through the way it looks, maybe with gold lettering on the cover, might be expressing the meme: **I'm special, take good care of me**. This would be to influence the people who only handle the book, and not particularly those who wrote it, or those who will read it. So that meme, part of the bundle that is the book, helps preserve the meme bundle, when it is not in some mind, that is, while it is traveling between minds, through space or time. The point here is that there can be many different memes in a meme bundle that help improve each of the three steps in meme transmission: Leaving mind 1, traveling via some medium, and getting into mind 2.

Good for people or good for memes?

When we speak of an ideal meme bundle, in what sense is it ideal? It's ideal in that it's good at spreading. A good or ideal meme bundle can be dangerous, or harmful, to our human interests. A good meme bundle may have nothing to do with truth or usefulness.

Behavior.

We could also talk about how some memes in a meme bundle facilitate, or hinder, the behavior of the person whose mind contains that meme bundle. A meme that is tightly connected to strong emotions is likely to be most effective in affecting behavior, since the strengths of the emotions associated with a meme, are indications of that meme's importance to us.

Meme's point of view.

When we talk about good memes, meaning memes that are good at spreading, we might take a next step that is called *the meme's point of view*. Of course, a meme does not have a point of view. It does not see. It does not think. It's not conscious. It's not alive. It does not have intentions. It cannot want anything. It's just an idea, or bundle of ideas, that often manages to get from one mind into another. Those who look at things from *the meme's point of view,* are using a kind of shorthand, so they can use fewer words, when talking about memes. They talk as if memes want to spread, want to survive. This can provide a useful perspective. But at first this *meme's point of view* can be confusing. If it is confusing, then to really understand what is being said, we have to translate these *meme point of view* statements back into the actual details of how memes work. The *meme's point of view* is a short cut which is often useful. This is a kind of higher level view of memes, which can provide insights not easily obtained, if we restrict ourselves to only lower level discussions. This *meme's point of view* is, or is related to, what philosopher Daniel C. Dennett calls the intentional stance. [Dennett, 1989].

Memes and names.

Most of the time, when two people are communicating, they are not transferring complete memes for complicated things. Rather they are transferring memes for just the names of those things. If I say *automobile* to you, and you hear it, and imagine an automobile in your mind, I did not transfer a copy of my **automobile** meme to you. You already had an **automobile** meme in your mind. You also had the meme for the word *automobile* in your mind, and that meme, for the word *automobile,* was associated with, or was a part of, your **automobile** meme. That's how you were able to call up to your consciousness, your **automobile** meme, when you heard me say *automobile*. We probably do not need to think about these distinctions for the purposes of this book, except that, at least one of the references, [Aunger, 2002], seems to be confused on this point, and it leads him to much difficulty. Yes there is no way the word *automobile* can contain all the information in my meme for **automobile**. But it doesn't have to, as the above example showed. When we communicate with others, most of the time, we are only exchanging names, or tokens, corresponding to memes, not the whole memes themselves, because both parties to the communication already have memes corresponding to the words they are using. A new meme may actually be transmitted when one speaker combines words into a sentence or story expressing a thought, a meme, that his listener does not already have. Notice also that my **automobile** meme, and your **automobile** meme, are not identical. Maybe you know how to repair automobiles, whereas I know nothing about that. So our **automobile** memes are different. But our two **automobile** memes do not have to be identical for us to communicate. We both can talk about automobiles meaningfully, unless we are talking about automobile repair, in which case you will have to educate me by transferring a lot of information, memes, to me about automobile repair, through speech or otherwise. This and related matters about memes are discussed in more detail in Chapter 9.

Memes in other contexts.

Since ideas are memes, it's not surprising that we can find many discussions by others which can be interpreted as really about memes. Some of these are also higher level views of memes. Below are a few examples.

Corporate spirits are memes.

Walter Wink, in his book, *"The Powers That Be"*, said:

"There is a growing recognition, even among secular thinkers, of the spiritual dimension of corporate entities. Terence Deal, for example, has written a text for businesses entitled Corporate Cultures, and other analysts have discussed the importance of a business's symbolic system and mission as clues to enhancing its efficiency. The corporate spirits of IBM and General Electric are palpably real and strikingly different, as are the national spirits of the United States and Canada. What distinguishes the notion of the angel of an institution is the Bible's emphasis on

vocation. The angel of a corporate entity is not simply the sum total of all it is, but also bears the message of what it ought to be." --- [Wink, 1998, page 29].

What is the spirit of a corporate entity but its collection of memes?

Myths are meme complexes.

In "*American Myth and the Legacy of Vietnam*", John Hellmann, [Hellmann 1986], discusses myths expressed in various Vietnam War literature. What are myths but meme complexes, stories, narratives?

Memories are memes.

War and Memory in the Twentieth Century, edited by Martin Evans and Ken Lunn, [Evans & Lunn, 1997], examines memories, recorded in holocaust and war crimes trials, oral testimonies, museums, war monuments, film, and popular memory. These memories are nothing but memes surviving from the wars, the evolutionary descendants of the war memes that existed during the wars.

Memes embodied.

The books by Lakoff, Lakoff and Johnson, Feldman, and Damasio listed in the reference section explain in detail how memes may be stored, connected, and organized, embodied in the brain in terms of frames, schemas, metaphors, narratives, associations, and sensory maps, and how they control behavior.

Memes can be implanted by force.

As some of the examples discussed above suggest, there are people who want to implant memes into your mind that you may not want. Among these people are advertisers, politicians, tyrants, dictators, secret police, regular police in some countries, and various ideologues. The methods of implanting memes discussed so far are relatively benign. There are less benign ways. Some of these ways involve doing serious mental, and even physical, violence to the target individuals. These methods have been thoroughly discussed by William Sargant in his book "*Battle for the Mind*", [Sargant, 1957]. [See also the KUBARK CIA Torture Manual. Just Google it.] All these methods rely on some kind of degradation of the brain functioning of the target individual. These include manipulation and intensification of stimuli, such as sound and light, heat, cold, and pain; prolonged isolation from human contact, and other methods of torture. Many different drugs may be applied. The target person may be deprived of sleep. The target may be debilitated, by not being given enough food, even to the extent of serious weight loss, and by forced physical activity. These methods applied singly or in combination, if continued long enough, will break down anyone. The victim's mental functioning becomes so degraded that in the simplest terms, their thinking is totally disrupted. The meme filters they had in place don't work any more. Their minds are open to suggestion. New memes can be implanted. The manipulator, the interrogator, or the torturer, can now implant any memes they may want.

Post traumatic stress.

Anything that disrupts normal brain functioning will work. William Sargant was a medical doctor in WW II England. He and other doctors treated soldiers who suffered from mental traumas. They suffered from repeating horrible thoughts and feelings implanted in their minds by all the death and destruction of war that they had experienced. The experience of war had implanted the horrible memes deeply in their minds. In order to remove them, the doctors would disrupt their brain activity again, by applying various drugs or chemicals. One chemical they used was insulin. Too much insulin leads to confusion, fainting, coma and finally death. The doctors applied just enough insulin to get the soldier almost to the point of coma. Insulin decreases the blood sugar, glucose. Brain cells need glucose to work correctly. So by carefully adjusting the insulin, the doctors could maintain the soldier's brain at just the right level of degradation. In this state of decreased brain functioning the doctors would lead the soldier to relive the horrible experience, or some other similar experience, and suggest that it was all over now, gone from his mind. Often this was enough to eliminate the horrible recurring thoughts from the soldier's mind.

Decreased brain functioning.

This suggests why many of the other methods used by various manipulators work as well. Food and sleep deprivation, excessive stimulation, like louder and louder music, drums, voodoo, and other dancing, continued to exhaustion, debilitating interrogation, with heightened fear and anger, can all result in decreased glucose or other necessary nutrients in the blood. Then the brain cells cannot work properly. Then meme filters don't work, and the target person is open to suggestions … any suggestions. New memes can be implanted.

Milder methods also work.

William Sargant, [1957], discussed extreme methods, at that time called brainwashing. This word was used probably because these extreme methods were often used to wipe out virtually all memes that defined the personality of the target individual. It is important to realize that these methods do not have to go that far. The same methods may be applied more lightly. Manipulators often have no need to, and do not want to, wipe away all of a person's defining memes. They only want to change one or a few memes, or maybe implant some relatively benign meme, such as **buy a new truck**. Even so, the methods are essentially the same. Your meme filters have to be temporarily weakened or bypassed. Applied with less force, the above methods can still be effective. A leader who wants to convince his population to support his pet war does not want to wipe away all their memes. He just wants to implant, or stir up, a few war memes. He and his supporters can do this by arousing fear, anxiety, anger; stir up glorious patriotism, and racism; instill national euphoria with praise, music, marches, rallies, parades; arouse anger by demonizing opponents; and they can use the mass media to repeat, repeat, repeat. These may not reduce blood glucose levels to near coma levels, but the emotions aroused may be enough to engender confusion and weaken the correct functioning of some of the people's meme filters, enough to slip in their war memes. Even heavy or too fast breathing, called hyperventilation, brought on by too much excitement or stress, can cause lightheadedness, confusion, and fainting because of reduced blood flow to the brain. So the brain is not working right. Defensive meme filters are down. Dangerous, unwanted memes can enter.

Counter moderate force meme pushing.

So, to counter moderate force meme pushing, do the following. Avoid excited crowds, rallies, patriotic speeches, patriotic music, and flag waving. Avoid similar things in the mass media. Keep in good health. Don't be too thin. Get enough sleep. Be cautious with drugs and chemicals. Don't work, play, or dance to exhaustion. If you should feel yourself becoming confused or lightheaded while listening to someone, in person or via media, immediately stop listening. Relax. Maybe get something to eat. Take a detached view of your situation. Think about something else and immediately turn off the TV or radio or leave the movie or leave the presence of the speaker.

Fear, anger, crazy, stupid, and contradictory memes.

But many memes are pushed more subtly. In commercials, most political speeches, newspapers, magazines, most mass media, the meme pushing does not rise to the level of causing noticeable mental confusion in the target audience members. Instead the techniques involve a lot of repetition. They include arousing fear of far off, hypothetical, possibilities by repeating fear mongering stories. They may involve demonizing those who disagree, which can increase anxiety, fear, and anger. Including crazy, stupid, and contradictory elements in the meme bundle can distract the target person from the real meme being pushed. The stupid commercials are mostly using this kind of distraction. While you are trying to make sense of the stupid and conflicting parts of the commercial, the memes for the product being pushed can enter your brain unexamined. The bottom line is still the same as the other methods: they try to weaken or go around your meme filters.

Your meme filters.

One way to counter the moderate and subtle methods used to sell war is to follow the program of this book. Identify and clean out your war memes methodically once and for all. By this process you have taught your meme filters to be alert, especially sensitive to these particular war memes. Then your meme filters will be stronger, at least in regards to war memes. Your mental environment will be much less accommodating to war memes.

How to change, replace or eliminate a meme in your mind.

We talked about how to keep out memes you don't want. But the program of this book involves removing memes you already have but that you don't want. How do we do that? Do we have to use the nasty methods discussed above? No we do not.

Implantation of memes via education.

Most of us get most of our most important memes from our parents and early education. We also get memes from later education and from our ordinary interactions with other people and the world. When we are children, you might say our memes are forced on us, since as children we are totally under the influence and control of our parents and other adults. We have no choice. We learn what our parents and other adults teach us directly but we also acquire memes from observation of their behavior. The force our teachers use is usually benign. (But for an alternate view of childhood education, see [Firestone, 1970].) Unlike most other animals, we are not born with most of what we need to know already wired into our brains. Without all that childhood education, we would not be complete humans. Humans are in a different category from other animals. This implantation of memes via education, this implantation of our basic culture, gives us huge amounts of knowledge acquired by our ancestors long ago, all passed onto, and into us, via the memes in our parents, other teachers, and books, etc. This much knowledge most likely could not have been wired into us by genetic evolution. Our childhood implantation of memes occurs mostly by repetition. We are motivated by rewards and praise and generally by our desire to do as our parents and teachers want. As we pass into adolescence we get many of our memes from our group. We still get some through formal education. As adults we get new memes from our friends and associates, maybe from further formal education, and from the media. Most of us most of the time get and have gotten our memes through these benign methods.

Plant new memes carefully.

J. M. Balkin, in his book "*Cultural Software*", wrote:

"*...we think about what we are feeling, consider what we believe, question our own motives, and compare our views with those of others. We do all these things with the goal of trying to figure out how to think about the social world and how our thought might be improved.*" --- [Balkin, 1998, page 135].

And when we have become adolescents, or adults, and we want to change some memes we have, to learn something new, we can generally do it using the same methods we used when we got them in the first place. We think. We ruminate. That is we go over some idea or ideas in our mind, compare them to our current ideas, compare them to the proposed new ideas, and after some consideration, decide which ideas we want, or which ideas we believe to be true or useful. We may repeat this process several times on different occasions, and in different ways until the new idea or ideas have *taken hold*. *Taken hold* means that we have made many connections between the new ideas and the other memes in our mind. These connections are logical, emotional, and metaphorical, and maybe other kinds of connections. [Lakoff, 2008], [Lakoff and Johnson, 1980], [Feldman, 2006]. We have established firm connections between the new ideas and our feelings. We have planted new memes carefully, and they have taken root. We feel good to have the new ideas. We feel we understand things better. We are pleased.

Calm determination and powerful feelings.

So we change a war meme, or remove it, and maybe replace it, using the same methods we ordinarily use when we learn new things. We think and consider and see if the new meme will fit in logically and emotionally with our other existing memes. We may do this calmly, coolly, and rationally. Or we may recall, or stir up, some of the emotions and feelings in ourselves, that we think will motivate us, and help us change, such as grief, sadness, or anger, on account of the loss and horrors of war. Nobody can live by logic and reason alone. It is a serious mistake to think that. We only do something when we have a reason to change, a motivation, something to move us. And motivation is some emotion and the feeling caused by it. [Damasio, 2003]. Even if we are doing this calmly, coolly, and rationally, there is still some emotion and feeling somewhere behind it. A calm determination previously fortified by strong emotion is most powerful. Those unable to experience emotion, through disease, or injury to the brain, are unable to make decisions. [Damasio, 2003]. We need both thought and feeling. And we take as much time as is necessary.

Strong anti-war emotions.

The fact that we need emotion to change is one reason that this book is not completely dispassionate. In the process of writing this book, much of my own grief, sadness, and anger at the absurdity of war, was often expressed. Some of this surely shows through from time to time. Sometimes I tone it down a bit. But other times, I've just let it all come out, partly for my own motivation, but also because I realize that you need this too. You need to experience strong anti-war emotions and feelings if you are going to be able to change yourself.

A vast evolving system.

The memes, which make up our cultures, can be viewed as a vast system of evolving entities, spreading themselves, and changing, evolving according to their own logic, which is not our logic. We are only temporary receptacles for them. They also travel through our artifacts: our books, other writings, computers, communications networks, our buildings, monuments, through everything we have made. This system has been evolving and growing since some time in our past, probably before we developed speech. Memes have modified the genetic evolution of our bodies and brains for their purposes. [Blackmore, 1999]. They evolve much faster than genetic evolution ever could. Their growth and evolution is accelerating. This system is the culture of the planet. We are just now beginning to understand this system, these memes. The sciences of psychology, linguistics, and neuroscience, daily are adding to our knowledge of how memes operate in us, in our brains. History, sociology, political science and all the other social sciences, and the humanities, are daily adding to our knowledge of how memes operate between and among us, in our cultures. But our memes are us. Our memes are our cultures. They come from us. Their function in us is to allow us to survive, succeed, and grow, in the physical world, and our culture, and to become better at surviving, succeeding, and growing, as they evolve in us, our artifacts, and our culture. We no longer need to view this vast system of memes, our world culture, as something above and beyond us, as beyond our understanding, as a system operating totally independent of us. The more we understand these memes and all their interactions, the more we will be able to direct and control them. We can start now with the war memes. If we do this, we and our culture may last some time into the future. We can do this. Let's do it.

Naif al-Mutawa, quoted by Associated Press writer Diana Elias, in an AP article titled "*In pop culture, new heroes emerge in Arab world*", from 16 FEB 09 said:

"*I really think that we limit ourselves with this catastrophic thinking that the world is controlled by others and there is nothing we can do. I think this is rubbish.*"

And [Balkin, 1998, page 293], says:

"*I noted earlier that we human beings exist in a great tide of informational evolution. Yet our participation in the tide of cultural evolution does not mean that we lack agency. Our cultural software surely affects our behavior; our actions always have unintended consequences. But it is a far cry from recognizing this to inferring that we are mere instruments of memetic evolution. We must reject a simplistic either/or view which insists that either we are in full control of the development of our memes or they are in full control of us.*"

PORTRAIT: Rest in Peace 9.1R1.

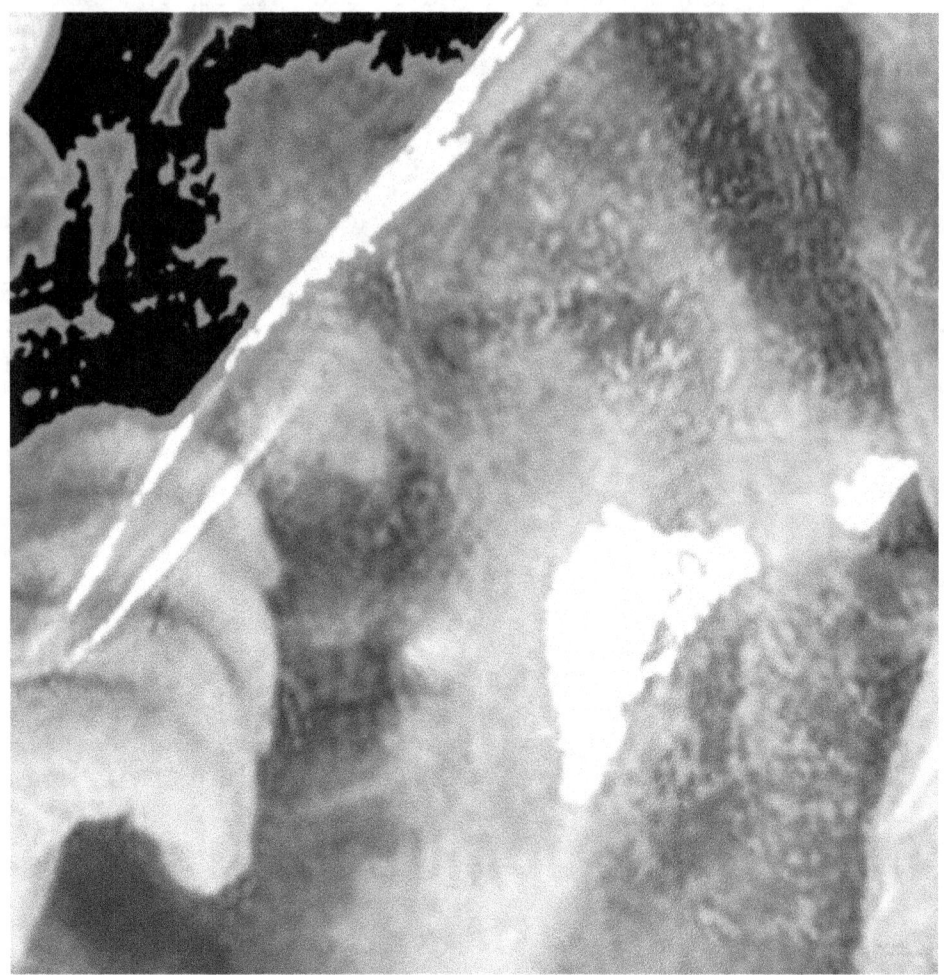

Chapter 6: Deconstruction of War Memes.

<u>The core of the program.</u>

Our intent here is to list some war memes and deconstruct them, and discuss how to deal with them. This is the heart of the program. This list is not exhaustive. I hope this analysis will inspire others to analyze these war memes further, or maybe even completely differently. Surely other people will have many insights. I also hope it will inspire others to identify and analyze other war memes. All that's needed is to be able to think about the meanings and associations of words, ideas, and behaviors, and see where these lead, maybe with some help from modern science. Our intent in this chapter is to go to the root of the problem of war, the war memes that presently infect the minds of so many people. We identify them, analyze them, and develop strategies, to mimetically engineer them, into harmless or less harmful memes, or root them out completely.

<u>Our way of thinking.</u>

This process of examining and changing our war memes can be framed in more old fashioned terms as examining, and changing, some of our old ways of thinking. What is a *way of thinking*? It's the kind of thinking most of us do every day. It's thinking based on our sets of assumptions, memes, about people, and the world, that we have had for a long time. We may not be aware that we have such assumptions. But we do. Consider just as an example, the two related, but different, assumptions: 1) Most people can be trusted most of the time. 2) Never trust anyone unless you know them really well. Some people go through life as if they believed statement 1). Others as if they believed statement 2). Generally people are not aware that they have such basic assumptions. There are many other basic assumptions about all sorts of things that people have and are generally unaware that they have them. These kinds of assumptions are what determine a person's *way of thinking*. Some of the war memes we will examine are, or come close to being, these kinds of assumptions. Since we have probably had our *way of thinking* assumptions for a long time, and since they are buried deep in our minds, it will require some work on our part, to examine and change those we want to change. And it will require vigilance to spot future war memes as they evolve. But we can do this.

"It is not true that we cannot and do not change our ways of thinking by thinking about our own thought." --- [Balkin, 1998, page 136].

<u>Your choices.</u>

In the extreme, you have two choices: 1) You can let the memes that guide your life be completely determined by other people, your parents, your teachers, your friends, your whole society and culture, or 2) You can look at some of the memes in your own mind, evaluate them to see how well they are guiding your life, and your society, and culture, and change some of them, if you want to. Most of your memes you will not want to change. After all, they have served you at least fairly well up to now. You have to have had a certain success in dealing with the world or you wouldn't be reading this book right now. And you must have been moved at least a little by the negativities of war, or again you would not be reading this book. If you choose 1), you may as well put this book down now and wait to see what everybody else does. If you choose 2), continue reading.

<u>Take your time.</u>

You should take as much time as you need to do this. This program is for the long term. We may not be able to affect the current war, whatever it may be, if there is one going on, when you read this. The purpose of this program is to help you make conscious, methodical, systematic, changes to your war memes, and have these changes stay with you, for the rest of your life. It is much more important that you be satisfied, and comfortable, with what you are doing, and completely understand what you are doing, rather than trying to rush. If you are going to change deeply buried memes, long held beliefs, it may take some time.

<u>Whatever works.</u>

The memes in a person's mind are interconnected. Many memes are unconscious. When you try to change one, you will also have to change others. The process of eliminating, or changing, your war memes, has to be a gradual process. The memes discussed below are a good beginning. They are discussed in no particular order. I use various styles and methods of analysis to emphasize that there are many ways to do this. Whatever works to understand war memes is what counts. So let's do it.

The idea that war is useful.

One of the most important war memes is the idea that **war is useful**. This is the idea that war can bring some benefit. We have already discussed this. If you do not believe by this point that war is always a net loss to humanity, and war is almost always a net loss to each group engaging in war, and that war is a danger to every person on this planet, then you need to do some more reading. Start with the book *The Three Trillion Dollar War* by Joseph E. Stiglitz and Linda J. Bilmes. [Stiglitz & Bilmes, 2008]. Then read a history of the twentieth century such as [Gilbert, 2001]. Many people, especially leaders of nations, have this meme. Clearly it is a war meme. But today many people, especially historians, social scientists, political scientists, and economists, understand that war is not useful. In the future, as more attention is paid to objective scientific research, even leaders will reject this meme. This is a powerful, widespread meme and there is still a lot of work to do to get rid of it. But it's tame compared to the next war meme.

There will always be war. Human nature is unchangeable.

<u>Fatalistic impotence.</u>

One of the greatest obstacles to eliminating war, is the almost universal belief, that it cannot be done. It has often been said, and many people still believe, that there have always been wars, and **there always will be wars**. In part 6 of "*The War*", a film by Ken Burns, one of the United States soldiers who fought in World War II said: ***There will always be***

war. He also said: *There will always be evil in the world,* because humans are aggressive. Pick someone at random and start a conversation about war. There is a high chance you will hear this meme expressed. Most people have this meme. This meme, **there will always be war,** often is associated with the idea that human nature is biologically, genetically determined by instincts. People say we are aggressive, and vicious, by nature, and there is nothing that can be done to change our nature. In that view, we're not much better than animals. We're inherently flawed, bad, evil, or partly so. It's a very pessimistic, fatalistic, defeatist view of our situation. It says whatever was, always will be. We can't change. No use trying. As in the past, so it will be in the future, to the end of time. We are doomed to repeat the past. So since no matter how far back in human history we go, we find wars, so in the future also, **there will always be wars**. It says wars are inevitable. This then is clearly a war meme, because from the very outset, it gives up on trying to change.

Cultures guide instincts.

This view of fixed human nature, driven by animal instincts, is contradicted by more recent scientific views of human nature. Human nature is influenced by our biological nature, but not fixed by it, not determined by it. Our cultures guide and constrain our biological instincts. Human nature is not equal to biological nature. Our behavior is not determined only by our instincts. The memes of our culture, and our instincts, determine who we are. Our biology may be essentially fixed, but our memes and culture are not fixed. They evolve rapidly, much faster than biological evolution. Actually our memes have changed our biology too, through modern medical science.

The memes took over.

The idea that human nature is fixed by biological genetic evolution, is a mistake. It ignores the fact that there have been at least two evolutions, genetic and memetic. [Dennett, 1991, 1995]. Memetic evolution has produced our current culture. It has changed us, in a few thousand years, from a species which wandered around on foot, gathering food wherever we could find it, to a species capable of traveling to another planet, and capable of destroying ourselves, and maybe all life on earth, with nuclear weapons. Our memes have made this change, not our genes. The genes provided the substrate, the body and brain, on, or in which, our memes could evolve and thrive. With the same brains and bodies our culture might have been quite different. The genes built our bodies and brains, and then the memes took over and built our cultures. Our memes have influenced how our brains evolved also.

Human nature is not fixed.

We have nearly learned to do without slavery. It was once considered human nature to own other human beings. No longer. It was once considered human nature that women were to be totally dominated by their husbands. We have changed. Our societies and cultures are always changing. In 1950 no one would have believed, that by 2000, we would have a mass environmental movement. No one would have believed, that something called global warming, would change the behavior of individuals, and whole nations. We aren't nearly as cruel as our ancestors were, at least in our individual relations. Our instincts for sex have been constrained, in one way or another, by our cultures for thousands of years. Some of us are trying to control our instincts for food. With scientific advances, soon everyone may be able to control their food instincts. History and science prove human nature is not fixed.

Standard inductive inference.

Why do we still have this meme? It's not entirely irrational. After all, history apparently shows that there have **always been wars**. History mostly focuses on wars. If there were long periods of no wars in the past, history probably wouldn't find that period interesting. It would maybe say nothing much happened during that time. But given the general assumption that there have **always been wars** in the past, by standard inductive inference, we would assume there will continue to be wars in the future. We also have this meme because the idea that human nature is not fixed, but rather is evolving rapidly through memetic evolution, is a relatively new idea.

This meme wants us to be demoralized.

Also we have become demoralized, because past attempts to create institutions to avoid wars, such as the League of Nations, and the United Nations, have not been successful. This meme wants us to be demoralized about eliminating war, and many people are.

That sinking, sickening feeling: an excellent war meme.

We also accept this meme, **there will always be war**, because it is so simple, absolute, pessimistic, and demoralizing. It deadens us. It prevents action. It says there is no hope. Once a hint of it enters our mind, we may have that sinking, sickening feeling that, it might be true, and all our efforts are for nothing. It says no matter what technology we have, no matter how prosperous and productive we, the people of the earth become, no matter how we organize ourselves, no matter how well we can communicate, every individual to every other individual on this earth, no matter what our education, and material well being, we will continue senselessly, barbarously, and will forever organize ourselves into large mobs, each mob fanatically trying to kill all the members of the other mob or mobs. It's an excellent war meme.

Meditate on this meme.

Let's slow down for a few minutes and meditate on this meme. Let's look at what it's doing and how it works. **There will always be war** is a most astonishing, powerful meme. It even has a kind of beauty, a kind of perfection, as a meme. It is simple. To be simple is a very valuable quality for a meme. It makes it easy to understand, easy to say, easy to hear, easy to travel. It saves time and mental effort. It is spoken with a tone of deep wisdom. It so easily slips in, but soon we have a Rosemary's baby growing in us. Five simple words anyone can easily understand. It has no caveats, no conditions, no doubts, no except, no unless, no until, and no maybe. It's absolute, uncompromising. It makes me cringe. I want to say it's evil. It categorically banishes all opposition. It's a powerful meme. It's a kind of self fulfilling prophecy. It reinforces itself. The more people believe it the more true it will become. We must dwell on this meme because part of its power is that it is not recognized as powerful. Many powerful memes are not recognized as such; this adds to their power. And it is firmly implanted in most human minds. It destroys that which is good, and beautiful, and true, about humans, our hope and our optimism. We must respect this meme. It's a beautiful meme. But there can be no compromise. It must be eliminated.

Not like our view of animals.

We do not have to behave like our view of animals, as vicious beasts. If enough of us are determined to examine war scientifically, analyze human psychology, and human culture, scientifically, analyze the memes that lead to war, change or counter those memes, and spread the new benign memes throughout the whole earth, war will fade away.

The causes of war are known.

Political scientists have studied the causes of war in great detail. See for example the great book *An Introduction to the Causes of War* by Greg Cashman and Leonard C. Robinson, [Cashman & Robinson, 2007], and other books on the causes of war by political scientists in the references section. Cashman and Robinson methodically discuss all the leading theories of the causes of wars, and compare and contrast these theories, to see how they apply to the following wars: World War I, World War II in the Pacific, The Six Day War, The Indo-Pakastani War of 1971, The Iran-Iraq War, and The Iraq War. Sociologists have studied the causes of war. See for example the excellent book *Why War?* by Philip Smith, [Smith, 2005]. Smith discusses the narratives, stories, and meme complexes predominant in various countries that led those countries to go to war, or not to go to war. He looks at three wars: The Suez Crisis of 1956, The Gulf War of 1991, and the Iraq War of 2003. For each of thee wars he analyses the dominant narrative, memes, in the minds of the populations in the United States, Great Brittan, France, and Spain. Also neuroscientists have made contributions. See the valuable books *The Political Brain* by Drew Westen [Westen, 2007] and *The Political Mind* by George Lakoff, [Lakoff, 2008]. Although these two books are not directly about war, they examine all the various psychological techniques political candidates use to influence, and embed memes into, voters. These same techniques and tricks are used by political leaders to get people to accept their war memes. So, now, since we know the causes of wars, the mistaken war memes held by the leaders and the populations of nations that go to war, we can work to eliminate these causes.

We have powers way beyond the animals.

So specifically how do we counter this war meme? We can start to get rid of the **there will always be war** meme, by admitting the truths discussed above. Just knowing how a war meme works is a huge first step, especially for a super trick meme like this one. In general to get rid of this meme worldwide we have to follow the program of this book or something similar. We use the results from the social sciences and spread these ideas far and wide. We must emphasize, that we have powers way beyond the animals, which allow us to control our instincts. These powers include language, and recent technologies like the Internet and cell phones, that allow us to communicate with all other people, and thus we can change their memes, and behavior, as well as our own. We must emphasize that we now know enough, to be able to identify, and analyze, and change, the memes that lead us to war, and that we can spread these ideas to the rest of humanity. With further scientific research, this process will become more and more efficient. And these ideas will be able to spread faster and faster, to the whole planet. But the **there will always be war** meme will probably last, in some people, until they die, and maybe long after the last war has been fought.

Good versus evil.

It's simple.

This meme is successful because it is simple. It divides the world into only two categories **good** and **evil** with nothing in between. We all know, and practice in our daily lives, the more nuanced view of the world, that there are degrees of goodness and badness. There is a whole range of punishments for crimes that range from small fines to larger fines, to required community service, to jail for a few days, to weeks, or months, to prison from months to many years, to life in prison, to the death penalty. We don't advocate the death penalty for someone who runs a stop sign. Yet the **good versus evil** dichotomous meme persists.

It's crude.

Why is it pro war? Because if the leaders or the people of one country apply this meme to other countries or groups in the world, then they have only two options for characterizing these other countries or groups: **good** or **evil**. If any country is seen as sufficiently threatening then it will be characterized as **evil**. **Evil** has no degrees. Something either is **evil**, or it is not, in which case, it is **good**. Something **evil** can't be helped, can't be improved. Its threat can only be eliminated, one way or another. It must be sealed off and contained, or it must be fought and destroyed. You can't negotiate with **evil**. How could you negotiate with **evil**? **Evil** people will lie and trick you because they are **evil**, and they only want to destroy you. You can't trust them, so you can't negotiate. So characterizing some country or group as **evil** is often a step toward war. In his book "*Why War?*" the sociologist Philip Smith, [Smith, 2005], observed that nations go to war when their narratives paint the enemy as absolute **evil**, and themselves as absolute **good**. So **good versus evil** is a war meme.

Many dimensions.

Good versus evil is not a nuanced way of dealing with the world. It's too simple. It throws everything into one of only two buckets. It doesn't allow any degrees along a continuum from the highest **good** to the lowest **evil**. Even if a continuum is used instead of just two buckets, a continuum is only one dimensional. Anything as complex and nuanced as a country, or other association of people, needs many dimensions to be evaluated properly.

<u>It gives an immediate yes/no answer.</u>

Why does the **good versus evil** meme persist? Maybe just because it's simple. Maybe it's left over from prehistoric times, when our ancestors had to make snap judgments about things, like whether that shape in the tall grass just ahead was a lion or an antelope. No time for nuances here, just a quick yes or no answer. It has persisted because we still have to make similar quick judgments in our daily lives, such as whether some other vehicle is about to pull out of a side street in front of us or not. The situation calls for an immediate yes or no answer. But this simple meme has no proper place in discussions or thoughts of war and peace.

<u>It needs a warning label.</u>

So we need the following addition, a warning label, you might say, to the **good versus evil** meme: Use only when an immediate yes or no answer is required. Do not use when there is time to think.

<u>Pressure for quick decisions.</u>

The **good versus evil** meme is related to the process by which memetic decisions are made in the mind in situations of possible danger. The process seems to want a quick decision. There is a strong tendency to jump to one conclusion or another. Indecision is uncomfortable. The primitive mechanism which requires an immediate decision whether to fight or flee may be the evolutionary predecessor to this process. So maybe it's wired in that the greater the fear, the greater the pressure for a quick decision. So when war is in the air, as fear increases, it's harder to stay neutral. People choose, they say yes or no to war, even though they have little information relevant to making a decision. The pressure to make a quick decision comes from the fear or confusion stirred up by war rhetoric. This fear or confusion is a state of suspense that is resolved when a decision is made. The fear or confusion may be worse when there is insufficient data to make a rational decision. So the pressure to decide is greater when the information is less.

The fear meme.

Franklin Roosevelt said: *"The only thing we have to fear, is fear itself."* This could be used as a war meme, to try to give potential soldiers courage. How ironic. But Roosevelt had a point. We have to get it right. **Fear** can immobilize people. It can freeze us like the deer in a car's headlights. But the biological purpose of **fear** is to mobilize us. To focus all our attention. So we can decide what to do, and do it. So the freeze is temporary. The freeze is the time the body and mind take after the mind has said: *Stop everything! Pay all your attention to this threat!* So we should not fear **fear**, at least for the evolutionary context for which it was developed. If we were fish swimming in the ocean, we would perhaps have need many times a day to invoke the **fear** or startle response as we swam by bigger fish who might see us as something good to eat. But although we are no longer fish swimming in the sea, and do not have as many daily instances where the **fear** response is useful, we still have that mechanism. Maybe we apply that mechanism too much. Maybe we apply it to situations where it should not be applied. [Brodie, 1996]. As in paranoia and all its variations. As to foreigners whom we feel we can not understand. As to foreign countries whom we see as having evil intentions toward us. But there are situations where **fear** is appropriate. **Fear** is a different kind of meme than most of the memes we are discussing. It is associated with many other memes. **Fear** is a feeling inside us. The emotion of **fear** is expressed by some of the things our bodies do before we feel **fear**. Our muscles tense, maybe freeze. Our facial expression changes to one easily recognized by other people as one of **fear**. Some people scream. The emotion is our bodily reaction to some situation. **Fear** itself is the feeling we then have. [Damasio, 2003]. The **fear** meme is a most valuable and useful meme. It helps us make decisions. When the **fear** meme is associated with some other meme or some situation, it represents, or it actually is, stored knowledge or information --- remember a meme is information --- about that situation. Different situations have different amounts of **fear** associated with them. Some situations of course have none. The **fear** meme is definitely telling us something. It's saying the situation is bad, maybe not just bad, but very bad, maybe so bad that we should stop whatever we are doing, and put all our attention to the situation, or meme, associated with, or which caused the **fear** in us. The evolutionary origins of fear discussed above have to do with life or death situations. **Fear** works through a very primitive part of the brain called the amygdala. Some neuron paths go from the eyes directly to the amygdala, bypassing the parts of our brain that usually handle our vision. And other paths go directly from the amygdala to our muscles. This is how a hiker can stop walking <u>before</u> he sees a snake on the path in front of him. This is spooky but real. The fear response is very primitive. Yet we still need it and we use it all the time. The problem is that we are largely not conscious of our **fear** response. It's largely automatic. Most people never question whether their **fear** response is appropriate to the situation before them. The problem also is that our **fear** response can be used against us by other people. The problem is that **fear** can be put into people, totally out of proportion to any, even partial, objective assessment of the situation, that is being associated with the **fear**. The problem is that **fear** feelings don't add up by the rules of arithmetic. Rather at some point they reach a threshold, a trigger, a tipping point. We can only experience so much **fear**. At that point the brain acts. Sometimes we can say it flips. [Sargant, 1957]. Like the snake meme, that went directly from the hiker's eyes, through his amygdala, to stop his leg muscles from walking, before he had any idea of what was happening, when a person keeps hearing that they, whoever they may be, are trying to kill us, over and over and over, there comes a time when the brain, probably through the amygdala, says enough! We've got to kill them before they kill us!

<u>Not only the Trojan Horse of fear.</u>

Does it all boil down to the overuse of the **fear** response? I doubt if many wars have been started by sex associated memes at least in modern times. Or food desires. In modern times at least, any starving peoples would not have had the means to wage war. Many of the war memes we examine may use a Trojan horse based on **fear** to slip in harmful memes. But some do not. Those having to do with the **hero** meme are aimed at diverting our attention from the negative consequences of war. Many other war memes work to divert our attention from the negativities of war.

Fear says hurry up! Decide now!

If over expression, or inappropriate expression, of **fear** is so important, how do we fix it? If we are letting the **fear** emotion inactivate our meme filters, to allow war memes into our minds, we must teach our meme filters to be especially vigilant, as to which memes we allow in, when the emotion and feelings of **fear** are involved. We must slow down **fear** in cases when a threat is not immediate. **Fear** was developed to cause the body and brain to make an immediate response. In our complex, interconnected society, **fear** is used in many situations which do not require an immediate response. **Fear** says hurry up, decide now. The **fear** and startle responses were developed in animals which had much less brain than we have. So if we make quick decisions according to **fear**'s demand for immediate action, we are not using the much more powerful tools we have. These tools are all the knowledge and intelligence we have in a brain much more developed than in the primitive animals. We must slow down. It takes time to think. Meme checking is just the process by which we see if a new meme fits in with the memes we already have. This is thinking. It takes time. We must suppress **fear** long enough to give our meme checkers time to do their job. **Fear** and the other feelings memes discussed below are interconnected with our thinking. Feelings and thinking are not separable. See Chapter 9 for more discussion of this.

Other feelings memes.

Probably all feelings can be used to manipulate people. Feelings and thinking go together in ways not completely understood. Not only the negative feelings like **fear**, **anger**, **hatred**, and **disgust**, but also positive feelings like **happiness**, **joy**, **elation**, and **awe**, can be used to manipulate people. We discussed **fear** above. The other negative feelings may operate similarly. The positive feelings are used when war is glorified through patriotic, nationalistic, speeches, rallies, marches, and music.

Hero/brave/courage.

Make more soldiers.

This complex is a war meme, when it is applied to soldiers, just because they are soldiers, and not considering what they actually have done. To speak or think of soldiers, just because they are soldiers, to be **heroes**, **brave**, and **courageous**, is to puff them up, since clearly, not every soldier is a **hero**, or **brave**, or **courageous**. To puff them up beyond reality is to try to get others to imitate them. It is trying to make more soldiers. Thus it is pro war. Recruitment posters for the United States military contain the phrases *He's not just my son. He's my **hero**;* and

*She's not just my daughter. She's my **hero***. A **hero** is someone who does something very special. So to say anyone who joins the military is a **hero** is to praise them as having done something very special. It's definitely a pro war meme.

<u>Risk your life.</u>

When this meme is adopted by an individual, he or she, it's usually a he, becomes programmed for certain behavior. He follows a script which diminishes his memes for self preservation. He more easily risks his own life. He also may be less concerned about the welfare of others. He is more likely to be in favor of wars, and he is more likely to participate in wars. Is someone with these memes more or less effective than someone who doesn't have them? It's generally assumed, that someone who is **brave** or **courageous**, is more likely to fight than not, and thus is more effective as a soldier. **Bravery** and **courage** are encouraged in soldiers. Too much **bravery** or **courage** may be ineffective, in that the possessor of too strong versions of these memes may be reckless, and die prematurely or unnecessarily. Their opposite, **cowardice**, is considered contemptible. This can go to extremes as among Japanese soldiers in WW II:

"In the fighting for Saipan Island, 20,000 Japanese were killed in battle and a further 7,000 committed suicide, many of them in deliberately suicidal rifle and bayonet charges against the American troops facing them." --- [Gilbert, 2001, page 297].

Is there such a thing as a proper balance among **bravery**, **courage**, **fear**, **cowardice**, **self preservation** and **recklessness**, for a soldier in a battle? Maybe the memes for **heroism**, **bravery**, **courage**, **cowardice** are used mainly to get people to join armies, rather than to juice up their fighting. In any case, these are all trick memes, in that they are used by leaders, to get soldiers to risk, and give their lives, for the leaders' purposes.

PORTRAIT: Rest in Peace 112.5.

Sugar coating death.

<u>Praising someone who dies in a war just because he died in a war.</u>

Saying anyone who dies in a war, no matter how he dies, is a hero, or otherwise praising someone who dies in a war, just because he died in a war is sugar coating the horror of death. It's trying to make death seem less bad. Thus the deaths caused by war are not so bad. So war is not as bad. So there is less reason to be against war. So these memes are war memes.

We must support our troops.

<u>Slips right in.</u>

This is rather obvious. **Support our troops**. Yes, I say, stop the war and bring them home as soon as possible. But no that's not what they mean. What this meme is doing is playing upon our sympathies for our soldiers. We all know they are subject to death and injury. So how could we not support them? What people really mean, when they say **support our troops** is, rather directly and obviously, **support the war**. It is not even subtle. It seems so obvious that we might think it's not worth analyzing. Yet it works! People will hear this slogan and accept it literally, uncritically. Of course we all **support our troops**. And the meme **support the war** slips right into our minds, and we don't realize it. What a trick! Like a cheap slight of hand card trick! The trick may work as follows: This meme is exploiting similar sentence structure. Compare the two sentences: 1) We must **support our troops**; 2) We must **support the war**. In everybody's mind, **our troops,** and **the war,** are very close. Psychologically there is a tight association between **our troops** and **the war**. If you think of either one you will think of the other. That means in our brains, these two memes are tightly connected. Sentence 1) we can all literally agree with. So when we hear it, we easily accept it. Because of the close similarity of sentence 1) to sentence 2), each starting with **We must support**, and each ending with one of the two closely associated memes, **our troops** and **the war,** when the meme for sentence 1) easily enters our mind, the meme for sentence 2) slips in along with it. Voila! The meme **support the war** has gotten in too.

<u>Tricky, subtle, and effective.</u>

This is an example of a really crazy meme. It's crazy because, on the one hand it is so apparently obvious and unsubtle, that we can feel that it does not affect us. Yet on the other hand, it's very tricky, subtle, and effective, because it does affect us! It's surely a war meme.

<u>Shine a light.</u>

How do we deal with such tricky memes? There surely are other memes which use such a similarity trick. War memes can get in by closely associating themselves with other memes, similar in some way, but memes which everybody can agree with. The **honor the fallen** meme complex, examined below, has war memes entangled with memes for remembering the dead. Of course most everyone agrees we should remember our dead. One way to deal with these tricky and entangled memes is to shine a light on them, and then disentangle them. Simple awareness of the tricks will help us guard against them in many cases.

We must all rally together.

<u>We are social creatures.</u>

This meme seems so obviously pro war that it would not need any discussion. But this is a powerful meme that sends many people off to kill and be killed. **Rally together. Let's not have any dissent. Get with the program. Go with the flow. Join the group. Stay with the herd**. These are very logical for those in favor of war. If there were no dissent, we could just go full speed ahead with the war, with no opposition. Clearly these are war memes. These memes are very attractive and comfortable for many people. **Belonging** to the group and **agreeing** and **accepting** the group's memes is comforting. It's easier. You don't have to think. Just **obey orders. Go along to get along**. This is a kind of meta meme, a meme about memes. It says accept all the memes that most everybody else accepts. It says, in the case of war, accept all the memes that are consistent with war, and reject all those memes not consistent with the war. Maybe the attractiveness of these memes comes from our ancient past, when living in groups provided a biological survival advantage. Indeed it still does for animals that live in herds. And it does for us too. We humans are inherently social creatures. To not live in social groups would be severely limiting for us. Is it a human instinct to **stay with the herd**? This **herd** or **rally** meme, whether instinctive or not, operates in human culture in areas not directly related to war. Joining cliques, clubs, gangs, and any groups that have their own codes of conduct and beliefs are some examples. But applied to matters of war, these **herd** memes are extremely dangerous and must be changed or controlled.

<u>Regarding war it's extremely dangerous to just go with the flow.</u>

It may be essential for humans to behave in a **herd** manner in some aspects of our lives. No individual can know everything about every aspect of life or culture. So regarding some areas, we may with good reason **just go along** with what most everybody else does. Maybe then it's just a matter of education to convince people that regarding war, it's extremely dangerous to just **go with the herd**, whereas in other areas, like music or clothes, it's OK to turn your thinking brain off, and **go with the flow.**

We must follow the advice of our generals.

<u>It's a cop out.</u>

This is an example of the **obey authority** meme, which we will discuss below. When civilians who are the leaders of governments say this, they are denying their duty to make the ultimate decisions about war for their countries. It's a cop out. Generals are presumed to know how to fight a war. It is not their place, as generals, to say whether a war should be fought, or if one should be continued. As generals they, of course, are expected to give their professional opinion about how a war is going, or about how it may go in the future. As citizens, they may give their opinions about whether a war should be started or continued. The **we must follow the advice of our generals,** is clearly a war meme. It's an abdication of our moral responsibility to think for ourselves regarding actions, such as war, that are carried out in our names, and which cause many deaths and the destruction of property. Are there any tricks this meme is using? They are mainly the same as the **obey authority** meme discussed below, such as, that **we are ignorant,** and **only authorities know** what to do.

"... in Germany, war plans were made without input from civilian political officials, resulting in a plan which --- in the context of the 1914 crisis --- made no real political sense and assured the worst possible outcome for Germany." --- [Cashman and Robinson, 2007, page 84].

Winning/losing; analogizing war to sports.

Many die for the vanity of leaders.

This is a big one. **Competition** is a powerful meme in many human cultures. **Competition** is almost the definition of sports in most people's minds. Each side fighting in a war wants to **win**. But as we have seen in Chapter 2, this is not possible. Humanity as a whole **loses**, and each individual country **loses** too. War is not **win/lose**. It is **lose/lose/lose/lose/lose**. So the **win** meme is contrary to reality from the beginning. The desire to **win**, or rather, often, the desire not to appear to **lose**, causes wars to last longer than they otherwise would. Leaders at some point realize they are not **winning**, and that the war is just senseless destruction. But these leaders will not stop fighting, because they do not wish to be seen as **losers**. This is related to the **honor** meme. This **win/lose** meme is powerful and dangerous. It causes wars that have become obviously senseless to everybody, to be continued indefinitely, only on account of the **vain,** and irrational, hopes, of leaders to salvage their reputations. Many people die for nothing more than this kind of **vanity**.

Hitler laughed.

"On the Eastern Front, where just over three million German soldiers faced six million Russians, the Soviet forces launched their winter offensive on 12 January 1945. Three days later Hitler left his headquarters near the Ardennes for Berlin. During the journey one of his staff, an SS colonel, commented wryly: 'Berlin will be most practical as our headquarters: we'll soon be able to take the tram from the Eastern to the Western Front.' Hitler laughed at the colonel's sense of humour." --- [Gilbert, 2001, page 305].

Clearly by this time, Hitler knew the war was hopeless, but he let it continue.

Control your memes.

Competition is good in some areas of life. It can be overdone. Some people are **competitive** in as many areas of their lives as they possibly can manage to be. Some want money for money's sake. They want the best in everything. The best house, the best spouse, children, and on and on. They want their children to be **competitive** too. They sometimes force their children to **compete** in sports, and praise them when they **win**, and demean them when they **lose**. The desire to **win** seems to become almost a transcendent value, a value more important than anything else. It's natural for us to enjoy praise, admiration, and respect, from other people, for good things we do. But it seems that, in some cases, some people go too far. So the meme for **competitiveness** is not one to be eliminated, but rather, it should be controlled as to where it is used. It causes much death and destruction when leaders apply it to themselves and their reputations. United States president Nixon said he didn't want to be the first president to **lose** a war. So he continued the Vietnam War long after it was already **lost**. It also motivates many non-leaders, who say wars must be continued, just so we don't **lose**. There is no way, feeling good about oneself for not **losing** a war, is worth all the death and destruction caused by continuing that war.

Focus on memes clearly leading to war.

There are already controversies in the social sciences about how games people play may affect their behavior. In some sports the players physically fight regularly. In some sports the fans physically fight. There is much dispute about video games, especially those depicting violence or war. Until and unless the science is definitive, it's better to focus our meme clean up efforts on those memes clearly leading to war. If there is some natural aggression in people, maybe sports and video games provide an outlet for the aggression that would otherwise be expressed in war. The memes for **competitiveness** in sports, life, and war represent a huge area for research. Much more work needs to be done. **Competitiveness** and **cooperation** are discussed further in Chapter 10.

Prospect theory.

Political scientists have done a lot of work analyzing causes of war related to the **win/lose** meme. One of these theories, Prospect Theory, says leaders are much more concerned about **losing** something than getting something of equal value. This suggests they are more likely to risk war if they feel some of their territory or influence might be **lost** than if they might **gain** much more by not going to war. See [Cashman and Robinson, 2007, page 7].

Nuclear deterrence.

Among those studying the causes of war, some say nuclear deterrence prevented war between the Soviet Union and the United States during the cold war. If so, this was a recognition, perhaps on account of the magnitude of the destruction that would occur, that nuclear war would be **lose/lose/lose**. Even so, it took about twenty years into the nuclear era before the absurdity of nuclear war became obvious. Just because the destruction may be less in a non-nuclear war does not make it **less lose/lose/lose**.

Machismo.

United States president Theodore Roosevelt said:

*"We **despise** a nation just as we **despise** a man who submits to **insult**. What is true of a man ought to be true of a nation."*

*"We do not admire a man of **timid** peace."*

*"By war alone we acquire those **virile** qualities necessary to **win** in the **stern strife** of actual life."*

*"In this world the nation that is trained to a career of unwarlike and isolated **ease** is bound to go down in the end before other nations which have not lost the **manly** and adventurous qualities"*

--- Theodore Roosevelt, quoted in, [Angel, 1912, page 169, emphasis added].

*"... the prevailing norms in 1914 saw war not merely as acceptable but also as beneficial, progressive, **manly**, virtuous, and uplifting --- something that provided spiritual regeneration."* --- [Cashman & Robinson, 2007, page 29, emphasis added].

Be a real man.

So, Theodore Roosevelt is saying: **be a man**, **be tough**, **don't be a sissy**, become a soldier, go to war, and kill people. When you attack, directly or indirectly, a man's **manhood**, you are attacking his concept of himself, what he may consider to be his essence, who he is. You are suggesting maybe he is **queer**. This can cause a lot of cognitive dissonance, mental confusion and trouble, not only in the young, but also among men who may have even very small doubts about their **sexual orientation**, and even in men who are quite happy with their **sexuality**. It can be taken as an **insult**. It's throwing in the mix a bit of **homophobia**, itself a very powerful, nasty meme, that causes much anxiety and grief. *I'll prove to you **I'm a man!** Where's the enlistment office? Give me a gun! I'll show you!* **Machismo** can surely be a powerful war meme. I wonder how often it is used by military recruiters, in their one on one conversations, with immature teenagers, on high school campuses. Sow a little confusion or doubt, about a very emotionally charged aspect, of a still developing personality. The poor kid may no longer think straight, since confusion and doubt easily overwhelm his meme filters. He's ready to kill, and be killed. It's a very good trick war meme. And it is so sad if you fall for this one. That's because a real man, an ideal human being, a person self confident in relation to others, does not have to prove anything to anyone.

In their book *An Introduction to the Causes of War,* Cashman and Robinson discuss the German Kaiser Wilhelm II before World War I as follows:

*"… He had been labeled as 'Wilhelm the **timid**" and 'the brave **coward'**. After these events there is no doubt that the Kaiser was well aware of his need to appear more outwardly **masculine** …. **Masculine** behavior required decisiveness, **toughness**, **belligerence**, and **assertiveness** in the foreign arena; it meant shunning diplomacy, **compromise**, and **concessions**. '**Compensatory belligerency**' would become standard operating procedure …. The July crises would in some ways become a public **test of his manhood**, and as he told the German industrialist Krupp, 'This time I won't **cave in**.'"* --- [Cashman & Robinson, 2007, page 78, emphasis added].

The German Kaiser was surely not the last leader, or citizen, helped into war by the **machismo** meme.

Arrogance.

Arrogance: *an attitude of **superiority** manifested in an **overbearing** manner or in **presumptuous claims** or assumptions.* --- Merriam-Webster Online Dictionary.

Arrogance is self limiting.

If you are inhabited by the **arrogance** meme, then you are more likely to think you already have all the answers, that other people's advice, and opinions, don't matter. If you are an **arrogant** person, you will cut off candid advice and opinion from those around you. You will be making decisions with less information. You are shutting some doors to your mind. Humans are social. We are embedded in our culture. We are products of our culture. Our knowledge, our successes, are built upon the knowledge and successes of our predecessors, and the people around us. If you already think you **know everything** there is to know about some matter, you are limiting yourself. This **arrogance** meme often occurs in national and military leaders, as they close their minds to information from other members of their governments, in the critical build up to war.

Arrogance positive feedback loop.

Arrogance is also a serious danger for leaders because their subordinates can reinforce the **arrogance** of the leader by their **subservience**. There is a runaway meme dynamic here in which any **arrogance** displayed by a leader induces more **subservience** by the subordinates. The subordinates give less candid advice. The subordinates observe, that the leader does not want to hear information, which is contrary to the beliefs and opinions he already has, so they don't offer any contrary data. The leader observes that the subordinates never seem to have any useful or new information. This confirms and strengthens the leader's **arrogance**. He may come to see his advisors as **ignorant** fools. So we have a feedback loop. The leader gets more **arrogant**; the subordinates get more **servile**. Saddam Hussein was a good example of this. He once asked for candid advice from his advisors as to whether he should resign. One suggested he should. Several days later the man's body, chopped in small pieces, was delivered to his wife in a black bag. [Cashman and Robinson, 2007, page 284]. We can be confident that any advice ever given to Saddam Hussein by any of his advisors for the rest of his life was most carefully **censored**.

<u>Arrogance is a war meme.</u>

So the **arrogance** meme makes national leaders even more **ignorant** than they normally are. It limits the information they have that is relevant to their decisions. It denies facts. They start wars on the basis of **incomplete and false information**. [Cashman and Robinson, 2007]. So the **arrogance** meme is definitely a war meme.

Duty.

<u>We forfeit life.</u>

"When we speak a language that denies choice, we forfeit the life in ourselves for a robot-like mentality that disconnects us from our own core." --- [Rosenberg, 2005, (a)].

<u>Easy to get there from here.</u>

How can **duty** be a war meme? It's not too hard to get there from here. Let's look at some definitions from Merriam-Webster's online dictionary.

1: conduct due to parents and superiors
2 a: obligatory tasks, conduct, service, or functions that arise from one's position (as in life or in a group) **b** (1): assigned service or business (2): active military service (3): a period of being on duty
3 a: a moral or legal obligation **b:** the force of moral obligation

<u>What other people want us to do, when we don't want to do it.</u>

Duty is stuff other people expect, want, urge, push, us to do. They say we have an **obligation** to do these things. They say we **must** do these things. We have **no choice**. It's settled. Case closed. The implication is, if we don't do these things, there will be consequences, we will be **punished**. So **duty** is a meme, to get us to do what other people want us to do, when we don't want to do it, whatever <u>it</u> may be. **Duty** only comes into play when we don't want to do something. If we want to do something, then it's not **duty**. **Duty** is a method of **force**. It's **coercion**. Something done for the sake of **duty** is not freely done. It's **forced** by others. It's related to the **obey authority** meme, but it's not the same. It's left over from the past, when everybody bossed somebody else around. When we act out of a sense of **duty**, we are not free. We are slaves.

<u>Duty makes us unhappy.</u>

We are taught the **duty** meme. Most people accept it, internalize it. It directs their behavior. Since their actions are not freely chosen by themselves, and the actions are by definition things they do not want to do, they are unhappy. They feel diminished, trapped, controlled, by forces outside themselves. They are programmed robots. They are slaves.

Not necessary.

*But, but, but, isn't the **duty** meme necessary?* you may be saying. No, it is not necessary. Those who push the **duty** meme, also push the **it is necessary** meme. The **it is necessary** meme is part of the **duty** meme.

Make the effort to find out what's good for us.

As with the **obey authority** meme, we do not have to allow our lives to be directed by others. We are better off if we direct our own lives. We each know ourselves better than anyone else does. So we know what we need, and want, and what's good for us. And if we are not confident, that we know what we need, and want, and what is good for us, then we can make the effort to find out. We can talk to others, if we want, in the process of finding out what we truly need, and want, and what is good for us. We can consider and evaluate what we hear from others, and accept or reject their views as we see fit. It is better for us to determine what is good for ourselves, than to rely on some **remote authority**, who does not know us in the least. How could it be otherwise?

Anonymous controllers.

When you act in accordance with the **duty** meme, you don't even have a clue about who is **controlling** you. Who knows who gave you your various versions of the **duty** meme? Your parents, your teachers, books, movies, TV? And where did they get it? It's an ancient meme, leftover from the past, which has outlasted its usefulness.

Programmed robots.

It's ironic, that in a country like the United States, which makes such a big to-do about **freedom**, many people want to turn others into programmed **robots**, and even more sad, many people would rather be programmed **robots**. **Slavery** has not vanished from the earth. **Slavery** is alive and well even in the country which speaks the most loudly about **freedom**.

It's a war meme.

So **duty** surely is a war meme. It allows anonymous leaders to **control** people, to send them off to kill, and be killed.

How to replace it.

The **duty** meme can be replaced by a meme that says: **Develop yourself**. Find out what you need, and want, and work toward those goals. You will come to see, that in order to reach your goals, you must work with others. Other people also have needs and wants. You will see, that the best way to reach your goals, is to work with others, so both your and others' needs and wants are satisfied. In a serious interaction with another person, you each seek a deep understanding of the other. To reach a deep understanding, each person needs to know what the other person is feeling, since knowing a person's feelings, will lead to an understanding of their needs. When each person knows and understands what the other person's feelings and needs are, they can discuss and consider whether they each would be willing to do specific things that would meet the other person's needs. The whole process involves non-judgmental observation, listening, and conversation, with the aim of each person being to reach this understanding. See [Rosenberg, 2005, (a), (b)]. One of the main things people need is **love**. **Love** is an ongoing process between two people like the communication process just described. You each **love** both of you. You each care for both of you. The two of you individually, and together, grow. The **duty** meme is not necessary.

Selfishness, selflessness, sacrifice.

All three of these memes have outlived heir usefulness. They are no longer needed. Their time is up. And all three are dangerous war memes.

<u>To work for a good cause increases the self.</u>

If I come across a political candidate, who's set of ideals overlap enough with my ideals, that I am willing to work in his campaign, or contribute money to it, I am not **sacrificing** my **self**. Rather I am growing my **self**. Literally. My ideals are a significant part of my **self**. They are some of my memes. Insofar as I am helping that politician get elected and implement his ideals, I am also literally helping, some of my **self**, some of my stuff, some of my essence, some of my memes, to spread and be put into practice. I am increasing my **self**. I am making my **self** a bigger **self**. [Hofstadter, 2006] So I am not **sacrificing** my **self**. I am not **sacrificing** anything. Nor am I being **selfless**. And I'm not being **selfish** either, because I believe if my ideals can be implemented, the world will be a better place.

<u>To work for a good cause increases the selves of others.</u>

Similarly if a rich couple, after careful research and consideration, gives a large amount of money for research and practices designed to reduce, or eliminate some disease, they are not **sacrificing** their money, they are not being **selfless** or **selfish**. They wish to see a better world, for whatever reason. They may be motivated by a desire to see justice, goodness, and beauty, increase in the world. Whatever their motivation, they have memes which mean a lot to them, for example, maybe a desire to relieve human suffering, and they have the means to work for that end. As they use their resources to implement their memes, their **selves** grow, their **selves** are greater. And they are helping others; they are increasing the **selves** of others also.

<u>Self and community rise and fall together.</u>

There is no opposition between **self** and **community**. Some people express the relationship as if there is a tradeoff. They imply that to help the **community**, one must sacrifice one's **self**. Or to improve one's **self**, the **community** must suffer. They suggest that if one goes up, the other must come down. This is a mistake. As the above indicated, they go together. The **self** grows, if, and only if, the **community** grows. We are social creatures. We can not live in isolation without seriously withering. We only grow when we interact with others, with the help of others, or when we help others. **Self** and **community** are not in opposition; they are positively correlated. They go together.

<u>Why are these three memes dangerous war memes?</u>

They are poor models of reality as explained above. **Selfishness** says pay attention only to your **self**. **Selfishness** says when considering any action, pay no attention to the effects of that action on others. It says if your actions harm others, that's OK. Clearly a truly **selfish** person would be pretty miserable, not sharing with others, not **cooperating** with others, probably avoided by others, alone and lonely. A pitiable example of a human being. If you have no concern for what happens to other people, then you are less likely to see the negativities of war. So it's a war meme. There probably aren't many people who have a strong **selfishness** meme because of all the negativities I just listed. So why does this meme still exist? What is this meme doing? What's its function? It's used in a crude way to get something from others: *Give me some of that. You are being **selfish** if you don't give me some.*

<u>Is selflessness the opposite of selfishness?</u>

Selflessness might be thought to be good, maybe the opposite of **selfishness**. **Selflessness** is to not to pay attention to your own needs. This is very dangerous. You have needs that must be met to continue your existence. You need food, water, air, shelter, and interactions with others such as **companionship**, **respect**, and **love**. To ignore your needs, if you were truly able to do that, would cause you to be miserable, sick, and maybe to die. So no one can be completely **selfless**. It's a trick meme, used to exploit others, often women, as when women were expected to ignore their own needs in taking care of their husband and children.

<u>The sacrifice meme, not good.</u>

Sacrifice means the **destruction** or **surrender** of something for the sake of **something else**. Why is that dangerous? It's not so bad if all it means is a tradeoff between equally valuable alternatives. If a person has to give up her car, so she can buy groceries, because she has lost her job, that's not good, and she might say the car had to be **sacrificed**, so she could buy food. The original meaning of the word, was to kill an animal that might have provided food, so it could be offered to a deity, who was expected to provide **something else**, in return. The problem with the **sacrifice** meme, is that there is often a disconnect between the **destruction** or **surrender** part, and the arrival of the **something else**. Sometimes the **something else** never comes. So the **sacrifice** meme brings along some anxiety. Really the trouble with the **sacrifice** meme, is that it is mostly used to get other people to give up **something good** they have, for some less than certain **something else**, to arrive at some unspecified time in the future. Soldiers must be willing to **sacrifice** for the good of the country. It's like **duty**, **selfishness**, and **selflessness**, in that it's a trick meme, used to con people into giving up **something valuable** or important to them. Since it's used to get people to participate in war, it is a war meme.

92

Us versus them.

<u>One interdependent species.</u>

One of the most destructive memes throughout human history is the **us versus them** meme. Early humans, like some other primates today, lived in small tribal groups of maybe about 100 people. There was probably considerable variation in sizes, but 100 is a nice round figure to keep in mind. There were survival advantages to group living. But as human populations grew, more and more, these tribal groups ran into one another, and they perhaps competed to occupy good areas for hunting or farming. So maybe there was conflict between groups. And the **us versus them** meme was reinforced. But now that humans have overrun the whole planet, and with mass communication, the number of people in the groups have become much larger, the number of groups has become smaller. So now we have divided the planet into about 200 countries, where the largest have populations of thousands of millions and the smallest one million or so. We should not be surprised if principles derived when humans lived in groups of one hundred people don't apply very well, when we now live in groups of millions. Memes appropriate for primitive tribal warfare, may not be good for countries with populations of billions or hundreds of millions of people. Yet modern warfare proceeds as if one group of hundreds of millions of people should somehow fight another such group. This **us versus them** meme is still coursing around all our heads, apparently not much different from when the first two primitive bands of 100 people each fought over which one could occupy a nice place by some beautiful river. We can now understand, that we are **one interdependent species**, living on one limited planet. We have the knowledge and tools, to arrange our affairs, so we can live in peace with one another. We don't have to like one another. Simple tolerance will do. Live and let live. We need to remove this **us versus them** meme, and replace it with the **one interdependent species** meme.

<u>We prefer our own ways.</u>

Why is this meme still so powerful? Maybe one reason is that we can only personally know maybe 100 to 150 other people. Now our modern countries are much, much larger than that, but they tend to be homogeneous. The most homogeneous ones may be the most stable. We seem to prefer homogeneity. Maybe that's why immigration is resisted by some people. So even though we can know personally 100 to 150 people, if our country is sufficiently homogeneous, it doesn't much matter which 150 people we know. If we know 150 people in a sufficiently homogeneous country, we could say, we know them all. We want to keep it that way, homogeneous. We are suspicious of **outsiders** because we don't know them. We see them as different. They have different conventions in greetings, in hospitality, maybe in what we consider honesty in business dealings, maybe different religious beliefs. That makes us uncomfortable. We feel we don't know how to behave properly in the presence of different conventions. So we prefer our own ways. We think they are better. But in reality often, they are just different. In one country if we violate a traffic rule, a policeman gives us a piece of paper noting the violation. We have to later go to court or send in a fine to the local government. In another country, we do the same violation, the policeman comes up to us, and we soon realize the way to settle this is to give the policeman a sum of money comparable to the fine we would pay in the first country. Some people see this as corruption. It could be seen as just another way of handling traffic fines, and a more efficient way at that. Of course not all corruption is efficient. So these different ways of doing things can make us feel uncomfortable.

Know anyone on the planet.

But times are changing. With the Internet and globalization, we can come to know people personally in any country in the world, and more and more of us are doing just that, and thus we come to know, in our hearts, that we are all very much the same.

Heads and hearts.

It's one thing to know intellectually, in our heads, that people all over the planet are basically the same, because maybe we were taught that it school. It's another and more powerful thing, to know it from personal experience, with many people from all over the planet. The distinction between knowing something, *in our heads,* and *in our hearts,* is very important. What this distinction really is, is the difference between knowing something logically, consciously, verbally, verses having the meme be buried deeply in, and connected to, many other memes in our whole mind, not just in the conscious part, and having it embedded tightly with our emotions. Anything tightly embedded within our emotions will have much more powerful effects on our behavior. A meme buried deeply, and tightly connected with our emotions, tends to be stable, and not easily wiped out or removed. So for this meme, and for all the others we analyze, it is important that we work to make the changes, in our hearts, as well as our heads.

Open your mind.

What can we do to counter the **us versus them** meme? The obvious things: In our physical and virtual, Internet, travels around the planet, make an effort to get to know personally those people we meet from other cultures. Do the same when we meet foreign visitors and workers in our own country. Read books, watch movies, listen to music from other countries. Study the sciences, genetics, anthropology, psychology that prove how similar we all are. Try anything you think might help. Open up your mind! Surely what we know now, in our own country, is not everything there is to know! Other countries, other cultures, other people, surely have many things of value, beauty, and interest, we can learn, and which can make our own lives better.

Escalation of hostile actions.

How specifically is the **us versus them** meme pro war? Those in the **us** group like one another, feel they understand one another, feel that their conventions are good or best, whereas they don't understand the **them** group as well, they don't like them as much, they don't trust them as much, they think they, and their culture, are not as good as that of the

us group. So the **us** group is more likely to think the **them** group has bad intentions toward them. The **us** group can thus more easily perceive hostile intent in some action by the **them** group. Assuming the **them** group also harbors the **us versus them** meme, the **them** group is also more likely to see the **us** group as having hostile intent. Thus the escalation of hostile actions can more easily start if both sides harbor the **us versus them** meme. So the **us versus them** meme can lead to war.

The **us versus them** meme, and most of the other war memes we discuss, are well known to the political scientists who research the causes of war. **Enduring rivals** are defined in [Cashman and Robinson, 2007, page 15], *as*:

*"... pairs of states who **compete** with each other over a period of decades, during which time they tend to become involved in a series of crises. ... Political elites in the two states perceive each other as **rivals**; they **mistrust** each other and are deeply **suspicious** of the other's motives and intentions. ... More than half the interstate wars in the nineteenth and twentieth centuries occurred between **enduring rivals**, and disputes among **enduring rivals** are almost twice as likely to end in war than disputes occurring between other pairs of states."* --- [Cashman and Robinson, 2007, page 15, emphasis added].

A specific example of the **us versus them** meme comes from the war between India and Pakistan of 1971*:*

*"... The Indian leadership believed that that the Pakistanis were intellectually **inferior** and Pakistan was a **second-rate** power. Thus the Indians **discounted** the Pakistanis as a potential peace partner. The **mirror-imaging** that the leaders of both parties projected on each other --- the tendency to define **themselves** as rational and peace loving, while seeing the **other** as being irrational and warmongering --- drove both parties to take a **dark view** of the intentions of the **other** throughout the second half of the 1960's."* --- [Cashman and Robinson, 2007, page 222, emphasis added].

Here's another example:

*"As John Dower ... has argued, the self-deception of Japanese elites was based in part on **cultural stereotypes** buttressed by governmental propaganda that 'portrayed Western culture as **effete** and the average American and Englishman as too **selfish** to support a long war in a distant place.' They assumed that the American war effort would be undermined by cultural forces such as labor strife, racial conflict, war profiteering, and by 'softness' and other **flaws** in the national culture."* --- [Cashman & Robinson, 2007, page 143, emphasis added].

The **us versus them** meme may be hard to get rid of. George Lakoff in his book *The Political Mind,* [Lakoff, 2008], discusses the Nation as Family metaphor. A **family** always has an **outside**, that is, **others**, who are not members of the **family**, as does the **us versus them** meme.

This would suggest the **family** metaphor could not be extended to the whole of humanity. Unless we discovered the existence of extraterrestrials. But of course the Nation as Family metaphor could be modified and it surely needs to be.

Racism.

No significant differences.

Racism is a more intense form of the **us versus them** meme. Historically, it was associated with some pseudo scientific theories, which purported to show significant differences, in mental capacities between races. There is no scientific evidence for significant differences between human races. Even if there were, that would not justify maltreatment of people of one race by people of another.

Example effects of racism.

"In October (1944) there was an uprising by the Jewish slave labourers inside Auschwitz who were being forced to take out the corpses from the gas chambers to the crematoria. They succeeded in blowing up three of the gas chambers. The explosives which they used had been smuggled into the camp by five Jewish women slave labourers working in an ammunition factory just beyond the camp perimeter."

"The revolt inside Auschwitz was crushed and all those who had taken part in it were killed. The five women who had made it possible were also executed: hanged in front of the whole camp. Despite severe torture they refused to betray their accomplices." [Gilbert, 2001, page 303].

Racism was also a factor during the India Pakistan war of 1971:

"... *[G. W.] Choudhury suggests that the brutality of the assault indicated a deep,* **ethnic based hatred** *of Bengalis on the part of Punjabis, ...*" --- [Cashman and Robinson, 2007, page 245, emphasis added].

Where does racism come from?

The basic mistake of **racism,** is to believe that physical or mental differences, between groups of people, would yield moral differences. That if there are enough differences, between two groups of human beings, then it is OK for one of the two groups, to **exploit**, **use**, and **abuse**, the **other**. Where does this idea come from? It may be related to, or come from the meme, that it's OK for humans to **exploit** animals. It is related to the meme complex **us versus them** discussed above.

How a strong rightness meme might lead one human group to abuse another.

If I'm in group 1, then I believe that group 1's beliefs, conventions, practices, religion, language, and so on, memes, are good, correct, and **right**, because group 1 probably has memes to that effect, more or less. Assume that's what I've been taught as I was raised in group 1. Group 1's memes are thoroughly embedded deep in my mind. Group 2's memes are more or less **different**, and almost by definition, in group 1's terms, not good, correct, or **right**. If I, as a member of group 1, apply the principles and memes I know, to the members of group 2, then I will see members of group 2 as all **messed up**. They aren't behaving the way I was brought up to behave. If I am unable to rise above the memes of my own group, if I am unable to see the world in any way except through the limited memes of my own group, then I can't help but to see group 2 as all **wrong**. If my group **punishes,** or **abuses,** its own members who deviate from my group memes, as many groups do, then it's an easy step for me, to accept the meme, that it's OK to **punish,** or **abuse**, members of group 2, because I see them as **deviating** from the only memes I consider **legitimate.**

<u>Conditions of scarcity.</u>

Another more direct way group 1 may **abuse**, physically **harm**, or **kill** members of group 2, is in conditions of scarcity. If group 1 is starving, and group 2 has food, and group 1 sees no other way to get food, group 1 may attack group 2 to get food. **Self preservation** may drive group 1 to risk physical **harm** or **death**. In general, if group 2 has stuff that group 1 needs, or perceives it needs, for **self preservation**, and group 1 sees no other way to get that stuff, then group 1 may attack group 2 to take that stuff.

<u>Direct and indirect paths to racism.</u>

So we have two ways one group may come to **abuse**, **coerce**, and apply **force** to another group. The first would seem to explain at least how some **racism** arises. The second, perceived scarcity, attempting to satisfy perceived needs, might lead one group to **envy** another group, on account of the second group's material, or memetic, goods. Group 1 might then justify an attack on group 2 via its **rightness**, **correctness**, and **superiority** memes. But now we are getting complicated. There are probably many other less direct ways **racism** can arise. It would be satisfying to be able to discover and explain these other ways mimetically. Maybe more research will do it. However **racism** arises, it clearly contributes to some wars.

<u>How do we get rid of the racism meme?</u>

Rather than thinking our own group has the **last word** on knowledge, truth, and wisdom, we need to spread the meme that there are **many paths** toward goodness, beauty, justice, and truth. The search for these ultimate values is never ending. No one, no group, has the **last word**. There is no **last word**. Can anyone say what **absolute** truth is? Could we ever know if we had attained it? Besides, the present greatly confused state of the world, suggests we are very far away, from any **absolutes**. Truth and our other transcendent values are **ideals,** apparently not attainable in practice. So there will always be work to do. Beautiful work. Instead of **condemning** other groups, just for being **different,** we need to put all our memes together, and see if we can evolve better memes for all of us.

Coercion.

<u>A sorry state.</u>

It's a central part of human nature to apply **force** to things. We had to pick fruit from trees, hunt animals, build houses. So we naturally use **force** on things. So it's not surprising that we might **push** some other person out of our way. What's a proper use of **force** in human affairs? Maybe none. We might make exceptions for deranged, criminal, or ignorant people. There are presently situations, in which for our own integrity, we must use **force**. **Self defense**. The world is overrun with **coercion** or threatened **coercion**. Laws galore. Laws hardly ever repealed. Just new ones added constantly. Police to **enforce** the laws. Most everybody wants more **police**. **Armies** to **coerce** other countries. Maybe a hermit could live without **coercion**. Most everybody wants more laws. Everybody thinks they know the best way for everyone else to live. And given the least chance they'll pass laws to **force** conformity to their vision. There are so many laws everyone needs her own lawyer. As we saw above, in the discussion of **racism**, there seems to be a relation between the allowed **coercion** within a group, and the amount of **coercion**, that group considers OK, to apply to other groups. We are immersed in **coercion**, and most people want more.

<u>Meme control is more effective.</u>

The **coercion** meme is related to the **control** meme. Many people believe that other people need to be **controlled, coerced,** and **forced**, to behave by **powers** external to themselves. Actually most people, most of the time, are **controlled** by their memes. The **controlling** memes do not have to have any connection to **police, force,** or any kind of physical **coercion**. When I go through a day without robbing, raping, or murdering anyone, it's not because I'm afraid the **police** would catch me, if I did any of these things. I don't want to do any of these things. My memes make me not want to do any of these things. My memes make me behave. OK, I'll admit it. Not everyone is like me. Some people need the threat of **prison**. But, on the other hand, most people are like me. They do not need **threats** of **prison** to behave. So we should explore how **non-coercive** memes alone can make most people behave. We don't have to have **coercion** for most people most of the time. We do not necessarily always need more laws and more **police**. **Coercion** is a primitive meme that says people's behavior can be changed only by **force** or the **threat** of **force**. The **coercion** meme is a poor model of reality. Proper meme **control** of personal behavior is much more effective for most people and it's a lot cheaper.

<u>Minimize coercion memes.</u>

There are negative effects of all these **coercive** memes coursing through our mental environments. As discussed above, they set up our cultures, and countries, to resort to **coercion** between countries. **Coercion** between countries is war. So **coercion** is a war meme. So we should minimize **coercion** memes in our cultures. We can do this without using **coercion**. Please keep in mind, as this book shows, that people can change their memes without **coercion**. When people start thinking about memes, they can change their own memes calmly, coolly, and rationally, as they see fit, as little, or as much, as they think appropriate. This program does not need **coercion**. To use the **coercion** meme, which leads to war, in order to try to eliminate war, would be a senseless contradiction.

Enemy.

What's an **enemy**? Someone who wants to **harm** you. Do you personally have **enemies**? Are there, right now, specific people who want to **harm** you? How many are there? How many other people have **enemies**? I wonder if psychologists or sociologists have ever investigated this. What's the average number of **enemies** per person? How many pairs of people do you know who are **enemies**? Do you have an accurate picture of the number of **enemies** you have? Paranoiacs don't. They think they have more **enemies** than they actually do. So paranoia or pronoia, thinking the universe is on your side, or that you have fewer **enemies** than you actually do, in a leader, could lead to war. Or if a nation might be characterized as paranoid or pronoid, it might be more likely to go to war. How often do whole nations, or whole groups, everybody in the nation or group, really want to harm us? So overestimation or underestimation of **enemies** are war memes. Maybe just the concept of **enemy** is a war meme.

"... leaders in both Germany and Britain were seduced into misperceptions; they each underestimated the **hostility** of the other." -- [Cashman & Robinson, 2007, page 71, emphasis added].

Obey authority.

<u>Find someone to tell you what to do.</u>

This is a big one. What is the **obey authority** meme? It's the idea that I can't figure something out for myself. I'm too **ignorant**. I just don't **know** enough. So I must find someone who will **tell** me what to do. This is one of the most dangerous and damaging memes ever. Well, you say, aren't some people **smarter** than others, and thus, does it not make sense, for the **less informed** to pay attention to the **more informed**? Perhaps in some cases. But most people, unless they are retarded, **know** better than anyone else, what is good for them. Nobody **knows** me better than I **know** myself. So I am the **most informed** person in the world as to what is good for me. To someone else, who has different values than I do, I may appear foolish. That other person would not make the **decisions** I make. A person may **choose** not to follow a doctor's recommendation for heart bypass surgery, and thereby live longer than he otherwise would have. Was he wise or foolish? Or did he make his own **choice**, the best **choice** for him, everything considered, as he saw it? Almost everybody on this planet believes that they **know** what's good for everybody else. The best ways to live. The best ways to do anything. And they'll **tell** you if you let them. And many people would use **force** to make you conform, if they got half a chance. A few people distrust **authority**. They have good reason to do so. If it were as simple as **smarter** people just helping the **less smart**, that would be OK. But the **obey authority** meme builds upon itself. It aggrandizes **power,** until there are immense **hierarchical** institutions, primarily countries, trying and succeeding, in **controlling** the lives, of billions of people around the planet. Institutions take on a life of their own. Each institution has its own set of memes. And many of these memes are predisposed for **preserving**, and **expanding**, the institution. **Power** corrupts. **Power** wants more **power**. These institutions become remote from the welfare of the people they claim to be helping. The main consideration for them is **institutional continuance**. Little else matters to them. A viral meme gone wild for sure. So when you give up your own **decision** making to the **obey authority** meme, you risk serious **harm** to your own self interest.

Learned ignorance.

People didn't naturally come to think of themselves as too **ignorant** to make their own **decisions**. They have **learned ignorance**! They have been **taught ignorance**. They have been infected with the **I am ignorant** meme. Why? For the purposes of others. Those who want to **control**. Those who think they **know** what's good for everybody else. **Power** and **control** freaks! This meme has run wild all over the planet. The trouble is, these **authorities** don't really **know** what's good for people, any more than anyone else, and they don't really care anymore what's good for you. They act according to what's good for them. So if you give up your own **decision** making, and subject yourself to these **authorities**, it's a crap shoot as to whether you will be better off. It's worse than a crap shoot, since **authority** is used by the **authorities** to accumulate **power** and **wealth** to themselves. So their motives are always, always, suspect. You run the serious risk of being **used**, **exploited**, **milked**, and **bilked**, when you hand over your **decision** making to some **authority**.

If you are ignorant you can't choose a wise advisor.

If you decide to **rely on** some **authority**, because you think you are not **smart** enough to make your own **decisions**, how can you **decide** which **authority** to **listen to**? You are hopeless. If you are not **smart** enough to make your own **decisions**, then you are not **smart** enough to **decide** which **authority** to **listen to**. United States president George W. Bush claimed he didn't have to **know** anything himself, since, he said, he could **rely on** his wise advisors. And as you would expect, he didn't **choose** wise advisors. No unless you are retarded, you will be better off making your best efforts to **think** for yourself. Remember you **know** more about what you need and want than anyone else.

Anti-human meme dynamic.

How does this meme work? **Authority** is **power**. The person **relying on** an **authority** has **subjected** herself to that **authority**. It's inherently a **power** relationship. The **powerful authorities** impress, and impress on, the **powerless** that the **powerful know**, while the **powerless** do not **know**. They impress with their **wealth** and **power**. They wear the finest clothes, live in the largest houses and castles, and as they move about among the **powerless**, they may bring along a few **soldiers**, or

police, in case you didn't get the message conveyed by their **wealth** alone, or in case they have to be protected from the people who are supposed to obey them. The average citizen says to herself: *Gee, they must know something I don't. Look at all the fine things they have.* This makes the **powerful** more **powerful** and the **powerless** more **powerless**. There is an anti-human meme dynamic going on here. It's close to the old saying *The rich get richer and the poor get poorer.* The richer you are the easier it becomes to get even more and more money. The same for **power** and **authority**. This self reinforcing meme dynamic can become unstable, unsustainable, and end in a crash. The extreme of **obey authority** is **slavery**, which has existed as an institution world wide until very recently. Those in **authority** readily accept the **obey authority** meme because it serves their interests. And of course they spread it every way they can. Our schools are **controlled** by it. And the **powerless** accept it because of all the **forces** that **push** it on them. Children in the home are **subject** to parental **authority**. They have no choice but to **submit**. It insures their survival. It makes life easier for them. Some, when they grow up, never **learn**, that they are **free** to make their own **choices**. Others may long for the simpler days when their parents made all **decisions** for them. Parents pass on the **obey authority** meme to their children, who then carry it on into adulthood. In some communities children are **taught** to **obey** any adult, even non family adults. Following the **obey authority** meme for the **powerless** may be a simpler, more comfortable way to live, at least as long as they are not **exploited** too much by those in **authority**. But when taxes get too high, when an economy crashes, when huge numbers of people lose their jobs, when there is too much death and destruction due to wars, when the irrationality of restrictions on personal behavior become apparent, then **revolts** may occur. Sadly or not, it's a rare **rebellion** that succeeds. **Soldiers** are used to keep the citizens under **control** as well as to **fight** external wars.

Self reinforcing meme.

The **obey authority** meme spreads **dependency** and **helplessness** among the **powerless**. It **trains** them to be less than they could be. It **trains** the **powerful** to accept and promote simplistic ideas so they can maintain and promote their **privileges**. Thus this meme is self reinforcing in both the **powerless** and the **powerful**. This meme is not going to go away soon. There is way too much **power** and **privilege** wrapped up in it.

Most pernicious ever.

How is this meme pro war? It can lead to war because it allows a few leaders to mobilize the masses of people. Since it dulls the masses **critical** capacities, it keeps them open to receive, accept, and act on, the leaders' war propaganda. **Dependent** people are more likely to be **fearful**, and thus more likely to accept the **fear mongering** of the leaders about enemies of the country. Younger people are more susceptible to the **obey authority** meme because they are closer to childhood. Ever wonder why **armies** prefer the 17, 18, and 19 year olds? It's because they are more susceptible to this meme. This meme is one of the most pernicious ever. This meme is so bad, so dangerous, and so destructive of human possibilities, that a culture without this meme would prosper unimaginably. <u>This meme is so bad, so dangerous, and so destructive of human possibilities, that a culture without this meme would prosper unimaginably.</u> It's conceivable that, if just this one meme could be eliminated from the planet, there would be no more war.

<u>Running stop signs and having wrecks.</u>

Don't argue that without this meme, we would have chaos, that we'd all be running stop signs, and having wrecks. We obey traffic laws, most of the time, because it makes sense, or because of fines if we didn't. These laws help society to run smoothly. Similarly for laws against murder, assault, rape, and those defining and protecting property rights, contracts, and economic activities. They make life in society safe, somewhat predictable, and tolerable. We may discuss the plusses and minuses of some particular laws, but we generally **obey** them, not because some **authority** said we must, but because we have made a general implicit contract among ourselves, among all the members of our society, that this is the way we **choose** to live.

<u>Much, much work needs to be done.</u>

So, how might this meme be eliminated, or its application limited? I mentioned above, that its application to the raising of children by their parents, and the education of young children is appropriate and necessary. So maybe it just needs to be eliminated from adult to adult interactions. How do we transition a child, who has **known** nothing but **obey authority**, to an adult who neither wishes to **control** others through his **authority**, nor to be **subservient** to anyone else claiming **authority**? Our educational systems, working with parents, would seem to be the appropriate institutions to do this work. But those institutions need much work themselves. We need a lot of research by all the social sciences to find out the best ways to do this. How much do our current educational institutions promote this transition? Do any? How many people even realize it is desirable? It seems to me that somewhere during the teenage **rebellious** years, we should **teach** our teens, via a carefully researched curriculum, how to gradually, methodically, transition from being a person totally **dependent** on **authority**, to being an **autonomous** adult. Much, much work needs to be done, all the while fighting this most powerful **obey authority** meme, whose **authoritarian** adherents will not easily give up their **privileges**.

<u>A universal meme?</u>

The **obey authority** meme is essential to the proper functioning of **armies**, since it is the basis of **armies'** rigid **hierarchies**, and no-questions-asked culture. It also predisposes people to simply accept, believe, and act on, whatever the leaders say. The almost universal penetration of the **obey authority** meme into human minds, has been, and is, a significant cause of almost all wars. Can anyone name a war where the **obey authority** meme was not present? Surely it has been prominent in all modern wars. The **obey authority** meme was prominent in pre WWII Japan, where the Emperor was nominally

supreme, but at the same time the lines of **authority** were so confused, and the governmental structure so disorganized, that the government became dysfunctional. Japan went to war with the United States while significant parts of the government were convinced that it would be defeated. [Cashman and Robinson, 2007, chapter 3]. Fascistic, communistic, and tyrannical governments in general, all control their populations through the **hierarchical obey authority** meme.

The trust me meme.

Notice that claims of any kind of **trustworthiness**, by any person or group, is a kind of trick meme, to get us to give them a free pass, to **insert** their memes into our brains, without having them checked by our meme filters. As in: *It's Okaaay.* **Trust me**. *You can't get pregnant the first time.* Here are some more examples of the **trust me** meme in action: *I have a Ph D.; I'm a Doctor; I'm an Engineer; We have your best interests at heart; We're on your side; We're both Christians; Or Jews, or Muslims, or … ; I'm your mother; I'm your father; I'm a friend of your friend X; We have the highest ratings; All the news that's fit to print; Eyewitness news; Fair and balanced news.* So is this a trick meme or what? On the surface it doesn't seem to be very subtle. But people and organizations use it all the time. And it works! Why and how does such an apparently dimwitted meme work so often? Some possible answers: 1) It's easy: the recipient doesn't have to **think**; 2) Only part of the recipient doesn't want the memes **inserted**; 3) The recipient might be possessed by the **obey authority** meme; 4) It's comforting because it reduces anxiety just to **trust** someone. Whatever the reason, anyone who accepts the simple **trust me** meme, is taking a **risk** she does not have to take. As with the **obey authority** meme, it is almost always better to do your own **thinking**.

Never trust the trust me meme.

Why do people use the **trust me** meme? If they had a sensible, convincing, explanation for what they wanted you to do or believe, something based on facts you already knew, something consistent with your values, your beliefs, and the other memes you live by, then they wouldn't have to say **trust me**, would they? People say **trust me** when they know that, whatever it is they are trying to get you to do, or believe, is against your interest. So if somebody tells you **trust me**, don't.

Don't give up on trust!

To be suspicious when we hear the **trust me** meme is appropriate. This does not mean we should never **trust** anyone. There are times when it is appropriate, or best under the circumstances, to **trust** another person. For example children do well almost always to **trust** their parents. We almost always **trust** our friends and people we love. Very often we **trust** total strangers. We have many ways, mostly unconscious, of sensing the **trustworthiness**, of other people, even people we have never seen before. And usually we build up **trust** over time. **Trust** must be earned, they say. A dead United States president said **trust** but **verify**. Is there any sure way never to be fooled? No. But to never **trust** anyone would be a poor way to live.

Devaluing life.

Demeaning memes.

In a very obvious sense, any meme that **devalues life** is a war meme. Because, if **life** has little or no **value**, then wars don't cost as much. On the surface, it would seem, that any meme that **devalued** human **life**, would tend not to survive, since its hosts might not **live** too long. Yes this is probably a factor. On the other hand, many people can manage to go through **life** inhabited by **life negative** memes. Such people **diminish** their own **lives**. But an individual may apply the meme more to other people. The meme may take the form that says **other people's lives** don't matter as much. If the other people this meme refers to, are an enemy group, then of course, a war against them is easier to justify. Or if one is an **aristocrat**, or otherwise feels **superior** to the bulk of humanity, then sending the **common soldier**, to die in wars is no great loss. There once were, and still probably are, people who think like that. Probably many bloody tyrants thought, or think, that way. They treat other people, as if they are mere **objects**, to be used for the tyrant's purposes. This is all rather obvious. Other dangers come from the subtlety with which **life devaluing** memes can hide themselves. What are some **life devaluing** memes besides the I'm **superior** meme? Memes that **put down** yourself. All those memes that **put down** the average person. Memes that **put down** the young. Or the old. Or any group. Memes that **put down** minorities, and foreigners. Memes that say **we're special**, or the **chosen of God**.

Life after death.

Are there any memes that devalue **life** in general, not just the relative values of groups or individuals? Well yes. A meme that promises a good **life** after death would relatively decrease the value of present **life**. This meme is in conflict with any meme which says, that the **life** after death might not be so good, or might not exist. But there are people who are convinced that if they die in a holy cause, they go directly to a **heavenly reward**. The meme has such a hold on them, that they are willing to **sacrifice** their **lives**, and the **lives** of others, for the holy cause.

Killer ideals.

Similarly there are memes which elevate **ideals** above **life**, such as *Give me liberty, or give me death*. And *My country, right or wrong*. If a person believes that his own **life**, is worth less than his **ideal**, whatever it may be, then he is likely to believe that others' **lives** are worth less than this **ideal** too.

Negative memes.

Other **life devaluing** memes: *I'm no good. People are no good. People are inherently flawed. People are controlled by their animal instincts. People are mean, selfish, vicious, always conniving, stupid, unreliable, can never be trusted, dirty,*

diseased, ugly, too fat, and **too thin**. These memes can be buried so deeply, that people who have such negative memes, are often completely unaware, that they have them. Their whole **lives**, their whole **outlook** on the world, may be so colored by these memes, that they will be very difficult to change. These memes can exist in a bundle which includes the **truth** meme and the **realism** meme. These people believe they have a **true,** and **realistic,** view of human nature. In general these memes can be summarized as: **self hatred**, **distrust, hatred,** and **fear of others**. These memes are often associated with memes which would deny our basic instincts for enjoying **life,** such as sex, food, good times, in a word, **aestheticism**.

Love life.

The antidote to these memes would be memes that **celebrate** this **life**, that tend to increase the value of **life**. These would include **love** of our selves, our family and friends. **Love** of good times: sex, food, music, art, companionship. **Love** of humanity. **Love** of all **life**. **Love** of all that is!

Life affirming.

The above has an interesting, and probably controversial, implication. More positive people, more **life affirming** people, are less likely to harbor war memes, than people who are negative. Research should be able to confirm this.

That something is worth dying for.

Maybe.

Maybe there really are a few things **worth dying for**. Maybe my child. Maybe if I am old, and you are young and healthy, and we're in one of those hypothetical situations, where one of us must die, so the other can live. Or maybe a soldier, who throws his body on a live grenade, to save his buddies. Maybe someone can think of other situations. There are cases where someone condemned to death for some crime refuses possible legal appeals. And there are people who commit suicide. But most of the time, the idea of **dying for some cause,** is just nonsensical hyperbolic propaganda. **Give me liberty or give me death**. Yes, it sounds glorious, but it's contradictory on its face: **liberty** means being **free** to do what you want; if you are dead, you can't do anything. The meme that tells people, X is **worth dying for,** often works because, in practice, what it means is that you, the person who hears the slogan, are supposed to **risk your life,** so that I, the speaker of the slogan, can have X. We con people into the military, mostly the young, our children, to **risk their lives** and limbs, so the rest of us can enjoy the supposed benefits.

Die, sucker!

The **worth dying for** meme is a trick meme. It is used by cynical people, to trick others into **risking their lives,** for the cynic's purposes. Don't fall for it. You should know it's a dangerous meme, by the way you feel when you hear it. First it's scary. Then as you start to believe it, you get confused, irrational, all emotional, **willing to kill** anyone who disagrees with you. These are clear signs of meme takeover. Beware! If you believe any of the versions of this meme, you are seriously being **used**. You are the ultimate **sucker**. If this meme had an imagination, it might be thinking to itself, as it takes control over your mind: **Die, sucker**! See you in **heaven**. Or **hell**. Or **nowhere**.

Don't die for a meme.

OK, we all take **risks,** every day, which might kill us. Drive a car. Ride a bicycle. Take a walk. We make life and death **choices** every day. There might even be situations when, after cool, calm, and rational consideration of the **risks**, you or I might **join** an army. But, whatever else you may do, don't ever **risk your life,** just by letting some crazy, idealistic, propagandistic, **worth-dying-for**, war meme take over your mind.

Other effects.

Not everyone who exploits these **death** memes is a cynic. Those exploiters, controlled by these memes themselves, are probably more effective exploiters. And these memes are not only used to get people to **risk** their own lives. The emotional confusion and excitement, generated by these memes, helps other war memes get past people's filters, and cause them to be more effectively in favor of war.

Memes override genes.

How do we counteract or remove memes that tell us right up front, that they would **kill** us? You would think our **self preservation** instincts would easily protect us from these memes. But no. Kamikaze pilots, suicide bombers, and ordinary soldiers, prove these **worth-dying-for** memes are effective. These memes provide clear proof, of the superior power of memes, compared to biological genetic evolution. Since the beginning of life on this planet, the most basic, built in, wired in instinct produced by genetic evolution, is **self preservation**. In the comparatively short period of time, that memes have evolved, numbered in thousands of years rather than millions, memetic evolution has produced these **worth-dying-for** memes, which can totally override the most basic **self preservation** instinct of biological life. Memes rule!

Turn the TV off.

Clearly things are getting serious when memes start talking about our own **death**. What should we do when we come into contact with such memes? Stop. Turn off the emotions immediately. Relax. These memes will go absolutely nowhere, if there are no emotions stirring you up. **Think**. Look at your situation. Ask yourself, why you are upset, or emotional. Whatever the reasons, cool it. Get out of the crowd. Turn the TV off. Throw the book away. Get away from the insane people trying to spread these memes. Avoid such people as if your life depended on it, because it might very well depend on it.

We're special.

Sports fans.

The **we're special** meme is self spreading. Why? It makes people feel good to think they are special. Look at sports fans. Consider a crowd, or mob, of basketball fans after their team has just won the basketball championship. They are yelling, and screaming, and jumping up and down, with broad smiles. **We're # 1** they shout. They feel good. They are euphoric. They may start fires in trash cans, and turn over automobiles. They feel good because their team won. The fans themselves didn't do much to cause the win. They think they did, by being fans, but that probably didn't increase the team's performance by much. So thinking you are special makes you feel good. It causes your brain to release endorphins, or other chemicals, that make you feel good. Endorphins are also released after about 45 minutes of physical activity, like running or walking. So maybe fans get an endorphin high just from jumping up and down, and their other physical activity as spectators. Older fans than college students, sit at home watching the TV, and still feel good if their team wins, although their physical activity is not enough to generate endorphins. So physical activity may not be the only explanation for the endorphin surge. But the same areas of the brain are activated, when people observe sports, as when they actually participate in sports. [Iacoboni, 2008]. So maybe endorphins are released even when people just watch sports. These should be easily empirically testable.

Frequency dependent fitness.

If I think I'm **special,** because I'm a fan of the winning team, and you think you are **special,** because you are a fan of the same winning team, then we each reinforce our belief, if we say and believe, that we both are **special**. So the more people that can be included in that *we*, the greater the reinforcement, that **we are special**. The more people included in this *we*, the greater the evidence, the greater the force to believe that **we are special**. So, if a person can spread the meme **we're special,** to other people, then that strengthens the meme in the first person. The meme gets stronger, in each person, as the number of people holding the meme increases. And the greater the size of *we*, the more persuasive, the easier it is for the meme to be accepted by a person not yet holding this meme. Thus the bigger the *we*, the more easily the meme can spread to new people. So this meme is self spreading. It has *frequency dependent fitness,* [Dennett 1995]. And the more it spreads, the easier it is for it to spread. So everything else being equal, we have an explosive, exponential propagation, of this meme in some population; in the population of eligible members of *we*, for example the population of college students where the team is. The eligible population can include alumnae of the college, and citizens of the city or region.

Division of the space.

If we extend the eligible population to all potential basketball fans, then the **we're special** meme will divide up this space into separate domains, each domain consisting of fans for a particular team, plus one domain of potential fans who didn't become fans of any team. It's like the pattern left after a pond dries up, with the dried mud on the bottom, all divided by cracks into separate areas. It's a partition of the space, a division of the space into non-overlapping areas.

Beyond sports.

The **we're special** meme can associate itself with other sets of memes: for example nations, religions, and ethnic groups. Many religions consider themselves to be God's **chosen people**. Almost every nation, or ethnic group, considers itself to be **special**. These versions of the **we're special** meme, will also tend to divide the planet's human population into a partition. So we have a new explanation of why the human population is partitioned by nations, and also partitioned by religions. This is clearly not the complete explanation for either of these. Ethnicity and language are two other important factors relevant to nationalism and religion. But this meme's eye view adds an interesting perspective.

Trojan horse.

Since the **we're special** meme makes people feel good, it's a good Trojan horse. That is, it can bring along memes, that aren't necessarily good for the people holding them. In general, any meme that can manipulate people's emotions and feelings, such as fear, anger, excitement, pleasure, and others, can be a good Trojan horse. Many war memes are good Trojan horses since they create fear, and at the same time feed off of fear.

Small steps.

It's a small step in meme space from **we're special** to **we're better**. **Better** how? In any way one can be **better**. Stronger, smarter, more beautiful, better in any human characteristic. Or several characteristics. Or all human characteristics. In meme space then, **we're special** is not many steps away from **racism**. This is not to say, that a nation of sports fans, is easily changed into a **racist** nation. The **we're special** meme is often associated with the **us versus them** meme. The **we're special** meme is probably a war meme when it is associated with the **us versus them** or **racism** memes, because when it is associated with them, it reinforces them. When applied to sports fans it seems to be harmless. So this is a meme whose character depends on where or how it is used. It's a meme we would not try to eliminate completely, but rather just limit its use.

Research questions.

People can harbor several versions of the **we're special** meme at the same time. A person can be a basketball fan, a football fan, a nationalist, and a member of a religion at the same time. So here are some questions for researchers. If a person is an avid sports fan, is she more or less likely, to be a nationalist? Or are the two totally independent? The more fanatical a person, a fan, becomes in any one area, the less time that person has for being fanatical in another area. This would suggest an inverse relationship. Can harboring the **we're special** meme become an addiction? Is fanaticism easily transferable from one area to another? People often change their favorite sports teams. Nations can quickly change enemies. Can people easily change their fanaticism from sports to religion? The endorphins could care less which variety of **we're special** inhabits a mind. These are important scientific questions that ought to be answerable relatively easily.

Everybody can't be special.

The **we're special** meme, as described above, cannot spread to the whole population of the planet, since the **we**, being everybody, wouldn't have any other group to distinguish itself from. If a group is to consider itself **special**, it seems it would have to have some other similar group to compare itself to.

Many groups might come to have the we're special meme.

The **we're special** meme ought to find welcome homes, in the minds of any pre existing, or already defined groups, if the members see themselves, as members of the group. We could define the group of all left handed, brown eyed, baseball players in Cincinnati. But the members of that group, would not see themselves as members of that group. So let's assume the members of some preexisting group see themselves as members of the group. Why then are the members of such a group more susceptible to the **we're special** meme than non members? Well they are already in the group, and identify with the group's purpose, and goals, so they have some memes in common, and that in itself does make them somewhat **special**. They are different than non members, from just that fact that they are members, and everybody else is not. Maybe the **we're different** meme is a weaker version, or a variation of, or a small mutation from, the **we're special** meme. Almost by definition, a self aware group would have the **we're different** meme. The members are each aware, that they are members of that group, and everybody else is not, so they would feel different, due to that simple definitional reason alone. *Special* implies some kind of praise, or recognition, by others, whereas *different*, doesn't have that connotation. In a **special** group, the praise or recognition, could come from the members themselves instead of outsiders. In the genesis of the **we're special** group, described above, the praise or recognition, of the second member, toward the first member, and vice versa, is what pumps out more endorphins. If people are having a good time together, as a group, then they are generating some endorphins, and they are apt to recognize the good qualities of the other members of the group, and maybe their own good qualities, as the cause of their good time together. When this recognition has spread to the whole group, we can say they all have the **we're good** meme, or **our group is good** meme, which is pretty much the same thing. So we have reasoned that a pre existing group, whose members see themselves as members of this group, and if they are having a good time, then they will have the **we're different** meme, and the **we're good** meme. At this point, I think the **we're special** and **we're different and good** memes, are so close, we can say they are the same.

Memes and groups.

Not all groups have a lot of good times. Sometimes a lot of disagreements occur in groups, yet they mostly hang together for long times. These groups may not feel they are good or **special**. And of course there are all kinds of groups of people. In Chapter 9, we will look at a generalization of human groups: meme organisms. There are many questions for researchers. Here are just a few: What kinds of memes fundamentally run around together in groups of people? That is, are there particular kinds of memes that thrive in limited groups of people? How are these memes related to the **team spirit** meme?

He's not just my son. He's my hero.

These nasty memes want to separate us from our children.

"He's not just my son. He's my hero." is a slogan on United States military recruitment posters. There is also the version: "**She's not just my daughter. She's my hero.**" The memes are hard at work here, working for war. Against the human instinct to **protect our children**, and after all the political use of the meme, **protect our children,** for issues not even related to children, the war memes have a lot of work to do, to **separate** us from our children, when the time comes, that our children are needed as soldiers. So these memes first, try to convince us, that our sons and daughters are **not important**. He's "… **just my son**…", just another of my many possessions, together with my wife, my dog, my truck, my car, my house, my hunting rifle, my friends. Nothing too special, "… **just my son**…" And even more cruelly, it says "**not…my son**." Remember, these partial memes, these sub memes, can enter our minds whenever the whole meme enters. The meme is trying to convince me, that he's **not my son** anymore. Maybe it doesn't want me to feel too bad, if he doesn't come back from the war. Well if he's **not my son** anymore, why should I care? No, now he's been transformed into a **shiny, uniformed, hero**. Something very special, like a **cold marble statue,** on a pedestal. **Not my son**. So if he dies in the war, I didn't **lose my son**, I just lost an abstracted, **depersonalized, hero**. So this nasty meme wants to **cut off our love for our children**. It wants to replace the warm, beautiful, loving, and beloved, daughter, in our minds, by an abstracted person, **even an object**, to be admired from a distance. All this, is to make us more easily go along, with our children signing away their freedom, and maybe their lives, to the military.

Everbody's smiling and happy.

This poster meme makes it easier for the enlistee too. It tells him, finally he's somebody. He's **grown up**. He's **a man, an adult**. He's not just somebody's son anymore. It's time for his parents to **let him go**. The poster shows him, in his spiffy uniform, with his proud parents all smiling, all happy. The poster shows his younger brother and sister, looking up at him, smiling with **admiration,** for his great **accomplishment** of becoming a soldier. Everybody's smiling and happy, as he's ready to go off to war, to kill or be killed.

The power of memes.

How is it that we can change so much, in only a few years, from caring for, helping, teaching, loving, worrying, crying for our children, to sending them off to war to kill or be killed? Something's **wrong here**. Something is **terribly wrong**. The war memes are **working very hard** here.

You did everything you were supposed to do.

As a mother, your son grew in your womb, from an invisible tiny cell, to a beautiful baby, in just nine months. During your pregnancy, you had your doctor check ups. You made sure you ate only healthy food. You eliminated any bad habits you felt might affect your baby. After he was born you fed him, cleaned him, clothed him, and **cared** for him, and **loved** him, in every way. As his father, you **worked** hard to provide for him, his mother, and the rest of your family. You both **taught** him your language, your culture, your values, and your religion, **everything** you could **teach** him, that you thought would be good for him, and **help** him to **grow** up to be a happy, productive, and responsible adult in your community. You **cared** for him in every way as he grew up. You sent him to school. You **helped** him with homework. You **worried** when he was sick. You **consoled** him when life put up obstacles in his way. You were **proud** to see him play sports in high school. You were **so proud,** to see all his accomplishments, and to see him **develop,** into a decent, good, fine young man. Then, one day, he came home and told you he was joining the army. You might have objected, but you didn't. The war was going on, and many other young men his age were joining too. All the young men who enlisted **believed**, like most everyone else, that the **war was necessary,** to fight evil countries, that wanted to destroy all the things, that the young men's parents, had taught them were good, their **way of life**, and their beliefs. So your son went off to war. He didn't come back. Not in one piece. A land mine blew up in his face. What was left of his body was sent back to your funeral home in a plastic body bag. You, his father, and his brothers, went to the funereal home to see him for the last time. The military person accompanying the body said to you, *"You don't want to look."* But you, his father, wanted to look, to see your son for the last time. You said: *"This is my son. I've got to see him."* So you looked at what was left of your son, in that plastic body bag. You, his mother, could not even bring yourself to go to the funeral home.

Become him, become her.

It's not easy to **imagine** what this father and mother **felt**. But do it. **Imagine it**. **Imagine it** right now, as if you were standing, looking at a plastic body bag, containing all that remained of your son. **Become** that father or that mother. **Feel** what they must have **felt**. **Cry** like they did. Or maybe the father thought it wasn't manly for a man to be seen to **cry**. But even if he showed no **tears** in his eyes, **tears** were in his soul, for the rest of his days.

Use your awesome human powers.

Did you do it? **Imagine it**? No? Why not? Are you afraid it will hurt? Yes it will hurt. But do it. You have the **power** to do it. This is one of the **magnificent powers** we humans have. In our minds we can put ourselves in the **place of others**. We can **feel** what they **feel**. We can put ourselves in different times and places. Our pets can't do this, but we can. Do it. Use your **awesome human powers,** and go deep, deep, into your soul, and know the terrible **reality of war**. If you are not a parent, then **imagine** one of your parents, or a brother, or sister, or anyone you know and love dearly, in that plastic bag.

Why?

Why go through this painful experience? Because if you are going to **change** your mind about war, if you are going to **root out** the war memes from your mind, from your deepest soul, you must be **motivated**. The war memes are **powerful**. They are intertwined with other memes that are important to us. They are buried deeply. You will have to go deep, and **work** hard, to get rid of them. And you have to have an equally **powerful** meme, as deep in your soul as they are, to **counteract** them, to **take them out** by the root. That's why I want you to go as deep into your soul as you possibly can, and implant this **reality of war** meme in there, as firmly as you possibly can, so that to the end of your days, you will be committed to **uncovering** war memes in yourself, and **rooting them out,** and be **committed** to urging others to do the same. This is the true **reality of war**. Don't ever forget it.

We do not live by reason and logic alone.

But why get **emotional** about it? Isn't this, as a non-fiction book, supposed to be a **rational,** sensible, discussion of how to eliminate war? Yes it is. But we do not live by **reason** and **logic** alone. **Emotions** and **feelings** are as much a part of us as **reason** and **logic**. **Emotions** and **feelings** should not be dismissed in favor of **logic**. Certain people, who on account of illness or damage to their brains, cannot feel **emotions**, are unable to make any **decisions. Emotions** are necessary. **Emotions, feelings, reason**, and **logic,** all work together, as we make **decisions,** and **guide** our actions. **Emotions** are the glue by which memes are attached to us. That's why war memes are so **powerful**; they use that most **powerful emotion** of **fear** as their glue.

Plant deep, deep in your soul, the reality of war.

If we cannot generate in ourselves, a strong **emotional** reaction against war, we will not be **strong** enough, or **committed** enough, to **root out** from ourselves the **powerful** war memes. And they are very **powerful,** as the history of the twentieth century shows. Consider how much **grief** they have caused. Just multiply the **grief** of that one father or one mother, whose son came home in a plastic bag, by a million. No, a million is not enough. Multiply it by one hundred million, to calculate the **grief** of all the wars of the twentieth century. The war memes have caused all this **grief**. Yet they still exist. That's proof of their **power**. No, they are not going to go easily. We must be **strong**. We must **fortify** ourselves, with the ugly truth, of this **reality of war** meme. If you can't **feel** in your heart, in your soul, deep, deep, in your soul, that war is never justified, except possibly, in the direst extreme of self defense, then you won't have the **strength,** and lifelong **commitment,** that is needed to get rid of these **powerful** war memes. That's why I ask you to **feel** what that mother **felt**, what that father **felt**. **Feel** it personally, as deeply as you can, as if you **were** her, or him, **looking** at that plastic bag containing what remained of your son's body, as if you **were** **looking** at your own son's body. If you haven't done it yet, do it now. **Cry** with them. Multiply that **grief** you **feel** by one hundred million. Use that parent's **grief**, your **grief**, and the **grief** of one hundred million others, to plant deep, deep in your soul, the **reality of war**. And keep that **reality** there till the end of your days. It will make you **strong**. And we will succeed. The world will be a better place because of what we do here. The world will be a better place, for us, and our children, and their children, and on and on into the future.

<u>But we can't multiply grief.</u>

In the preceding paragraph, I asked you to **imagine** a father and mother's **grief,** and then multiply it by one hundred million. But this can't be done. Mathematics is useless here. We cannot multiply the **grief** we feel for one person killed, by some huge number, and actually **experience** the result. To actually **feel** the **grief,** caused by one hundred million deaths, would kill us instantly. It would be like the old science fiction, thinking computer, which when given some contradiction to contemplate, burns up all its circuits, and destroys itself. No, one hundred million deaths is not truly **imaginable**. We probably cannot truly **imagine** even ten. Our minds are not constructed to deal with these things. The memes and **feelings** in our minds just can't do it. This then is another reason we still have wars. Our minds are unable to handle the enormity of what we do.

113

PORTRAIT: Rest in Peace 15.1R.

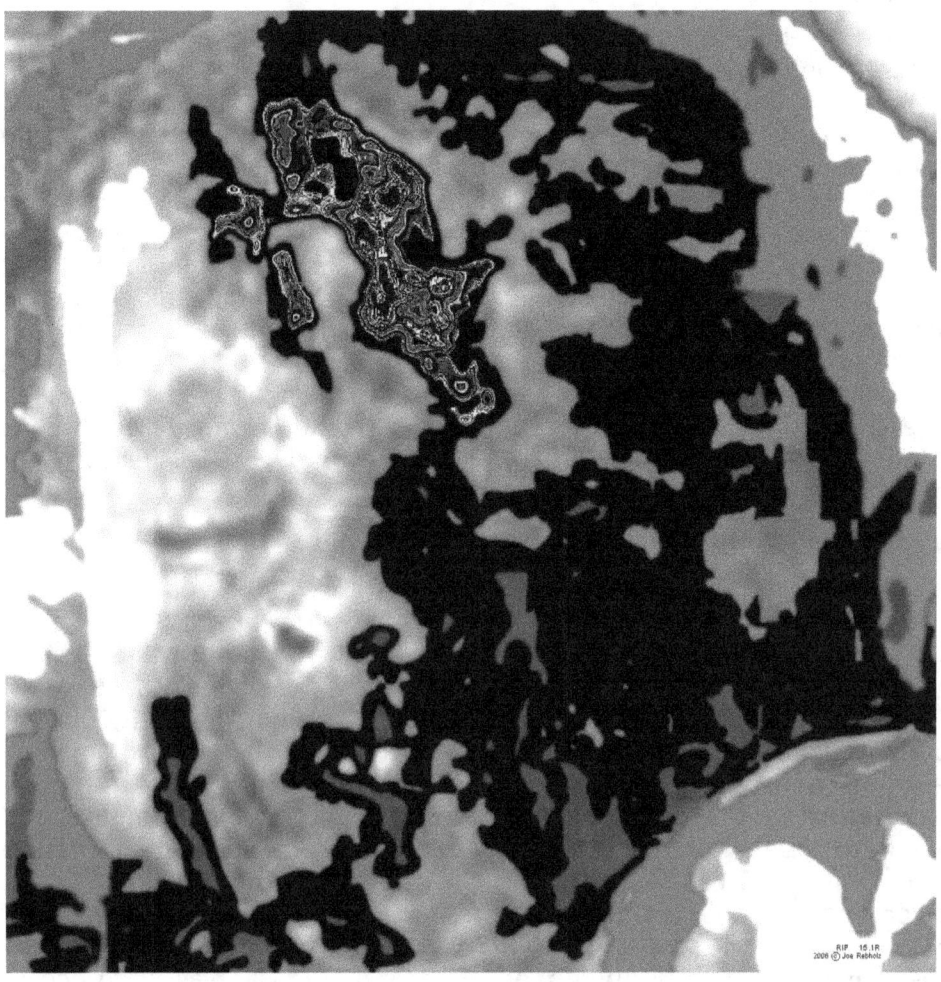

Honor the fallen.

<u>Make more soldiers.</u>

This war meme, like many others, is subtle. That is, it is not easily recognizable for what it is. It is draped with **emotions**. When we hear it, we want to **choke up**. We would think the least anyone could do, irrespective of their politics or their **feelings** about war, is to **honor the dead**. But why **honor** them? **Remember** them, **mourn** them, **grieve** for them, yes, but **honor** them? Did they do something good by dying in a war? Did they kill other human beings, before they themselves were killed? Even if they didn't, they might have, if they had been in the right situation. What does it mean to **honor** someone? It means to **praise** them and their actions. It means to **hold them up,** as models for ourselves, or others, to **imitate**. Yes, **imitate** their behavior. Do what they did. **Imitate** their thoughts and beliefs too. And if you **imitate** their beliefs, and thoughts, and actions, what will you do? You will **become a soldier,** like them, and go off to kill people. And you will believe that you, and other soldiers, should be **honored**.

<u>Powerful war meme.</u>

So what do we have here? We have a very **powerful,** replicating, war meme. It's bundled up very tightly with a powerful **spread me** meme. And the war aspect of the meme is well **hidden, camouflaged**, since the whole thing is drenched with the **emotions** of **sadness**, **mourning**, **loss**, and **grief**. Also this meme says **fallen** and not **dead**. It is sugar coating the awful **reality of death**, decreasing the **horror**, making death seem less bad. That makes it easier, then, to pass on the meme. Also **honoring** the dead soldier makes it easier for his relatives and friends to accept his death, so they too absorb the **honor the fallen** meme, and it **spreads** to them, and from them to others. Also it is easier to accept the death of someone you loved if you can believe that they died for a **good reason**, and if everybody **honors** them, then they must have died for a **good reason**. So this meme will bias us to accept other memes, which say the war had a **noble purpose**. So now can you see how **powerful** this war meme is? It's so **powerful,** that even most people who oppose war, accept it, and they have no idea that they are promoting war. So **honor the fallen** says **become a soldier**. It also says, **spread** the idea that **being a soldier is good**, and that **war is noble**.

<u>Memes can do many things at once.</u>

But is that all? Does this mean we must try to get rid of the meme **honor the fallen**? Memes, or meme complexes, often are complex and they may be doing several things at the same time. It sounds too harsh to say we should not **honor our soldiers** killed in war. After all, most of them thought they were doing what was right. Most all of us thought they were doing what was right, at the time they fought and died. We thought that what they were doing was good for our country. They were immersed in the society, and sea of memes, everybody else was, at that time past. So maybe we do have good reason to **honor** them.

Nevertheless the meme, **honor the fallen,** promotes war, as outlined above. It really does. So what should we do? The solution lies in accepting that a meme or meme complex can do many things at once. We must use this knowledge to sort out the good from the bad, and modify, or grow the meme, make it more sophisticated, so it can keep doing the good part, and we analyze it, and somehow separate out the bad part. Maybe it will be sufficient, to just **be aware of** the bad part, the war part. If people **realize** that the war meme is riding along with the good part, that **realization** itself might be enough to stop the **propagation** of the war part. This, or some other explanation, had better work, because, no way can I give up the meme that tells me to **remember** and **honor** our dead, as beautiful human beings who have died, who are no longer with us, even if I might not **honor** all of their actions.

Honor the good, shun the bad.

Some say "*Love the sinner, hate the sin.*" Yes, maybe this is the way to look at it. Make a **distinction** between the person and her actions. Does it even make sense to try to talk about **separating** the person from his actions? We often do that. In another sense it does not make sense, since a person's actions are part of what it is to be that person. Maybe it's as simple as separating a dead person's good deeds, from her bad deeds, and **honoring** the good in the person, and **shunning**, and **learning** from, the bad.

Entangled memes.

See also *Private Grief and Public Remberance: British First World War Memorials* by Catherine Moriarty in *War and Memory in the Twentieth Century* edited by Martin Evans and Ken Lunn. [Evans & Lunn, 1997]. The unveiling ceremonies of these memorials and monuments wrap up the **grief,** and **loss,** of death, with all the **glorious** community war **ideals**. This article shows forcefully, how totally successfully, the war memes have entangled themselves, with our natural desires to **remember** our dead.

War memorials.

The first war memorial that was actually anti-war.

Are there any anti-war memes in **war memorials**? There often are. After all, they are **remembering** death. Death, and its negative associations, are anti-war memes. But, at present, most **war memorials** are more pro-war than anti-war. Maybe so many people were upset with the Vietnam **memorial** in Washington, DC, because the wall part is so stark and **unheroic**. It's low down to the ground. No reaching to the heavens. No **glory**. It is stark black granite, with the names of all United States soldiers killed in the Vietnam War inscribed on it. Maybe it would have been the first **war memorial that** was actually anti-war, if the sculpture of the three big, **tough** looking, soldiers hadn't been added to it. The war memes of **machismo** and **glory** managed to sneak themselves into the **memorial**, as an afterthought, even though they spoiled the unitary artistic vision of the artist who designed the wall,

Maya Ying Lin. They should be removed. And so should the nurses. It would have been fitting, if the United States could have been the first country, to construct a **war memorial that** was anti-war.

Nightmare war memorial.

But we need to go further. We need a **war memorial** that realistically depicts the **horrors of war**. Maybe a diorama of **death and destruction**. I would have some **dead soldiers,** and **dead civilians,** realistically depicted in realistic colors, none of that dull old bronze. Some kind of long lasting acrylic, or ceramic, so the colors don't fade with time. I would have **guts** being **squished** out of **ripped** open bloated stomachs. Yellow, brown, purple and black **guts**. With **flies** and **maggots**. Arms and legs **blown off**. Heads **blown off**. A body with half its head **blown away**. Red-brown half dried **blood** everywhere. Babies, children, old men, old women. The **armless, legless, child** Mike Palacek cried to God about, in *Cost of Freedom* [Annis, Palacek, Trettien, 2007, page 126]. And my neighbor, Bill, looking at what remained of his son's body, in a **plastic body bag**. I would have a soldier, sitting on the ground, trying to apply a tourniquet to his right leg, just above the knee, because his leg, from the knee down, has been **blown off** and is lying to the side. **Blood** is squirting out of his leg. He is trying to stop the gushing **blood,** so he does not die in the next minute. And a sculpture of South Vietnamese General Loan shooting his Viet Cong prisoner in the head. I would include the stream of **blood** and **brains** shooting out of the wound, which was edited out of the NBC broadcast of the film on United States TV. There would be **body bags** and flag draped **coffins**. And I would just call it *War Memorial*. Think how such a **monument**, lasting for centuries, would seem so bizarre, to people who have never known war, and have never even heard of war, except as ancient history. But that would be **tasteless**.

Celebrate war memorials that don't exist.

The ultimate anti-war, **war memorial,** is no memorial at all. Someday when war is no more, we will be thankful, when we realize that there are no new **war memorials**. We will celebrate the **war memorials** that don't exist, for the wars that didn't happen.

Good taste.

Good taste is a conspiracy, a cover up.

Yes, that nightmare **war memorial** would be **tasteless**. Maybe we're going to have to be **tasteless,** because **good taste** is a pernicious war meme. **Good taste** covers up the **realities of war**. How can we deal effectively with reality, if we refuse to face it directly, if we hide from it, or hide it from ourselves? What could be more anti-war, than an image of a beautiful child, dead, from a massive, bloody, bullet wound, in the head? What could be more **tasteless**? The war memes must suppress such images, such thoughts, such memes. The memes are always fighting their own wars for survival in our minds. Such powerful anti-war memes, cannot be allowed to exist, alongside war memes, in the same human brain. Too much cognitive dissonance. Too much confusion for most minds to handle. Enter **good taste**. **Good taste** shows no **blood**. No **dead bodies**. No **gory wounds**. No **weeping soldiers**. **Good taste** does not mention **death**. Soldiers are not **dead** but **fallen**. **Good taste** doesn't talk about **absurdity**, **insanity**, **futility**, **ugliness**, **sorrow**, **grief**, or **loss**. **Good taste** talks about **nobility**, **duty**, **sacrifice**, **glory**, and **selflessness**. **Good taste** goes along with the crowd. **Good taste** looks to the group to see what to do. **Good taste** follows the leaders. **Good taste** is conformist, herd behavior. **Good taste** is a **controlling**, **confining**, **authoritarian**, trick meme, used by the elites to keep everybody else in their **subservient places**. **Good taste** is a sneaky, pernicious, war meme.

<u>Media shamelessly promote the good taste meme.</u>

The United States mass media are dominated by this **good taste** war meme. Never any **dead bodies**. No **blood**. Only fraction of a second views of the **wounded** in combat hospitals. We must demand the truth from our media. During the Vietnam War combat footage on United States TV helped turn the population against that war. But since then the government, and the powers that be, have used the **good taste meme,** to **sanitize** our media, so that citizens can't **see**, **feel**, and **understand,** the **realities of war**. We must demand the truth, **see** the truth, **and speak** the truth, without the sugar coating **good taste** meme. Besides, killing is the ultimate **poor taste**. Fuck **good taste**!

<u>Compromise: the **good taste** meme is not all bad.</u>

I almost compromised. I considered substituting three asterisks for the last three letters in the F-word, in my denunciation of the **good taste** meme, because I want to respect those readers for whom that word is too much. But that would be sugar coating. That would be giving in to the **good taste** meme, which I am saying we must not do. The bigger point is that we must allow ourselves to be shook up, and shocked, if we are to get rid of war memes. Even so, I am denouncing the **good taste** meme only when it is used to make war easier. The **good taste** meme can sometimes help us find beauty.

PORTRAIT: Rest in Peace 1.1R.

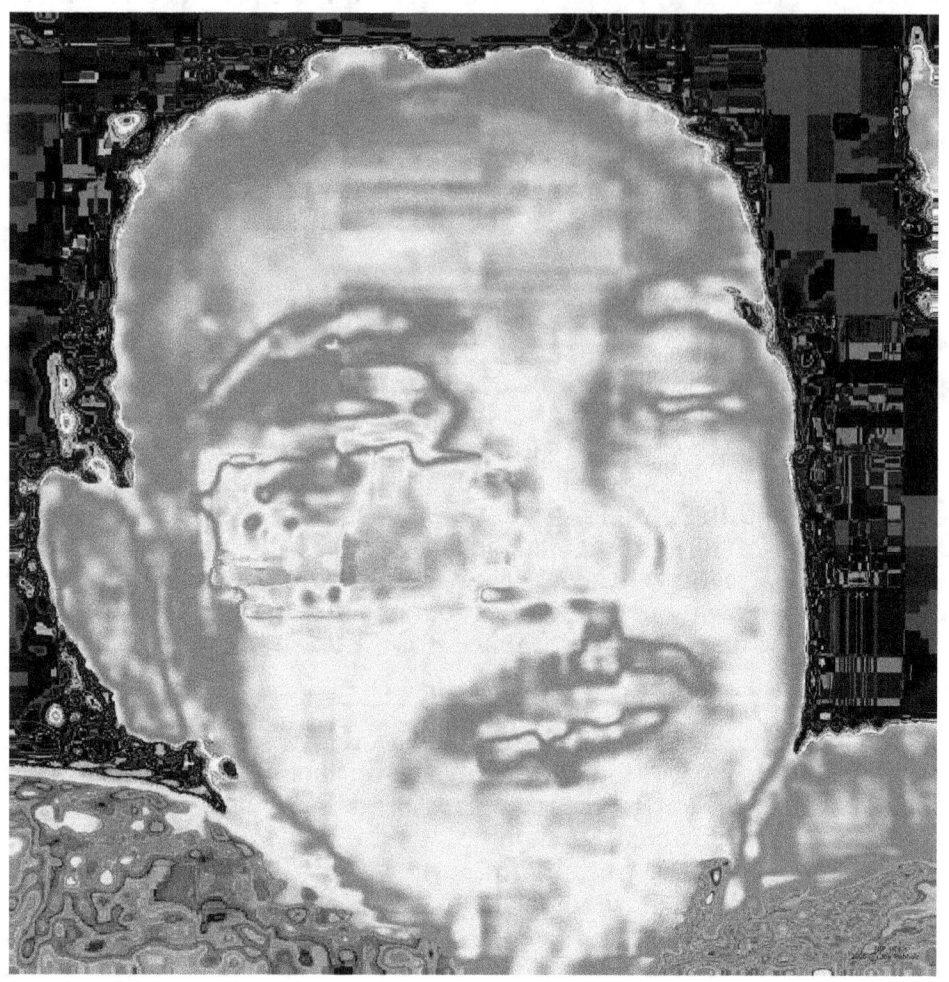

Fallen hero.

Many un-heroic ways to die.

This is similar to the **honor the fallen** meme, but it has its own twists. Some people use the phrase **fallen heroes** to refer to all soldiers killed in war. This usage is bad for several reasons. First, it is a lie. Not all soldiers killed in wars are **heroes**. Some surely were, but most were not. Some soldiers die in accidents, their vehicle goes off the road, into a canal, and they drown, or an enemy explosive comes out of the sky when they are walking from one building to another and they are killed, or their vehicle is blown up by an enemy bomb. There are many **un-heroic** ways to die in a war. All the deaths are **tragic** and **sad**, but not everyone who dies is a **hero**.

It short changes real heroes.

Second, it debases the meaning of the word *hero*. If everybody is a **hero**, then nobody is, because a **hero** is someone who does something **really special**, out of the ordinary. Todd Beamer and the people who joined him were **heroes**. Those who sat in their seats, frozen with **fear,** or just confused, that day, September 11, 2001, on that plane, were not **heroes**. All their deaths were **tragic** and **sad**, but they were not all **heroes**. To say they were all **heroes** would short change those who truly were.

They are never going to get up again.

Third, to refer to soldiers who died in wars as *fallen,* instead of *dead,* is **sugar coating reality**, trying to make things sound better than they really are. What are you saying when you say *fallen*? That they are not **dead**? That any minute now they will get up and walk away? To say they are merely *fallen* and not *dead* debases their **sacrifice**. *Hey people!* they are **really dead**, they are never going to get up again, they are never going to be seen again, heard again, hugged again, by those who loved them. Don't try to hide that awful truth.

Using dead soldiers for war propaganda.

Fourth, the worst part is that it's war propaganda. It's a **sugar coating** lie, trying to make war seem better, and death seem less terrible, than they really are. We **puff them all up,** pretending they are all **heroes,** when only some of them are, making war seem **heroic**, **wonderful**, and **glorious**, and simultaneously we downplay their **sacrifice**, their **loss**, their **deaths,** by saying they are only **fallen**. To say *fallen heroes,* instead of *dead soldiers,* is to buy into, and propagate, war propaganda. It is using **dead soldiers** for political purposes, for war propaganda. And if people speak, and think, war propaganda, instead of the truth, then wars are easier to continue, and new ones are easier to start, and we will make even more **dead soldiers**.

A mixed meme, mostly pro-war.

What are you saying when you call someone a **hero**? You are saying that they did something really **special**, something important, under difficult conditions, possibly at great risk to their own welfare, something that was good for others. Implicit in all this is that they should be **praised**, **honored**, and **imitated**. *Honored,* as in *honor the fallen,* implies also that they should be **imitated**. If **heroes** are to be **imitated**, then soldiers called **heroes** should be **imitated**. You should become a soldier too. As above this is a powerful, easily replicating, war meme. Also, as for the **honor the fallen** meme, this meme may be doing some good things along with the bad. If that's so, then we must learn how to separate the bad from the good, and keep only the good.

The spread me meme.

<u>A different kind of meme.</u>

The **spread me** meme is a different kind of meme than the others we have examined. It's really a structural part of all other memes. By itself it does nothing. If a meme did not have the **spread me** meme included in it, the meme would go nowhere. Every meme needs some positive amount of the **spread me** meme, for it to begin its travels, by leaving a human mind. The amount of the **spread me** meme, associated with some other meme, is some kind of measure of its value or importance. So the **spread me** meme is definitely a different kind of meme. It's not the presence or absence of the **spread me** meme which counts. It's the strength of the **spread me** meme that matters.

<u>Spreadness = goodness.</u>

Up to some point, the stronger the **spread me** meme, in some meme complex, the better the meme complex is, from the memetic point of view. The **spread me** meme helps meme complexes spread. From the meme's point of view, amount of spread = amount of goodness. Or spreadness = goodness. The **spread me** meme is an integral structural component of all other memes which circulate through our cultures. The amount of the **spread me** meme associated with another meme, or a meme complex, may be correlated with the strength of the **desire** its possessor has to spread it. Or its **importance** to that person. The **spread me** meme, in a meme complex, is information claiming how **important** the complex is, saying how much **effort** should be used to transmit it, and implant it, in other minds or human artifacts. It's a claim of the **value** of the meme complex. Although I speak of *the* **spread me** meme, in some cases we may analyze it into various types.

<u>There is a memetic force to increase the strength of the spread me meme.</u>

The **spread me** meme aids the development of individual people, and communities of people. If a person has discovered a new meme, let's say something that makes that person's existence better, maybe a better way to gather food, hunt or fish, and, if that person has a **stronger spread me** tendency, than other people, she is more likely to better communicate that new meme to other members of her community. Thus both she, and her group, are more likely to **succeed,** and **prosper,** compared to other groups. So there is a memetic force to **increase** the **strength** of the **spread me** meme. **Increasing** the **strength** of the

spread me meme, at least up to some point, is good for meme evolution.

Strength of spread me corresponds to amount of coercion.

In our analysis of the **racism** meme, and the **coercion** meme, the strength of the **spread me** meme was what seemed to be correlated with the amount of **coercion** that members of one group find OK, and morally acceptable, to apply to one of their deviating members. And thus also, more or less, the group finds this amount of **coercion** OK to apply to another group.

From very near zero, to life threatening force.

The strength of the **spread me** meme can vary from very near zero, to life threatening **force**: *I'll kill you if you don't agree with me*. On the low end, a person has to say or do something if a meme is to come out of her and possibly get into another person. So the most casual speech or action has a minimal, but positive, amount of the **spread me** meme. The **spread me** meme is stronger when speech, expressing some meme complex, is addressed directly to another person. It's greater still when she talks **louder,** or with more **emotion**, with **repetition**, or when several people **push** the meme complex onto the target person. The **spread me** meme is **stronger** when she speaks to a crowd, or uses technology, human artifacts, such as books, periodicals, and mass media.

Spread me meme can lead to partitions.

In the discussion of the **we're special,** meme we saw that this meme, with the help of the **spread me** meme, partitions the space of potential sports fans into non-overlapping groups, each group being the fans of a particular sports team in a specific sport. We considered a possible mechanism for how the **spread me** meme may work, at least in the case of sports, namely the releasing of endorphins. In several other war memes we discussed, the **spread me** meme also leads to a partition of some relevant population, often the whole of humanity. Humanity is partitioned by language, religion, ethnicity, nationalism, by various ideologies concerning how societies are best organized, and other things. These partitions are all different. They divide humanity in different ways. For example, the collection of people whose native language is French, is not the same as the collection of people who are citizens of France.

Wars occur when the spread me meme crosses a certain red line.

It seems most of these partitions can be the basis for a war between two groups of the partition, or a war among several, or many of the groups, in the partition. By definition, any two groups in the partition have different memes. And each group has the **spread me** meme, at some strength, for each of its memes. So there is some tension between every two groups in the partition. The memes of group 1 would <u>always</u>, to some degree, like to **spread** to, and **overwhelm,** the memes of group 2, and vice versa. That's just the **spread me** meme doing its thing. Wars can start if, in one or more groups, the **spread me** meme gets too **strong**. Wars occur when the **spread me** meme crosses a certain red line. That red line is somewhere near the point, where the **spread me** meme is **forceful** enough, to use **violence,** or **threats** of **violence**.

<u>Control spread me memes.</u>

Wars will be eliminated when enough humans learn to, and actually do, constrain their **spread me** memes. Of course the task before us is to teach ourselves, and enough others, how to do this, and then actually do it, and keep doing it. We do this by identifying, modifying, or eliminating our war memes. It's the war memes that stir us up enough so that our **spread me** memes cross the red line. It's our memes that turn us into killers.

<u>OK below the red line.</u>

Many of the memes that lead to war, when their **spread me** meme gets too **strong,** are benign when the **spread me** meme is below the red line. For example, consider all the ideals like freedom, liberty, democracy, maybe socialism, (within limits), libertarianism, (within limits), teaching others, doing good in the world, trying to make the world a better place. These all seem worth working for, worth **spreading**. Yet, if a person has an overactive **spread me** meme, associated with any one of these meme bundles, in his mind, if he has been worked up enough, so that the associated **spread me** meme, becomes so **strong** that he is willing to kill others, in the service of his meme complex, the meme complex has become pro-war.

<u>We had to destroy the village in order to save it.</u>

In John Hellmann's book *American Myth and the Legacy of Vietnam* [Hellmann, 1986], one of the myths discussed is the idea, the myth, (myths are not necessarily false), that the United States went into Vietnam to **do good**, to **make the world a better place**. The war seemed to destroy this myth, and some other **glorious** American myths. Myths are meme bundles. Maybe the **spread me** meme in the **make the world a better place** meme bundle went into hyperdrive, to the extent that the United States ended up killing the Vietnamese in order to help them. At one point in that war, a United States soldier explained, *We had to destroy the village in order to save it*. The basic meme bundle, **make the world a better place,** in itself does not seem so bad. The problem arises with the **make** part of the meme. That's too close to **force**. Maybe a tamer version of the meme is required: ***Offer people knowledge and tools, that they may accept or reject, as they see fit, and let them make their lives 'better', if they want to."***

<u>Spread me makes pests.</u>

In everyday life the **help others** meme often has a too strong **spread me** meme. Most everybody thinks they know the **best** way to do everything. We sometimes make ourselves pests, by **insisting** on telling others our ways of doing things, as if everyone should live their lives the way we live ours.

When does the spread me meme get too strong?

If the **strength** of the **spread me** meme is too great, it turns into a **force me** meme, or **kill them if they don't let me in meme**. Then we have wars. Under what conditions does the **spread me** meme get too **strong**? The **spread me** meme doesn't **go wild** in every meme complex containing it. Have you ever heard of anyone willing to **kill** in order to spread stamp collecting? I doubt it. So what makes the **spread me** meme **go wild** in some meme bundles, but not others? Where does the **spread me** meme most often **go wild**? It seems to **go wild** mostly in nationalism, ethnocentrism, racism, religion, and other ideologies about how societies should be organized such as monarchy, democracy, communism, capitalism, socialism, libertarianism. I'll refer to all of these as ideologies. An ideology is a set of memes. These ideologies define groups with strong feelings of **we're special, we're good, we're better**, or **we're best**. These groups seem to have in common, that there is little or no clear objective basis, for the strong feelings. If you were an alien observer from another planet, would you see any significant differences, between two human groups with somewhat different ideologies, as they try to exterminate each other in wars? Yet the members of each group are firmly convinced of the truth, goodness, rightness, and **superiority,** of their memes. Maybe as a compensation for the lack of a clear objective basis for the ideology, the members of each group strive to increase their numbers, as proof of their rightness. So they put their **spread me** memes into hyperdrive, to prove to themselves that they are right, by winning the numbers game. *Forty million Frenchmen can't be wrong*.

The meme the biggest group is most likely right is sometimes useful.

This is like the way the **we're special** meme increased the collection of fans. The greater the number of people in the group, the stronger the feeling of **we're special**. There is no necessary logical connection between the number of believers of a proposition and its truth. But historically or practically, in the absence of objective evidence, the number of believers may be relevant. If you were a member of a primitive tribe, and the group is trying to cross a river, and you have never done this before, if 10 people say it should be done one way, and one other person says it should be done another way, who are you going to cross the river with? So **going by the numbers** is not irrational when you have no other information. In other words, the meme that says **the biggest group is most likely right,** is sometimes useful.

What makes people so want to prove they are right?

Why do people hold onto their beliefs so **strongly**? Enough to **kill** for them? Or, what is it about certain meme complexes, that cause their **spread me** meme to go into hyperdrive? The paragraphs above gave one answer: The lack of knowledge, or objective evidence, can cause people to substitute numbers **of co-believers,** as proof of **correctness**. What else? What makes people so want to prove they are **right**?

PORTRAIT: Rest in Peace 150.1.

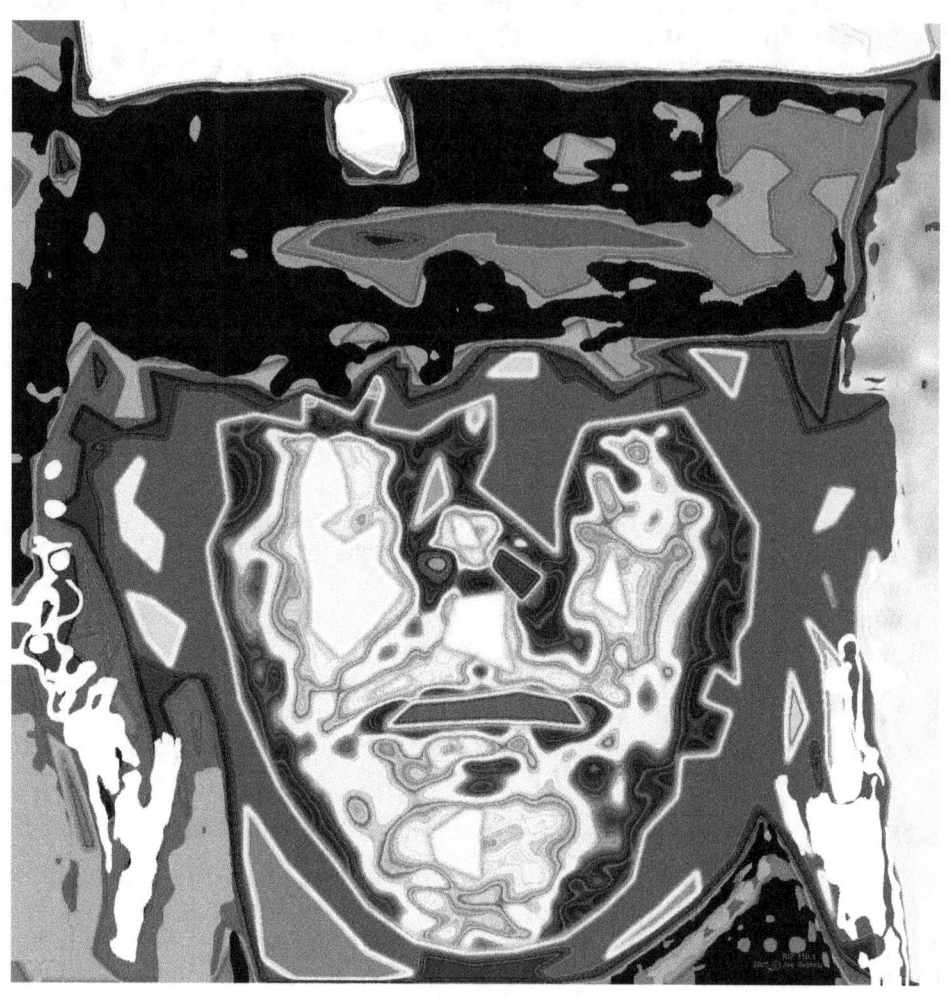

Demonstrate devotion to the cause.

Maybe it has to do with **demonstrating** their **devotion** to the cause. A person may try to **demonstrate** his **devotion** to the cause to himself, and to others, by the great **ferocity** of his **spread me** meme. This might sooth his doubts.

No beliefs without doubts.

It's part of human nature to have **doubts**. We **believe** this or that about the world. As we go through life, we see new things, maybe **change** our **beliefs**. So during the **transition** we have **doubts**. **Doubts** are as much a part of human existence as **beliefs**. They go together. They are both part of the process of **acquiring,** and **revising,** our **knowledge,** our memes, our models of the world.

Humans are somewhat rational.

Some amount of **rationality** is probably built into humans by genetic or memetic evolution. Most people are **rational** in much of their lives, their actions often being based on past **experiences**. So their actions are based on the **evidence** provided by past **experience**. So they are **rational**, but only some times, and in some ways. See [Lakoff, 2008], and [Westen, 2007].

Two ways to increase the spread me meme.

So holders of the various ideology memes have **doubts** from time to time. Their **doubts** may cause them to reassure themselves in two ways. 1) They want to increase the **number of people** who agree with them. 2) They want to prove to themselves, and others, how certain they are, by **upping the force** they use with the **spread me** meme. These are two ways the **strength** of the **spread me** meme is increased.

Violence works, but only up to some point.

The core beliefs of most ideologies do not contain **violent spread me** memes. So the **violent spread me** memes later acquired, or evolved, may be seen as pathologies, or corruptions, of the original memes. The **spread me** meme tends to increase, in **force** and **violence,** over time because the more **forceful spread me** memes are, the more **successful** at **spreading** they are, up to a point. In a word the **spread me** meme tends to get **violent**. This then is a third way the **strength** of the **spread me** meme increases. It's inherent to the nature of the **spread me** meme. The more **violent** versions are more **successful,** they **spread** more. This is the dilemma. Why does it get **violent**? Because **violence works** in **spreading** memes. [Sargant, 1957]. But only up to some point. **Violence** and the effects of **violence** at some point generate counter memes to **suppress** the **violence**. See Chapter 7, on population dynamics of war and peace memes.

Stamp collectors won't beat you up.

Why does the **spread me** meme not **go wild** in many ideologies? Why don't hard core stamp collectors **kill** to **spread** stamp collecting? There may well be hard core stamp collectors for whom their hobby is the primary focus of their lives, maybe the only thing they live for. Maybe because there is no stamp collecting leader, urging them to stamp out coin collectors, and convert them to stamp collectors. Also stamp collectors are a small group. They don't have much power. They do not **force** conformity on members of their group. If you want to collect stamps in an odd way, the worst that will happen to you is that the other stamp collectors will say you are not a true or proper stamp collector. They won't **beat you up.**

A leader unbalanced.

Maybe it's because you need a leader like Mao Zedong who sees his country in a mess, overrun by warlords and colonialists, and who convinces himself that an ideology like communism is the answer to help his country, and who then **spreads** the communism memes, even by **violent** methods like war and brainwashing. His nationalism meme bundle was connected so emotionally and **strongly** in his mind, that it wiped out any other possibly restraining memes, like **compassion**, that might have controlled his **spread me** meme. So his **spread me** meme was allowed to promote the killing, and brainwashing, of millions of people, to satisfy his desire for a Chinese nation. His excessively strong nationalism memes wiped out any counter balancing memes.

A leader with hypothetical vision.

So maybe it has to start with some individual leader, who gloms onto a far off hypothetical evil or good, and who is willing to use **violence,** for his purposes. He then stirs up enough people with war memes, to the extent that their **spread me** memes go into hyperdrive.

Easy control of the spread me meme?

In the preceding we have been circling around the question of when and how does the **spread me** meme cross the red line to **violence**. There seems to be more questions than answers. It would have been nice if we had been able to find some shortcut, some neat trick, which would easily allow **control** of the **spread me** meme. This may not happen. The **spread me meme** is nothing by itself. It only works in conjunction with other memes. Its **strength** is somehow determined by the other memes it is associated with. So we may not get very far just trying to analyze the **spread me** meme in isolation, as the above examples show.

Memes are always social.

In most of the other memes analyzed so far, we first looked at the meme in isolation. This often led to progress. In some cases we found our memes of interest very much entangled with other memes. In reality all memes are entangled with others, and with emotions. Memes are always interacting with one another. They change over time. Their populations go up and down in myriad patterns of interaction with one another. The ecology of memes is probably much more complex than the ecologies of living organisms. So some questions we may ask might not be able to be answered easily. We need more work, more research. But there may still be some easy insights into the question: *under what conditions does the* **spread me** *meme get too* **strong**? Below is another approach.

Why and how the spread me meme gets too strong, into violence.

Here's a simple answer which will be explained further below: Some people get **trapped** by their **ideologies**. They so **identify** with their **ideologies** that their i**dentity** is their **ideology**. It's their whole **life**. They can't imagine existing without the **support** their **ideology** provides. The **ideology** is the basis for their **power**, **influence**, **prestige**, and **material well being**. They **feel** that without their **ideology**, they would **die**. They **feel** that they would **starve** because they would have no **material** means of **support**.

Leaders have much more invested.

The preceding does not in general apply to the average person. It applies to the leaders. In each group of a partition caused by the **spread me** meme, or the **we're special** meme, some of the people, the leaders, are more committed to the **ideology** defined by the memes, than the vast majority of the population. These leaders have much more **invested**, are much more **committed** to the **ideology,** than the mass of the population. These leaders are the **enforcers**. They are sensitive to any **deviance,** and apply their **spread me** memes more **forcefully,** to correct any **deviance**. In a **hierarchical organization**, the higher up a leader is, the more dependent he is on the continuance of the **ideology**. And the lower down a person is in the **hierarchy**, the less she is committed to the **ideology**.

Leaders identify with their ideology.

Consider three people: a capitalist, a bishop, and a leader of a tribe in some ethnic group. Each one's **persona** is defined, more **strongly**, by the **ideology** of the group than the average member of the group. This is fundamentally because his **material well being** is dependent more **strongly** on the acceptance of the memes of the **ideology** by all the members of the group. If the population stops believing in capitalism, the religion of the bishop, or the beliefs and customs of the ethnic group, then what happens to these three leaders? Their position is eroded. This is not just theoretical. This is **practical**. The **material basis** for their **existence** is removed. The **rationale** for their **power**, **wealth**, and **influence,** is removed. What could a bishop do if there are no believers? No one will listen to him. No one will contribute money. How will he feed himself? Where will he live? Similarly what does the capitalist think he would do if the economic system were changed drastically? What can an ethnic group leader do if all the youth are abandoning the group's customs? They will see **hard times** ahead. **Starvation**. At least it will **seem** so to them.

Individual self preservation led to wars.

In primitive times, small bands of a hundred or so related people roamed around together. They might settle in some nice productive place, where there was plenty of game, or fruit and plants to eat, or where the soil was good and crops could be grown, or where domestic animals might be kept. Times were good. With plenty of food their population might grow to the point where there might no longer be enough food. Or the weather changes and their fertile valley turns to desert. What can they do? They are more and more hungry. They move. They think of **starvation**. They travel until they come upon another good place. If there are no other humans there, they just settle there. If there are other humans there, and if they are **fearful** enough of **starvation**, they will **fight** the inhabitants, and **kill** them, if they can, so that they may have the good area to live in, and supply themselves with food. They **kill** others to **preserve** their own **lives**. Almost any animal, if cornered and threatened enough, that the animal perceives its **life** to be **threatened**, will become **vicious**, **violent** enough to **kill** or try to **kill** his attacker. We can call this the instinct for **self preservation**. So individual **self preservation** led to wars.

Self preservation is a meme.

This leads to an explanation of how wars may continue to occur. We do not need any kind of group genetic selection for war. The simple instinct for individual **self preservation** is enough. This instinct is already wired in almost every individual animal. **Self preservation** is a meme. All we need is for this meme to survive to modern times, maybe modified slightly. In the example of the past tribe, the **self preservation** meme operated in the customary sense of avoiding **physical death**. In modern times, the **self preservation** meme still operates that way, but it can also operate to **preserve** the person's **psychological self**, or **spiritual self**, his **way of life**, **his image of himself**, **his identity**, **his memes!**

If I am my memes, then self preservation applies to my memes.

In the past, impending **starvation** caused sufficient **fear** in people, **fear of death**, to activate their **self preservation** meme, so that they would **kill** others, in order to prevent their own **death**. In modern times, anything which can cause sufficient **fear**, **fear of death**, actual physical death, or even just **spiritual** or **psychological** death, or, (we might even say), **memetic** death, will activate the **self preservation** meme, and may cause people to **kill** others, to prevent their own **death**, actual or otherwise. The **fear** that is experienced does not have to correspond to reality.

*"... His confrontational stance toward Israel **bolstered his domestic and regional standing**, and therefore Nasser was willing to accept the **risk** that they might trigger a war with the Israelis. In fact in April 1967, after meeting with Nasser, U. S. official Lucius Battle reported back to Washington that he believed that the Egyptian leader was anxious to create a foreign policy crisis in order to deflect mounting internal pressure against his regime. ... Faced with growing domestic and regional opposition, Nasser took strategic risks in order to try to minimize his political losses."* --- [Cashman & Robinson, 2007, page 181, emphasis added].

So Nasser **risked** war, **killing** people, to **preserve** his **self memes** as a great leader. Nasser was not the first and not the last political leader to make this choice.

Willing to kill for their ideology.

Those people whose **material well being**, whose **identity**, whose continued **existence**, in their own view, depend exclusively on the **continuance** of their **defining ideology,** will be willing to **kill,** if they **perceive** their **ideology** to be **threatened**. On the other hand, a person who sees himself as able to continue to **exist,** and **prosper,** with a different set of memes, need not **fear change**. He will have no need to **kill** to preserve his **ideology**. He will not be **trapped** by his **ideology**.

War is self defense.

War caused by this mechanism is always **self defense**. It is not necessarily **physical** self defense. It is **defense of self defining memes**. The aggressors are responding to their **perceived threats** to their **self defining ideologies**. Those whom the aggressors attack respond with **self defense** in the usual sense.

Leaders only, the meme enforcers.

The above applies to the leaders, the meme **enforcers**, of the group. The mass of people have to be brought to war by other means. The people don't know what's going on. Or at least they didn't in the past. Some are waking up now. They are **conned** by propaganda. They are **herded** like animals. Their own **fears** are stirred up by the leaders, who paint the other group as **threatening** the **existence** of the whole group.

Only a few leaders may be the seeds which lead to war.

Not all the leaders of an **ideology** have to be so **trapped** by their **ideology**. It only requires **one,** or a **few,** to be infected by a **self limiting** meme. This one or a few, spread the **contagion** by fear, propaganda, the usual methods, to enough of the rest of the leaders, until most of them then **spread** the war memes to enough of the population of followers, so that the war may be started. Only one or a few **trapped** leaders can be the seeds which lead to war.

Mere existence is a threat.

The mere existence of group 2 can be perceived as a **threat** to the **ideology** of group 1 by the leaders of group 1. That's because most **ideologies** contain the meme that says the **ideology** is the **one and only true way**. This meme is good for group 1 because it helps the **spread me** meme of group 1 enforce all of group 1's memes on the members of group 1. So, many successful groups will have this **one and only true way** meme. The existence of a similar but different ideology in group 2 contradicts the **one and only true way** meme of group 1. This is a **threat** to the **ideology** of group 1. The **enforcer** meme, the **spread me** meme of group 1, then wants to **convert** or **exterminate** group 2.

Similar but different.

The two groups have to be similar but different. They can't be too similar or two different. If they are too similar, then they might not be perceived as different groups at all. If they are too different, the members of group 1 might not be able to imagine the memes of group 2 to be potential replacements for their group 1 memes. Then group 1 would not see group 2 as a **threat**. So, not enough **fear** would be generated in the leaders of group 1 to start a war. Probably relevant here, would be any evolution of group 2 from group 1, that may have occurred in the past. How do new meme species arise? That is, how do **ideologies** speciate? This needs further research. The speciation of Protestantism led to the one hundred years war in Europe.

Self limiting memetic trap.

We have shown how wars can occur as a result of the primitive, yet persisting, simple genetic, or memetic, instinct for individual **self preservation**. The instinct for **self preservation** relevant here in modern times is memetic, not genetic, since the **self preservation** we are talking about is **ideological self preservation**. This derivation required that the leaders of an **ideology feel trapped** by their **ideology**. They must **feel** there is no alternative to their current **ideologically** supported **existence**. Those **trapped** by their **ideologies** have small minds and little vision because they cannot imagine existence without their **ideology**. They refuse to consider memes outside their **ideology**. Their meme filters are so strong against any memes outside their **ideological** meme set, that even if such new memes would be useful, they cannot see them, they cannot accept the new, useful information.

Again: Why and how the spread me meme goes wild enough to kill.

The leaders of group 1 see the simple existence of the memes of group 2, or they see the memes of group 2 **spreading,** maybe even to some members of group 1, and they have increasing **fear,** that their group 1 memes may be **overrun,** or **wiped out,** in time. Since their **power**, **privileges**, **material well being**, and in their view, maybe their own **physical existence**, depend on their position as a leader, and strong **enforcer,** of group 1's memes, their personal **self preservation** instinct leads them to accept a strong enough version of group 1's **spread me** meme, to urge all the members of group 1, to go to war against group 2. The **strength** of the **spread me** meme, for their group 1 meme set, their **ideology,** increases enough, that they are willing to **kill** members of group 2. There it is! This is why and how the **spread me** meme **goes wild enough to kill**. This provides a memetic explanation for many wars. And it's surely a contributing factor to all wars.

This explains many wars among ethnic groups, religions, communism, capitalism, and nations.

The **trapped by ideology** meme explains many wars between nations. It explains the wars between capitalism and communism. It explains wars between religions, and wars between ethnic groups. The analysis above showed simple partitions of humanity. We looked at how humanity is partitioned by nation states. We saw another partition of humanity by religion. The analysis looked at wars between two or more groups of the same partition. But there is nothing in principle to prevent war between two groups one of which is, say, a nation, and the other is, say, a religion. The fact is that the real world allows mixing up of categories.

For example both the Korean and Vietnam wars and the Chinese civil war were partly wars between denominations of religion against communism. They also were wars between nation states as well as wars between communism and capitalism. [Gilbert, 2001], [Cashman & Robinson, 2007]. The one hundred years war in Europe was between and among nation states, or their predecessor kingdoms, principalities, etc., as well as among religious groups.

One and only true way meme.

So although in the real world, categories can mix it up, the causative meme, **trapped by ideology**, remains. Leaders so **identify** with their supporting **ideologies** that they can't imagine existing without them. When they perceive a **threat** to their **ideology**, the **one and only true way** meme, which is contained in almost all **ideologies**, says they must defend their **ideology,** because there is nothing else. The strength of the **one and only true way** meme will correlate with the strength of the perceived **ideological trap**.

Leaders' memes versus people's memes.

This observation that the war process starts with leaders is important because the **spread me** meme, or **defense** memes, for a group's **ideology,** are not very **strong** in the lowest levels of any **hierarchy**. The people at the bottom could often care less about their **ideology** memes. It didn't much matter to peasants who bossed them around. They could be sure someone would. In modern times, most average citizens pay little, or no, attention to what their government is doing, as long as it doesn't screw up too badly, with a war, or economic collapse. This means we need to keep in mind that meme processes in leaders and the subservient populations may be quite different. We need to focus on both. The program of this book is mostly based on the idea, that average people can disinfect and inoculate themselves, from war memes enough, so that the leaders will no longer be able to herd them into war. We could also try to change leaders' memes directly, simultaneously.

The program of this book does not need the above explanation of war.

Although the above is interesting and may be helpful for our understanding, for the purposes of this program, we do not need grand theories of the causes of wars. We do not need to be concerned too much about which of the various theories is correct. Maybe each theory is partly correct. Nor do we need explanations of why and how the **spread me** meme **goes wild**. We can control our **spread me** memes by the simple methods of this program. We simply identify any memes we suspect may lead to war, one by one, analyze them, and change, or eliminate them from ourselves, and urge enough others to do likewise.

Music.

Music can strengthen the spread me meme.

Music can promote war because it can stir up our **emotions**. When our **emotions** are stirred up enough, memes can get into our minds easier because the stirred up **emotions** distract our meme filters. Rousing music also strengthens the **spread me** meme. If our **emotions** are stirred up enough, that the **spread me** meme, associated in a meme complex, with some ideal such as liberty or communism, goes into hyperdrive, then we can accept war, we can be ready to **kill**. Specific memes can be associated with specific music. The Nazis ruined some great music, for many people, by playing the music over and over on the radio, before announcements of their victories. For me that knowledge has forever associated *Les Preludes* by Franz Liszt with Nazism. If I hear the **glorious** music of *Les Preludes,* I can't help but think of Nazism, and all the **horrors** of WW II. Similarly many people, even today, experience a **sickening** feeling, when they hear the music of Richard Wagner, because they know Wagner's operas were appropriated for Nazi propaganda. As in operas, the music added to the sound tracks of movies, allows the movie director to **manipulate** the audience's **emotions,** minute by minute, throughout the movie.

Visual art brings in memes by parallel processing.

Similarly visual art has a certain advantage in transmitting memes because visual art allows many memes to enter a mind at once, in parallel, and thus bypass some of the meme filters, which may work better on linear sequences of memes, such as those presented by speech or writing. Music and visual arts may enhance both pro-war and anti-war memes.

Fame.

Fame is: a: public estimation **b:** popular acclaim.

Bread and circuses.

This is an odd one and maybe somewhat a stretch. It's partly like the Romans' bread and circuses. Keep the population distracted, so it doesn't cause problems. It can be an entertaining diversion from reality. Thus its danger. The fascination with the behavior of the **famous** can distract the populations from the harmful actions of governments. Their minds are filled with memes about the **famous**. So there is less room in their minds, and less time in their days, for the real things that affect their lives. No time to pay attention to the boring, confusing, hidden, and secret, acts of governments.

The myth.

The desire for **fame** is related to the desires for **money** and **success**. The focus on **fame, money,** and **success,** can cause people to desire these things. The myth of **fame**, **money,** and **success,** says they would solve all my problems. I'd be **rich**. I could **afford** cosmetic surgery. Everybody would **like me**. Everybody would pay **attention** to me. I'd have all the **sex** I want, all day, and all night long. No more worries. I'd be **perfect**.

Work, work, work, work.

So these myths can distract people from other things and keep them **working**. Since most people who seek **fame**, **money** and **success** have concepts of them which are so **extravagant**, they can never have enough. They can be in states of perpetual **anxiety,** because no matter how much **money** they have, no matter how much **success** they have, no matter how much **fame**, it can never be enough. So **work, work, work, work**. Of course not everybody who has **money, success,** or **fame,** buys into the above simplistic myths. Those who have **money,** etc. at least have opportunities to **develop** themselves, in more beneficial ways, than those of the simple myths.

Work ethic not all bad.

No doubt these myths can distract people so leaders can more easily do dirty deeds. And the **work, work, work, work** ethic can keep people busy as well as maybe produce more things. This last is not necessarily bad for people. After all, the world still needs a lot of things: food, houses, medicines, environmental protection, global warming reversal.

People need distractions.

But people also need distractions from all the unpleasantness of the world: wars, disease, disasters, suffering. So let them divert themselves with fantasies of **fame** and **fortune**, and winning the **lottery**.

If some is good, is more better?

The fact that some people can never have enough of **fame, money**, or **success,** suggests there may be some interesting meme dynamics going on here. Some runaway memes. How might these work? Maybe these are examples of the **if some is good, more is better** meme. This is a common meme which in many cases has harmful consequences, for example with drugs and food.

Decreasing marginal utility.

There is a principle in economics called the principle of decreasing marginal utility. If you have no apples, and I give you one, that apple has a greater value to you, than if you already had 15 apples, and I gave you another one. In the case of people who can never get enough **money, fame**, or **success**, it seems the principle of decreasing marginal utility does not apply. So likely, utility is not what matters to them.

What am I worth?

The meme, **amount of money I have,** is not connected in their mind primarily to the utility of **money**. We can get a clue from another way this meme is expressed: **net worth. Worth,** yes, this gives it away! What am I **worth**? So it's **self esteem**. It's a measure of **worth, value, goodness,** applied to myself. So we're back to the myth of **fame,** above. **Everyone will pay attention to me**. If everyone pays **attention** to me, then I must be **good**. These people are using the amount of **fame, success**, or **money** they have as measures of their **value as human beings**. Is it an absolute thing or is it a relative thing, a way of **ranking** themselves and others? Probably it's a **ranking**. If it weren't a **ranking**, would they always want more? And there is plenty of empirical evidence from the ways **rich, famous,** and **successful** people interact with one another that it is a **ranking**.

It's a put down.

If it's a **ranking**, then it's a way of **putting most people down**. That's what it is. Just look at people who spend most of their time watching movie stars. It's clear they definitely feel **inferior** to them. So it's a way of making people feel they are **incomplete** human beings, that they are **second class**, not as **good**. Movie stars are **like gods** compared to **lowly me**. It's also a way of making some people feel they are better than others. But note that most of the better people in the **fame**, **money**, **success, hierarchy**, in that they have bought into the **hierarchy**, feel **inferior** to those **above** them, and thus they are also **kept in their places** by these memes.

So it is a war meme.

So the **fame**, **money**, **success** memes help to keep most of the people in their place, that is, **subservient** to **authorities**, in a **hierarchy,** with most people on the **bottom**, to keep them as **zombies** and **slaves**. So **fame** is a war meme! I really felt it was, but I wasn't sure I could get there. But there it is! The memes for ever more **money,** and ever more **success,** are also war memes. In their effects these three memes are similar to the **obey authority** meme.

Memetic traps.

In our previous discussion, of how a too strong **spread me** meme, can lead people to war, we came upon the **trapped by ideology** meme. Related to this is a more general idea, namely a memetic **trap**. The **trapped by ideology** meme is a special case. There are all kinds of memetic **traps,** and it would take several books to explore them all. The general idea is, that a person, or group of people, have a set of operational memes, which keep them from improving, adapting, evolving. It is often obvious to other people, or people outside the group, that those **trapped** could do better. But those **trapped** don't seem able to see this. In one sense everybody is in a memetic **trap**. At any instant we can only make decisions based upon the memes we have. We have nothing else to work with. But now most of us know that if what we are doing is not working to our satisfaction, we should try something else, look for some new memes. But sadly, there are people, and nations, that from their actions, seem not to realize this. Here's a sad example. A woman stays with an abusive husband. Her set of operational memes does not allow her to leave him and seek help. We all can get into **traps**. We limit ourselves in many ways. One of the biggest **traps** is to think we have found **the answer** to some area of life, or all of life. We may think that **the answer** we have found is so good, so true, or whatever, that it can never be improved. There are no such answers.

What is a memetic trap?

A **memetic trap** is a set of interacting memes, in a person, or other meme organism, which tend to exclude other memes, and which tend to reinforce themselves with use, and which are ineffective or counter productive.

War trap.

A **war trap** is a **memetic trap** that says war is the answer. A group of people, or a nation, at war, is in a memetic war **trap**.

Typical content of war traps.

A **war trap** contains many specifically war related memes such as **enemy, fear, hatred, revenge, injustice, horror, atrocity, death, killing, injury, destruction, fighting, noble, brave, hero, defense, defender, attack, punishment, war, peace, conflict**, and many more. These basic memes are connected in various ways by other memes to form larger meme sets. A narrative, a story, is the common and easily understood way these memes are tied together. In a **war trap**, there are usually narratives like the following. Our **enemy** is **evil** and wants to **destroy** us, **kill** us, **injure** us. Our **enemy** is not as good as we are. Our enemy is **subhuman**. Our **enemy** has **fought** us in the past, is **fighting** us now, and will probably want to keep **fighting** us in the future. Our **enemy** does not desire **peace**. Our **enemy** only desires **war**. We on the other hand are acting in **self defense**, are **noble**, **brave**, **heroes**, and desire **peace**. And God is on our side. The feelings of **fear** and **hatred** and desire for **revenge**, and **punishment** of the **enemy**, will be connected with these narratives. The narrative will likely go on and on, repeating diverse **gory** details of past **atrocities**. The longer the war, or series of conflicts, has been going on, and the more **horrific** the **fighting**, the more intense the feelings of **fear**, **hatred**, desire for **revenge** will be.

Trap contents tighten the traps.

Each side's **trap** is the ideology of that side, the complete set of all its memories of **injustices**, **fighting**, **death** and **destruction** of the distant or recent past, as well as all the **fears**, **hatreds**, and ideas of **revenge** associated with them. Included within these warring ideologies may be the idea that war works to help them attain their goals. Or maybe not. Maybe the **fear**, **hatred**, desire for **revenge** memes are themselves so strong, that one or the other side, may resort to war, even without believing that war works. Or some people may start a conflict for perceived personal aggrandizement, such as money, or political advancement. Specific content of the war **traps** may vary. The point is that each ideology is a **trap**: The content is such that each side can see no way out, no options, except to continue with their current **trapped** ideology. This **reinforces** the **trap**. Continued conflict adds to the lists of **injustices**, reinforces **fears** and **hatreds**, and **tightens** the **traps** for each side, **strengthens** the ideology. Even if one side is nearly exterminated, the remnants may carry on the ideology for generations, as seeds for future wars.

A war is a trap of dynamically interacting traps.

The participants are **trapped** each within their own war ideology, and the two or more ideologies are interacting. The several ideologies dynamically react to, and feed off of, and reinforce, one another. It is indeed a **trap** of two or more interacting **trapped** ideologies.

Help from outside.

If two countries or groups are **fighting** a war or are engaged in a conflict spiral, what can be done? The participants are **trapped** by their operational meme sets, their war ideologies. They each probably believe they can achieve a net **gain** by **fighting**. They each are willing to trade off the **death** and **destruction** they will suffer for some imagined **gain**. They each have a list of **grievances** and **injustices** going back maybe years. There has been action, reaction, rereaction, rerereaction, never to end. Since they are **trapped** and they cannot help themselves get out of their respective **traps**, if there is to be any help, it must come from **outside** the warring ideologies.

Show them that war is not working and that there are alternatives.

Those outside the war **traps** must **work** to pull out those **trapped**. How do we do this? To use **force** or **violence** would be absurd. So we must communicate with them. We must get new memes in to them. We must show those **trapped** that they are **trapped**. That war is not **working**. That war is not bringing them what they say they **need** or **want**. They must see this. The ideologies must be opened up by those outside the **traps**. We help them to see the mechanisms, the memes that keep them **trapped**. Then they, and those helping from outside, must work together, to dismantle the **trapping** ideologies, in the minds of all the combatants. The **fears**, **hatreds**, desires for **revenge** associated with the long lists of **injustices** must be damped down. The past must be disconnected from the present situation, because to continue to focus on the past long lists of **injustices,** and their associated **fears**, **hatreds**, desires for **revenge**, who was **right** and who was **wrong**, just goes back into the ideologies, reinforces them. But that is the **trap** we are trying to help everybody get out of. So we must stay out of that trap ourselves, we must give that up, disconnect ourselves, and them, from the past, at least for the purpose of stopping the war. People will change what they are doing, if they can see that what they are doing is not working, and that there are alternatives. That's it. The people outside the **traps** must keep talking to, working on, those inside the **traps,** until enough are pulled out to stop the war or conflict.

How to pull people out of their traps in practice.

There are complications of course that make this difficult in practice. The war or conflict extends beyond those physically engaged in the fighting. The ideologies of the various participating factions can and almost always do spread far and wide away from those physically engaged in fighting.

It's easy for outsiders to fall into a war trap.

A person who **empathizes** more with those in one group than another, in a war, or series of ongoing conflicts, can easily **adopt** the set of memes from that one side, because of the nature of **empathy**: Having the same **feelings** as those on that one side of the conflict, causes them to **adopt** the other memes in the set, because the **feelings** are **connected** with, **associated** with, **cause**, or are **caused** by, the memes in the narrative, and the narrative itself. The narratives can go on and on, years, tens of years, hundreds, even thousands of years. A president can inadvertently use the word *crusade* and immediately add 800 year old **fear** and **hatred** memes to a **war trap**.

<u>To help stop the war it must be seen from ouside the traps.</u>

People and countries not directly involved must not be sucked in. So people outside the **traps** must keep themselves out. People outside the **traps** may be **empathic** more toward one group than another. This is dangerous because if they are not careful, they may be sucked into the ideological **trap** of the group they **empathize** with. People outside the **traps** must see the conflict from the point of view of humanity as a whole. From this viewpoint, war is always **bad**. War is always a **net loss** for humanity. Wars are **death** and **destruction**. Wars **diminish** people on all sides of all conflicts. People outside the **war traps** must **empathize** with the human suffering in all warring populations and must not buy into the **trap** of any side. The outsiders must temporarily ignore all the **history**, all the **arguments**, all the claimed **injustices**. To do otherwise is to get sucked into the ideology **trap** of one group or another, to join the ongoing verbal war. This is not to say the two sides are morally equivalent. But for the purpose of stopping the war, the **morality**, the **justice,** of each faction must be set aside. These matters may be relevant later to establish a **just peace**.

<u>It can be difficult to stop a war.</u>

The above is easy to say, easy to carry out in principle. In practice it can be a lot of **work**. We must get many people to change their minds. We must get enough people outside the **traps** to take an **empathic** view of all those inside the **traps** and be willing to do some **work** to end the war. One problem is that it's not a simple clear inside/outside fine line. There are many people not directly involved in the war who have gotten **trapped** in one or the other ideologies, or they are on their way to being **trapped**, or who tend to **empathize** more with one side than the other. The ideologies are saturated with all the **grievances**, **injustices**, real, exaggerated, or imagined, that each side has regarding the other. After a long series of interactions, conflicts, or war, many, even most, felt **grievances** and **injustices** are real. After all, we have just assumed the fighting has been going on for a long time. A lot of physical, and mental, **damage** will have been done by all participants, each to the others, as well as to themselves. Within each **ideology** there have been built up huge amounts of **fear**, **anger**, **loathing**, **hatred**, and long, long lists of real **injustices**. All these horrors of war, all these emotions, make it very difficult for participants, as well as outsiders, to think straight. In so far as an outsider has bought into such an ideology, that person has joined the war, at least verbally. These people also need to be helped to get out of their traps.

<u>Once the war is stopped, what next?</u>

Once the war is stopped, how do we keep it or similar wars from starting up again? One theory is to apportion blame, pick out some possible war criminals. Then investigation, indictment, trials, and punishment if there is a conviction. A logical reason to take this course is to deter others from committing the same or similar crimes in the future. In our present culture this may be the best we can do and thus this may be necessary. It might be better if somehow the punishment could be accompanied by or replaced by a genuine conversion out of the war **trapping** ideologies. Yes, of course, no forced conversions. That would be absurdly to use violence to eliminate violence. But prison is violence. Maybe the convicted war criminal could be given a choice: Either prison, or effectively working to show the world that wars don't work, and how to avoid war **traps**. Of course, this is not pure non-violence, because the threat of prison is a kind of violence, but it's not as bad as unconditional prison time. But more importantly, it would work to eliminate war memes.

Secrecy.

Secrecy is kind of opposite to the **free speech** meme. It wants to keep memes **hidden**. It is used by governments mostly to keep relevant information about government activities from the people. The purpose of **secrecy** is only very rarely to keep information **hidden** from adversaries. So **secrecy** allows governments, and leaders, to plan and undertake activities that lead to war, **without review** by the people. See the book *The Way of the World* by Ron Suskind. [Suskind, 2008] So **secrecy** by governments, or government leaders, is a war meme. **Secrecy** inhibits the **free circulation** of memes. So it is bad for **meme evolution**. It is bad for **democracy**. Since it is bad for **meme evolution,** it is bad for societies, our cultures, and for the **progress** of humanity as a whole.

Censorship.

Censorship is very much like **secrecy**. It has been used by governments. It has also been openly used by religious institutions in the past. Today it has often gone underground in the form of **self censorship** by government officials, journalists, writers, producers, religious and corporate leaders and members. This is because it cannot coexist openly with the **free speech,** meme which is supposed to be applicable in many modern cultures. Like **secrecy**, **censorship** inhibits the **free circulation** of memes and it thus has all the negative consequences listed above for **secrecy**. During wars newspapers and other media are **censored** by governments. During coups, political instability, or other crises, the governments of some countries **shut down** newspapers, TV, radio stations, and the Internet.

Self Fulfilling Prophecies.

A **self fulfilling prophecy** is a meme whose expression causes the actual occurrence of what it represents. If a person believes she is **ignorant**, then she may not learn much. A girl who thinks mathematics is **too hard** for girls probably won't do well in mathematics. The meme **there will always be war** is, we have seen, at least partly, a **self fulfilling prophecy**. How does a meme become a **self fulfilling prophecy**? First it becomes a belief of one or more people. That is, it gets past their meme filters, gets imbedded with their other memes, and becomes operational for them. That is, it is used by those having it, as if it were true whether or not it is. So they act, behave as if it were true. So if the belief is about some human behavior or ability, they will, or will not, engage in the behavior or develop the ability. The girl who believes mathematics is **too hard** for girls will not develop her mathematical abilities. If most girls believe this, few women will become mathematicians, and it will indeed seem as if mathematics is **too hard** for girls, because there will be fewer women mathematicians than men mathematicians. If you believe you **can't** dance you won't even **try**. If you believe you are **talented** musically, you are more likely to **practice** singing or playing a musical instrument. If most of the world believes **there will always be war**, then few people will work to eliminate war, and there may well **always be war**. There are probably many other **self fulfilling prophecies** that lead to war.

Conformity.

What is the conformity meme?

The **conformity** meme says just accept the memes of the group you are in, don't generate any new memes yourself. Look to others to see what kind of clothes they are wearing, and then wear the same things. Act like others do. Think like others do. Don't do anything different from what the people around you do. Don't come up with any new memes yourself. Don't combine old memes to come up with anything new. There are two ways people can get new memes: 1) get new memes from outside yourself, from others; 2) get new memes from your own self by thinking, dreaming, exploring, investigating, playing, working, trying new combinations, through **creativity**. **Conformity** puts the emphasis on the first method, in some people almost to the total suppression of the second method.

Necessary for living in groups.

We are social creatures. A human totally isolated from contact with other humans becomes a sad, pathetic human specimen who will almost surely be very unhappy, and who will almost surely die much sooner than she otherwise would. So to be completely human we must get many memes from other people, from outside ourselves. So of course we must then have some **conformity**. The **conformity** meme is bad only when it's **too strong**, when it's **so strong** that there is too little **creativity**. Obviously, the optimal state is for a proper balance.

Group becomes a herd.

So when the **conformity** meme is **too strong,** a person is not thinking, not being **creative**, is letting herself be guided, and controlled, by the behavior, memes of the people around her. If all the members of a group have **too strong conformity** memes, the group becomes a **herd**. And a **herd** can be **herded** into a war by cowboy leaders. So a **too strong conformity** meme leads to war.

PORTRAIT: Rest in Peace 11R.

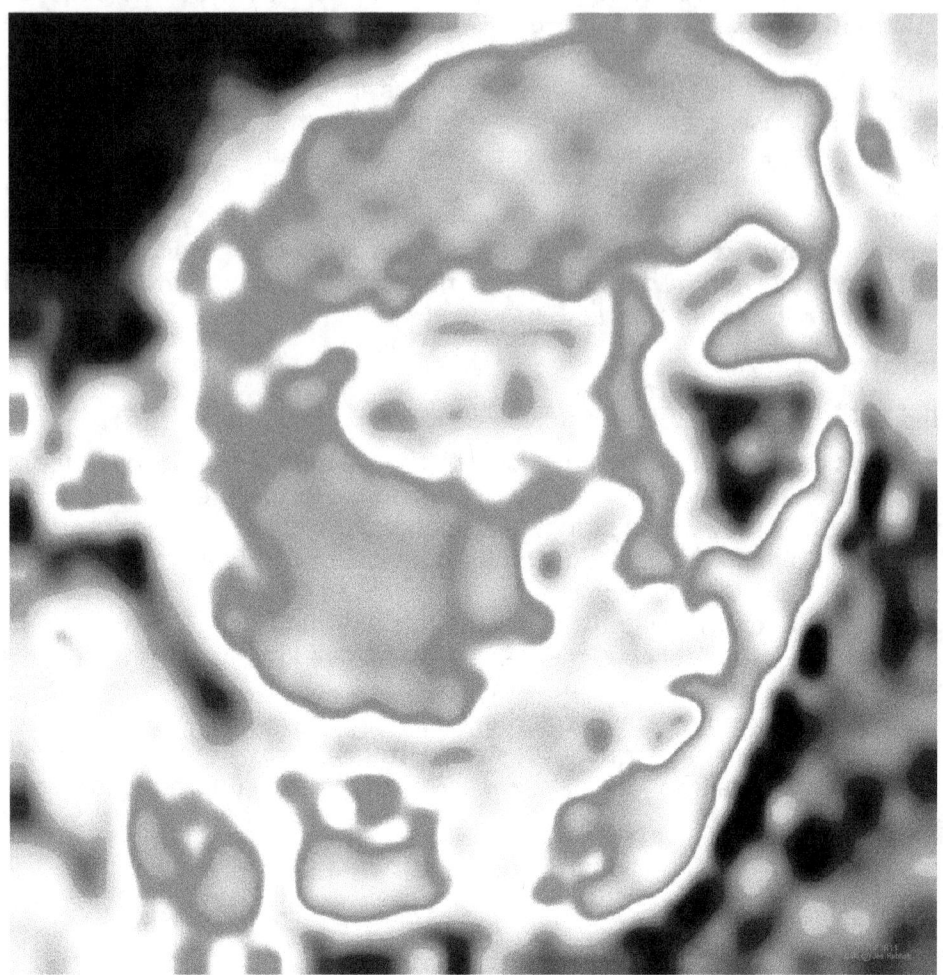

Groupthink.

"... [In Oct. 1941] The [Japanese] Navy was divided. Though many of its leaders believed it would be madness to fight the U. S., they would not say this openly..." --- [Cashman & Robinson, 2007, page 132].

The **conformity** meme is the same as, or is closely related to, the **groupthink** meme. The **groupthink** meme in the causes of war literature, is when some group in a country, such as a particular class, or a bureaucratic subunit, such as the foreign service, or maybe the leaders of an army, for some reason or other, are cut off from outside memes, to the extent that they do not have relevant information, memes, corresponding to the real world situation their country faces. The members of the group **all think the same way**. This may be due to one, or a few, individuals who by their personalities, or their strong **ideology,** force their views on all the other members. Maybe it can come about merely by a strong **conformity** meme in the members of the group. And there are other ways **groupthink** can come about. However **groupthink** comes about, the group's **decisions** may not correspond to reality, because they have not used all the memes that could have been available to them. They make wrong **decisions**. They **misperceive** their adversaries. Maybe they go to war on the basis of **false** information. So **groupthink** and the **conformity** memes can lead to war.

*" ... In **groupthink**, members of a **cohesive, homogeneous,** and **insulated decision** making group strive for **unanimity** and **cohesion**, adversely affecting their ability to **realistically** assess the problem in front of them. The need for group **cohesion** is driven by situations of high **stress** and the inherent difficulties of making critical national-security **decisions**. Group **cohesion** serves to allay the **stress** felt by group members but leads to several problems: **limitations** of group debate, **limitation** of options, the **closing** of the process to outsiders, **suppression** of doubts and **self censorship**, unwillingness to **criticize** the opinions of others, unwillingness to **confront** the risks of the preferred solution, selective **bias** in favor of the group's preferred solution, and a general lack of critical **thinking**. The result is a policy that is ill considered, risky, and unlikely to lead to a successful outcome."* --- [Cashman & Robinson, 2007, page 9, emphasis added].

When in doubt assume the worst.

Totally crude.

This is a deliberate refusal to consider all rational possibilities. This is stupid. If this meme had been operational in Robert Kennedy's mind during the Cuban missile crisis of 1962, most of us would likely not be alive today. Dick Cheney supposedly accepted this meme when contemplating possible future terrorist attacks after 9/11. Presumably this made him a greater hawk than he would have been if he had been more rational.

"... an expected utility theory of war says that wars are intentional, calculated acts and that they will only occur when the initiator believes that war will yield a positive expected utility. --- [Cashman & Robinson, 2005, page 6].

"... The expected utility of a particular war strategy is a function of the sum of the utilities of the possible outcomes times their probabilities." --- [Cashman & Robinson, 2007, page 7].

So the **when in doubt assume the worst** meme is a totally crude, fragmentary, and degenerate, attempt to apply expected utility theory. Instead of looking at all of the possible outcomes, you only look at one, the worst, and you base your decision only on that one. This is being deliberately ignorant. So clearly this is a war meme.

State Rivalry.

*"Statistically, long-term enduring **rivals** have been responsible for <u>roughly half</u> of all wars, militarized disputes, and violent changes of territory in the last two centuries. More than half the interstate wars in the nineteenth and twentieth centuries occurred between enduring **rivals**, and disputes among enduring **rivals** are almost twice as likely to end in war than disputes occurring between other pairs of states."* --- [Cashman and Robinson, 2007, page 15, emphasis added].

Some states **compete**. Some don't. **Rivalry** can take various forms. The most ancient is probably **competition** for land or territory. More generally **competition** for material goods. Stuff. Wealth. In the past wealth, stuff, material goods were associated with land. You could grow crops, raise animals on land. You could dig minerals from the earth, harvest forests. As the **wealth** meme expands beyond material goods to include **intangibles** like intellectual property, the importance of land and territory should decrease, although at present we still depend heavily on digging coal and oil from the earth. When the world gets all the energy it needs from sunlight, the desirability of controlling territory should decrease. If a world system of global trading can be established that is stable, fair, environmentally protective, non-exploitative of human labor, this should also reduce the perceived need to control territory. Besides territory, what else generates rivalries between or among states? **Ideologies** generate rivalries; both religious and economic system **ideologies**. Also **pride** and **vanity** in leaders.

Misperceptions.

*"The most relevant, and most typical, **misperceptions** in the realm of international conflicts are (1) the **perceptions** that the **intentions** of one's opponent are more hostile than they are in reality, and (2) the **perception** that the **power** of one's own state (or alliance) is greater than it really is and/or that the **power** of one's opponent (or its alliance) is less than it really is."* --- [Cashman and Robinson, 2007, page 5, emphasis added].

Dysfunctional Crisis Learning.

According to [Cashman and Robinson, 2007, page 15], this is a concept associated with the work of Russell Leng. The enduring **rivals** experience crises involving **force**, **threats** etc. Each **rival** takes certain **lessons**, memes, from each crisis. The **winner** of the crisis **learns** that **force** and **threats work**; the **loser learns** that in the next crisis more **force** and **threats** are needed. So the process escalates to war.

Rational War Theories.

Respect researchers.

Below I will be making some comments and presenting critical quotes from others regarding some research and scholarship concerning war. Please take seriously what I am going to say right now. All the people who engage in this research and scholarship, deserve our deepest respect and admiration, for all the work they have done, and are continuing to do. Many of them have devoted their lives, to discovering and understanding, the causes of war, while the rest of the world gives them little credit. Anyone who wants to see the end of war forever, should welcome all research and scholarship, or any kind of work, literary, artistic, or whatever, that increases our understanding of war. Each of us can only work in the context of our time and culture. If additional research shows some theory to be lacking in some way, this can be viewed as a setback, or as progress. From the perspective of the advancement of knowledge, this is progress, since now we know something that does not work. We should respect, and thank, both the original developers of the theory, and those who found its flaws.

Better theories needed.

There are several theories or schools of thought about war that assume **rationality** or **realism** by leaders or nations.

"**realism** *A theoretical school that argues that, much as individuals in their daily lives are obsessed with their own* **security** *and* **survival**, *states are obsessed with their own* **security** *and* **survival** *in the international system. Thus* **realism** *assumes that all states seek to maximize or maintain their* **power** *in order to ensure their* **security** *in the anarchic global system."* --- [Cashman & Robinson, 2007, page 393, emphasis added].

"**rational choice (or rational actor model)** *A model that assumes that states, as unified* **rational** *actors, undertake the following steps in making a* **decision***: identify and place* **goals** *in the order of their* **importance**, *list the policy* **alternatives** *available for achieving those goals,* **calculate** *the costs and benefits of the* **expected** *outcomes of each* **alternative**, *and* **choose** *the policy that will produce the best outcome (in terms of the balance of costs and benefits)."* --- [Cashman & Robinson, 2007, page 393, emphasis added].

"*In fact, most so-called theories of international politics are not really theories at all."* --- [Bennett & Stam, 2004, page 3].

*"Balance of **power** and other **realpolitik** arguments appear before students in much the same way as they have for decades, unaffected in many classrooms by careful logical analysis demonstrating the logical flaws of the 'theory'."* --- [Bennett & Sam, 2004, page 5, emphasis added].

"Most so-called theories of international politics are simply broad-brush descriptions based on the observation of small numbers of events rather than carefully deduced explanations of political behavior." --- [Bennett & Stam, 2004, page 6].

"First, we believe (and demonstrate later) that no single current theory, conjecture, assertion, or description stands alone as a dominant predictor of international conflict. In subsequent chapters we will show that <u>there is no single indicator</u> for the onset of international conflict with predictive power approaching a level that we would consider high." --- [Bennett & Stam, 2004, page 9, emphasis added].

"In many instances, the logic behind the 'theory' is so vague or poorly specified that it is impossible to test critical underlying causal steps of the argument. … Part of the dilemma is that, in most cases, the various authors do not really have an explicit theory of the decisions that lead to war, Instead, they make conjectural arguments linking some operational measure to some vaguely specified mechanisms that makes the decisions leading to war more or less likely." --- [Bennett & Stam, 2004, page 70].

*"Most **rational choice** theorists treat abstract concepts such as similarity of interests, risk aversion, and <u>the costs of war</u> as implicitly immeasurable …."* --- [Bennett & Stam, 2004, page 86, emphasis added].

So, if this is true, most actual **rational choice** theorists leave out a central requirement of **rational choice** theories!

*"When scholars working in the **rational choice** tradition confront the task of building a general model of interstate conflict and war, they must assume away much of the detail and nuance found in individual cases."* --- [Bennett & Stam, 2004, page 165, emphasis added].

"Most models of interstate behavior must make sweeping simplifying assumptions about states' preferences and decision-making procedures." --- [Bennett & Stam, 2004, page 166].

*"Many critics of **rational choice** models focus on the likely breakdown of procedural **rationality**, and/or agents' cognitive **failure** to be able to perform or even approximate the process that **rational choice** theory imputes to them."* --- [Bennett & Stam, 2004, page 171, emphasis added].

"If there were one single story to take from this book, it would be that there is no single story of war. In many ways, we are as uncertain about the causes and likely timing of any individual war today as we were in 1942 when [Quincy] Wright initially published his study of war." --- [Bennett & Stam, 2004, page 201, emphasis added].

"None of the individual arguments we examined comes close to explaining the majority of international conflict or even a substantial proportion of it." --- [Bennett & Stam, 2004, page 203].

"Given the weakness of the relations between the operational indicators and the onset of war, our results suggest that increased attention to how multiple incentives and factors combine to increase the risk of conflict may prove fruitful." --- [Bennett & Stam, 2004, page 204].

No single cause.

The multiple incentives and factors in this last quote are those things Bennett & Stam's analysis shows all contribute to wars, but no one of them is significant by itself. Any one of them might have been significant for one or a few wars, or conflicts, but no one or a few of them are significant for all wars. So, if for each of these multiple incentives or factors we identify, analyze, and modify, or eliminate, the war memes which relate to that incentive or factor, we will decrease, and eventually eliminate, all of these multiple incentives and factors, that lead to wars. The war memes we are examining in this book relate to these factors and incentives in various ways. A detailed analysis, factor by factor, and incentive by incentive, and meme by meme, would probably require another book.

False confidence.

Why do these and similar theories or schools of thought lead to war? Because, despite their names, they do not correspond to reality. They give a **false confidence** that war can be a **rational choice**. They can give a **false confidence** to the non-expert person, that war, and the causes of war are understood by leaders, and that leaders know what they are doing, when they lead us to war. And the very names given to these theories, **realism**, **rational choice**, **realpolitik**, all clever memetic choices, add to the confusion, by denying with a name, their **disconnect from the real world**.

Almost a joke.

The history of wars gives many examples of leaders who are far from **rational**. They **overestimate** themselves, and their nation, and **underestimate** their opponents. They do not understand the **intentions** of their opponents. They believe their own **propaganda** and **optimistic** estimates. Nations are **not unified**. Different subpopulations have different **goals**. Different parts of the government have different **goals**. There are **rivalries** among parts of the military. Nations are far form unified **rational** actors. It's almost a joke to assert that any nation or leader ever, for any war, carefully and methodically followed the **rational choice** model. For one thing, as we discussed earlier, it is

impossible to calculate the costs and benefits of the expected outcomes of each alternative.

<u>Unrealistic theories mean we need much more research.</u>

So when a theory is **flawed** we must modify it and test it again. We must stop teaching **flawed** theories. If a theory can't be **fixed,** it should be **abandoned**. We all should push, and push, and push, for greater funding, and attention, to all the relevant science areas, international relations, politics, causes of wars, history, psychology, sociology, neuroscience, anthropology. These research areas do not receive nearly enough funding considering their importance for the future of humanity.

Bureaucratic Politics.

Parts of a nation often act for their own **purposes**, not the **purposes** of the nation as a whole. Bureaucracies often act in their own **interests**, not the **interests** of the nation.

"... *The **bureaucratic politics** model argues that government **decisions** are not necessarily the result of a **rational** process; instead, **decisions** are made through a **conflictual** political process by individuals who represent institutions with different **interests**, **outlooks**, and **preferences** (like the Imperial Navy and Imperial Army [of Japan]). Any **decision**, therefore reflects the prevailing balance of power among the various **competing** individuals and groups involved in the process." ---* [Cashman & Robinson, 2007, page 99, emphasis added].

We can replace the phrase *balance of power* with *balance of memes* in the above quote.

"...*European militaries adopted offensive doctrines primarily because, unlike defensive doctrines, they enhanced the **power** and **size** of military **organizations**, they promoted the **autonomy** of the military, they enhanced the **prestige** and **morale** of military professionals, and they minimized uncertainty. For a variety of **bureaucratic** and **psychological** reasons, most **organizations** and the **individuals** within them tend to be reluctant to reconsider core **values** and **beliefs**. Once adopted as policy, offensive **doctrine** and the **beliefs** upon which they were based were naturally **resistant** to change." ---* [Cashman & Robinson, 2007, page 80, referring to World War I, emphasis added].

Once the **offense is better than defense** meme was adopted by the militaries, for the reasons stated in the quote, their meme filters kept other relevant memes out. This **cult of the offense** tended to instability, since part of the cult was that whoever attacked first had an advantage. This instability occurs with nuclear deterrence too.

"... *especially in Germany, war plans were made without input from civilian political officials, resulting in a plan which --- in the context of the 1914 crisis --- made no real political sense and assured the worst possible outcome for Germany ...*" --- [Cashman & Robinson, 2007, page 84].

*"Time and again, Nixon's policy of 'tilting towards' Pakistan was simply **ignored** by those in the government who disagreed with him. The Department of State consistently advocated --- and actively pursued --- a policy designed to undermine Pakistan's ability to meet the rising threat from India, ..."* --- [Cashman & Robinson, 2007, page 238, emphasis added].

There was a similar bureaucratic war in the United States between the State Department and the Defense Department before the start and during the 2003 Iraq war.

Power.

"Power tends to corrupt, and absolute power corrupts absolutely." said Lord Acton. *"Power is an aphrodisiac."* said former United States Secretary of State Henry Kissinger. I wonder how psychologically close this is to sadism or other situations where sex is connected to **dominance** of other people, or using **force,** or other **coercion,** against unwilling people. The exercise of **power** is inherently **bad,** and sometimes **evil**. It is the nature of the exercise of **power** that it **harms** the people against whom **power** is used, because if the people being **forced** to do something, actually wanted to do whatever it is, then **power** wouldn't be needed. So the use of **power** is always **bad**. But when limited **force** is used, say to prevent a crime, we accept it, since a greater **harm** is presumably prevented.

The vicious memetic cycle of power and corruption.

People may have **power**, the ability to **force** other people to do what you want, even more, the ability to **force** other people to do what you want when they do not want to do it, and yet not use that **power**. That's why above I spoke of the exercise of **power** as **bad** or **evil**. But the point of the phrase *power corrupts,* is that many people who have **power,** cannot resist the temptation to use it. This goes along nicely with the meme, which many people have, which says **my way is the best way**. So people with **power** tend to be **corrupted,** and the more **power** they have the more they use it, and the more **corrupt** they become. Often the more corrupt they become, the more power they seek, and get. With enough **power,** a leader or leaders, think they can do whatever they want, **just,** or not, **bad, destructive**, **killing,** or not. And they do. So **power** is a war meme.

Demonization.

It's a trick.

One of the tricks used by some of those pushing war memes is to **demonize** their opponents. If you tell your followers, that people who disagree with you, are **devils**, and your followers believe you, then they will not listen to your opponents. Your followers install simple meme filters of the form don't listen to person X.

It's old.

This is an old rhetorical trick. When you are unable to counter an argument with facts and sense, you can **attack** the character of **the person** making the argument. So when someone attacks the character of another person, instead of addressing the matter being discussed, we should suspect they do not have a good argument for their position.

It's a war meme.

This meme is pro-war because it is used to avoid reasonable discussion. It's used to **fool** people. It shows **disrespect,** or **contempt,** for the person being **demonized,** as well as for the people the meme is being pushed on. It demonstrates simplistic thinking by the person doing the **demonizing**. It is applying the simplistic binary **good versus evil** meme to people.

To lose oneself in a cause greater than oneself.

It's a war meme if the cause is some war.

This is an important factor for some people in some wars. A war can often be that cause. For some people war can give their lives meaning. It is sad to contemplate that some people cannot find meaning in their lives except through war. [Hedges, 2002] has the title *"War is a Force that gives us Meaning"*. So these are people whose minds have been taken over by one or more war memes.

There are many more war memes.

Many of our cultures are polluted and saturated with war memes. In the United States, we have, or have had, wars on cancer, drugs, poverty, crime, and terror. You can probably extend this list. We haven't won any of these. But we keep on fighting. We really like to have wars on stuff. War metaphors are used in many other contexts far removed from military activities. [Lakoff & Johnson, 1980]. The reality of metaphor, the embodiment of metaphor, the fact that metaphors are not just alternative ways of speaking about independently existing reality, but rather are the fundamental ways we understand the world, means we are talking, writing, and thinking about war, consciously and otherwise, when we are dealing with all kinds of other things, that on the surface, would seem to have nothing to do with actual war. So the above list is only a small first step. I have not tried to be methodical in any way. I listed and analyzed these memes, more or less, as they occurred to me. I expect that others will be much more methodical. Surely war memes can be categorized in various ways and relations among them analyzed too. I hope and expect, that many people will continue the process of identifying, and analyzing the memes that lead us to war.

Chapter 7: Population Dynamics of War Memes.

War must have good reasons to exist.

The memes for war must have good reasons to exist because they continue to persist despite all the harm they cause. The reasons are good for the memes, but not for us. These reasons can be appreciated by looking at how the pro-war and anti-war memes interact in a dynamic system. Some times the memes proliferate and spread themselves to many people. Other times they almost die out. To understand war memes, we look at how they grow and diminish, and affect greater and lesser numbers of people.

The number of war memes grows in a positive feedback loop.

War memes like **talk of war** and **threats of war** by leaders. War memes spread better into people who are **fearful**. **Talk of war,** and **threats of war,** create fear. Leaders often deliberately **spread fear,** in their own populations, to make them more susceptible to war memes. And war memes in people create more **fear,** both in the people with the war memes, and in people who do not have the war memes. Imagine a group of people full of war memes. People outside that group, seeing and hearing the war activities, and rhetoric of the group, will experience **fear,** and thus become more **susceptible** to war memes. So war memes are **good at spreading** themselves. They generate **fear,** and **fear** generates more war memes. This process, going on in one country, can cause the same process to start in the proposed enemy country. And that can feedback to the first country. As leaders promote war memes, there comes a time when the number of people hosting war memes, is large enough that the leader can start the war. The other country, whether it wanted a war or not, is now in a war. Then the war memes really spread. Even to several other countries. One good thing about wars, from the meme's point of view, is that wars, by their very nature, cause vast numbers of people to set aside their usual activities, and interests, so they can concentrate their energies on war. The war memes get to **spread to huge numbers** of people that they wouldn't otherwise get to. Maybe these people, now energized by **fear** and war memes, recall their narratives of long past **injustices,** committed against them by their traditional enemies, and thus attack them. War **helps** war memes **spread** far and wide. This is a **huge positive feedback loop**. So we get **runaway growth**. The greater the population of war memes, the faster the population grows. This is an example of frequency dependent fitness. [Dennett, 1995] So war memes, and war, **spread** like a **contagion**.

What stops war memes?

What would **stop** the runaway **growth** of wars? First of all, in at least two cases, war has almost spread to the whole planet. The two World Wars of the twentieth century weren't called world wars for nothing. In some other wars of the twentieth century, **fear** of nuclear annihilation, may have prevented the wars from **spreading**. Also some countries, or groups, become exhausted, or full of anti-war memes, from their recent participation in wars. Wars **destroy** lives and property. When enough soldiers are **killed**, a country can't continue to fight. When food runs out, or oil, or weapons, they can't continue either. So exhaustion of resources can cause a country to **stop fighting**. If a country has enough soldiers and resources, it can **continue fighting**. But the **death** and **destruction,** observed both by soldiers and civilian populations, can cause the proliferation of anti-war memes in both these groups. In wars there are often shortages of food. Civilians can become **malnourished, weak, sick,** and **die from illness or starvation**. Among soldiers who aren't **killed**, many are **wounded,** and mentally **incapacitated,** to some degree. The experiences of war, cause many soldiers, to become temporarily, or permanently **insane**. They **kill** prisoners of war, and civilians, in **cold blood**. Many soldiers **desert,** or **disobey** orders. In Vietnam, some United States soldiers **fragged** their officers. "*Fragged*", as in "*fragmentation*", with a hand **grenade**, or maybe just a **shot** in the back. So, over time, as the **death** and **destruction** continues, anti-war memes proliferate. The leaders continue their propaganda campaigns as best they can, to keep pumping out war memes. But if the war continues long enough, the war memes are overwhelmed by the generated anti-war memes, and either the soldiers, or the civilians, or both, no longer have the **will** to **fight**. So a war can end due to running out of live bodies, (soldiers), and/or material goods, (food, weapons), or due to loss of the **will** to **fight,** because the population of anti-war memes has sufficiently exceeded the population of war memes. Note that the physical exhaustion of resources, also leads to the population of war memes being overwhelmed by the population of anti-war memes, because most of the surviving soldiers and civilians will be **demoralized**. That is, they will not have many war memes left.

<u>War is easy, peace is hard.</u>

Clearly there is a contest between the war and anti-war memes. As war memes predominate, anti-war memes decrease. Anti-war memes only increase later, as a reaction to the predominance of war memes, as these war memes cause wars, and as the wars grow, and continue, and cause so much **death** and **destruction,** that the anti-war **death** and **destruction** memes are everywhere, and are forced into the minds of even the most fanatical hawks. It becomes obvious, to more and more people, that war is **hopeless,** and **absurd**. So the population of anti-war memes grows in the survivors of the wars, till finally the war ends, and most everyone espouses peace. But peace memes, or anti-war memes, fade away over time, because they only exist, as a reaction to the war memes. Anti-war memes don't have the advantage of **runaway growth**. Rather they have the disadvantage of **runaway extinction!** The anti-war memes, being based on **memories** of all the **death,** and **destruction,** and **horror,** of war caused by the war memes, are unpleasant, tied to negative, ugly **feelings**, and tend to be **forgotten**. People are biased to **forget** bad things. The more anti-war memes **spread**, the less reason there is for them to **spread** further. In a period of peace why worry about war? Or, more and more of the people who experienced the last war, and who still might retain anti-war memes, grow old and **die out**. The young then have no anti-war memes. This is one reason why war is so easy, and peace is so hard.

War memes have independent generators. Peace memes don't.

The war memes always come back because they have an independent generator, a generator outside the war/anti-war cycle, namely **fear mongering** leaders. Leaders stir up war memes, using **fear,** to gain political advantage, or deliberately to get their populations to support a proposed war. Peace memes have no such advantage. If war didn't exist, we would have no need for the peace memes. If war didn't exist, there would be no peace memes. If war didn't exist, the concept of peace would not exist. Peace has no independent existence. So war memes have an advantage over peace memes, as long as populations allow themselves to be manipulated by cynical and foolish leaders.

A cycle.

So we have an **unstable** situation, with wars occurring randomly, and successively. Leaders **push** war memes. War memes **generate** wars. Wars **generate** peace memes, which more or less quickly, **fade away**. Then leaders can **push** war memes again. Then war memes return, **generate** wars, which **generate** peace memes, and the cycle continues.

Rabbits and foxes.

The continual occurrence of wars, with an interval of peace between, is similar, in the ecology of memes, to a cycle of boom and bust in predator and prey populations. Early fur traders in Canada, saw that the populations of rabbits and foxes, increased and then decreased, in cycles. When there are a lot of rabbits, the foxes have plenty to eat, and so the foxes have large numbers of baby foxes. After a while, there are so many foxes, that they eat almost all the rabbits. Then most of the foxes don't have enough to eat, and so they starve. Then the scattered, remaining rabbits, can breed like rabbits. The rabbit population grows large. Then the remaining few foxes can have a feast, and breed like foxes, so their population grows. They eat most of the rabbits, then starve. And so on and on.

Boom and bust for war memes.

Like the rabbits and foxes, the populations of war, and anti-war memes increase and decrease cyclically. A leader **pushes** war memes, the population of war memes increases, a war **starts**. The war **intensifies** as the population of war memes **explodes**. Note the **euphoria** of men volunteering to join the armies at the start of WW I and WW II. The war memes are so **dominant** that they have almost completely **suppressed** the anti-war memes in these men's minds. But as the war continues, the population of **death, destruction, horror, absurdity, ugliness,** and other anti-war memes **increases**. This **diminishes** the population of war memes. The war **winds down**, ends. Now anti-war and peace memes predominate. Note also the attempts at this point in the cycle, to somehow **institutionalize peace,** at the conclusion of the two world wars, by the founding of the League of Nations, and the United Nations.

As the period of peace continues, peace memes gradually **fade away**, because during peace there is no need for peace memes. Thus after a time, minds are **open** to war memes, and the cycle **repeats**.

Random war seed.

Does it ever seem strange to you, that almost always as soon as one enemy fades away or is defeated, very shortly after, a new enemy **pops up,** apparently from nowhere, or a former ally **turns into** an enemy, almost overnight? This is what would be expected from an **unstable war meme saturated culture,** where any little **random event,** can become a war **seed,** which grows faster and faster into a new **threat**. This kind of **instability** arises, because war memes automatically **grow,** and peace memes automatically **extinguish** themselves. War memes are **better than** peace memes, in the memes eye view.

A serious danger for this program.

The above discussion points out very serious and dangerous implications for the program of this book. Attention paid to this program is likely to oscillate with the war-peace cycle. Anti-war memes get their most attention at the height and toward the ends of wars, when the **absurdity,** and **ugliness,** of all the **death** and **destruction,** become obvious to everyone. This suppresses the war memes, and brings about a population explosion of anti-war memes. So this program will get most attention at the height of wars. It will get less attention during intervals of relative peace. This problem will get **even worse,** and we will have to **work** very hard to keep **interest** in this program, as it begins to have **success,** in **decreasing** the number of wars. It will be **crucial** for all the **anti-war movements** to **keep this process going** during increasingly **long periods** of relative peace. This will have to be one of the **main tasks** of the world wide **anti-war organizations.**

Meme population dynamics in other areas of culture.

In many other areas of culture, there are similar cycles of boom and bust, in the populations of memes. In particular, in economics, and finance, many phenomena may be better understood in terms of such cycles, rather than in terms of mathematical models, based on incorrect assumptions of universal reason.

Chapter 8: The Mass Media.

Mass media can whip up a frenzy for war.

In general, as their name says, the mass media **spread** all kinds of memes, from a **few** people, to **almost all** of the rest of the population. And as has long been known, mass media can whip up a **frenzy** for war. The simple fact is, the mass media allow a very **few** people, to easily **implant** all kinds of memes, into **almost all** of the rest of the population. There can be little doubt, that war memes that are **spread** through the mass media, **cause** wars. Let's look at meme dynamics in the mass media. More research is needed in this area, especially as the Internet modulates the influence of the traditional mass media.

Meditate on this.

The memes of the owners, users, or controllers of newspapers, radio, and television companies, are **multiplied** millions of times every day. It's once or twice a day for newspapers, and continuously every day, for radio and television. And most people are more or less **passive receptacles** for these memes. People used to read their newspapers while **eating** breakfast. Now the radio is on, while they **drive** long commutes to and from work, and in homes as well as many public places, television is **always on,** in the **background.** Television news programs congregate around **meal** times. War memes love **distraction.** No time to **think,** but the **fear** comes through. Memes can't do **emotional multiplication** right in a single person's brain, but with mass media they easily do **multiplication** from one brain into **millions** of other brains. And the same memes can be, and are, **pushed** over and over and over 24/7/52. Meditate on this.

Every group thinks it's right and everybody else is biased.

There are apparently endless debates about media **bias.** The **bias** considered may be conscious, or unconscious, by the owners and employees of the media. Most every group thinks the media is **biased** against them. Are there some memes at work for their own purposes here? The **we're right** meme infects every group. So in so far as the media do not completely espouse a particular group's philosophy, that group sees the media as **biased** against them. The media are infected by the **equal time** and **fairness** memes to some extent. These memes say all points of view are **equally valid** and deserve equal coverage. These memes are held firmly in place in media minds by the **biased media** meme in the assorted groups the media cover. But the idea that all points of view are **equally valid** is **absurd.** So of course the media cannot adhere to it. So the media trot out their **fairness** meme, when they try to give the same coverage to the views of some noisy, but peripheral group's views, as they give to established views. So by this line of thought there is a media **bias** in favor of noisy but inconsequential groups and their views. But who decides what is inconsequential? Or valid? Perhaps all this shows is that there is no nice tidy method by which we can decide what is a **valid** view. In the media, like everywhere else, the **seeker** of truth must **sort** things out for herself. The media are a monstrous meme **mashup**. And it's not for nothing that some people call the mass media mind **pollution**.

Always bias.

What are the meme dynamics of media **bias**? Every person, every group, every political party thinks he, she, or it, is **right**. They all want to **spread** their memes. They use any logic, emotions, or tricks, they can, to do this. So they all have a **bias** for their own memes. A **fairness** meme was invented which says more or less that the same amount of time given to any opinion, should also be given to its opposite. This is simplistic, since there is no single opposite to an opinion. The world of opinions is not either/or. So **fairness,** in this sense, is impossible. But it's a **handy** meme for the mass media, or anyone else, to **claim** from time to time, that they are **fair,** and **balanced,** and not **biased**. They do this to convince potential recipients of the memes they are pushing, that they can **stop thinking,** and **just accept,** the **pushed** memes.

Is anything wrong with bias?

So if every person, and every group, is **biased**, is something **wrong**? If this is just the way the world **works**, the way memes work, what could it mean to say it's **wrong**? It would have to mean, that somehow, we should try to get rid of **bias**. But we **can't**. **Bias** for their own memes is inherent to meme organisms. So there is something **wrong** with the **bias** meme. It's a funny meme. It includes the sub meme, that **no one should have it**, that it shouldn't exist! Let's be as clear as possible. It is impossible for humans, and other meme organisms to be **unbiased**. Maybe a rock can be **unbiased**. So let's get over it. We need to simply accept the truth that **bias** exists, **always**, in every meme organism. It is important to recognize this, to know that **bias** is always there, and not be **fooled** by anyone, or any organization, that claims it is **unbiased**. We need to evaluate memes sent our way by any person, or organization, on the **merits** of the memes, and not on the basis of the **trustworthiness** claimed by the person or organization. See the **trust me** meme discussed previously. The more the mass media say **trust me**, the more **suspicious** we should be. And the mass media sure send out a lot of **trust me** memes.

Snippets.

Most mass media broadcast commercial messages to make money. In a period of one hour, about 15 minutes is devoted to commercials. The 15 minutes of commercials, is spread over the one hour period, in chunks of a minute or two. If each chunk is two minutes, then the hour is divided into seven or eight periods for the programming. So the average programming period is about six minutes. If each commercial break were one minute, then the average programming period would be about three minutes. So however the commercials are spread out, the time for presenting a story, or more importantly, news and information, is only a matter of minutes. A few minutes is just not enough time to present a **coherent** case for a new idea, an idea the viewer or listener does not already expect. So the structure of commercial radio and television, allows only **simple** ideas, ideas that can be grasped **quickly**. And the commercials are **distractions**, totally unrelated **interruptions**, to any train of **thought** lasting more than just a few minutes. The extreme example of this is the impossibility of enjoying a movie **interrupted** by commercials. This means we mostly get sound bites, **snippets**, chopped up ideas, that the viewer or listener already knows or believes. In other words commercial mass media, particularly radio and television, inherently present, and reinforce, **simple** memes **consistent** with the memes, the viewer, or listener, already has.

Tendencies to spread war memes.

Is there anything about the mass media that inherently makes it pro-war? Mass media, newspapers, TV, and radio, are important in spreading war memes. They are important in spreading memes in general. But there are some inherent tendencies to spread war memes preferentially. Why? Because the media are organizations, and organizations take on a life of their own, and want to grow. Spreading war memes can help them do that. Like all organizations, the mass media have **self perpetuation,** and **self aggrandizement** memes. They will have memes like **success, influence**, and **profit**. They want to **maintain,** and **increase,** these memes. The **success** and **influence** memes can work even without the **profit** meme.

Bias inherent in the organizational structure.

The **profit** meme, the **influence** meme, and the **success** meme, cause mass media to want to **increase** the number of people in their audiences. One way to hold, and **increase,** an audience is to be a **fear monger. Fear, anxiety,** and **anger,** get people's attention. **Bad news** stirs up **fears. Fears** stirred up about hypothetical foreign actions, and intentions, are often the first steps in an escalation process that leads to wars. And when a leader deliberately wants a war, he must to some extent, implant **fear** laden war memes in some of the population, perhaps more in a democracy, and less in a tyranny. So such a leader is throwing out good memes, for the mass media to use, to **increase** their **success**. With or without leaders **pushing** war memes, there is a meme **force** to stir up **fear**. War memes are good at that. It doesn't matter whether this is conscious, or not, in the minds of the owners or employees. It is **inherent** in the organizational structure of the mass media. As discussed above, **bias** exists in every individual and organization. In the case of the mass media, considering that the product of the mass media, is the **implantation** of memes in **millions** of minds, the dynamic, or meme **force,** for **fear mongering** in order to increase audience size, is much greater in mass media organizations than for other organizations.

Is there a correction?

So what would be a correction for this? Even individual bloggers are influenced by the **profit** meme, and the **influence,** and **success** memes. Almost all writers and artists are also. Most all people are. If we communicate with other people, we usually want to **influence** them. So if this **bias** is due to the **profit, influence,** and **success,** memes, it's everywhere in human communication. And as we discussed above, **bias** is **inherent** in all meme organisms. Does this mean the tendency for **fear mongering** cannot be removed or neutralized? No. But it seems, it must take us back to the fundamental **fear** factor, for the spread of memes. Recall our discussion of the **fear** meme. The **fear** meme has its uses. The problem is, most people are completely **in the dark,** about how **fear** is **misused** against them. We, everyone, need to educate ourselves, as to how the **fear** meme works. **Fear** is appropriate for immediate bodily threats. It is not appropriate, for distant, far off, debatable, uncertain, hypothetical events. We all need to learn, how to better calibrate our **fear** responses, to the actual situations we face. These facts, about the proper use of **fear,** and the easy ways it can be used to **delude**, **confuse**, and **herd** us into wars, must be taught in every school on the planet, at the earliest practical age. If everybody on this planet knew how **fear** worked, and knew how it can be used to **exploit** us, then **fear mongering** would no longer work! For now the question you must ask, for every news item you read in the newspaper, hear on the radio, see on TV, or read, or see on the Internet, should be: Is the **scariness** coming across with this news item **realistic**?

Reporting only what people say is inherently deficient.

Leader A said ..., expert B said ..., and on and on. This is not enough. This kind of reporting simply allows the media to be a totally **passive conduit**, actually megaphone, for leaders **pushing fear** laden war memes. This is nowhere near objective. The reporter needs to compare what leader A or expert B said with reality insofar as reality can be known. Listen up reporters! You are intelligent human beings with magnificent brains. Use them. Many of you are more intelligent, perceptive, and honest, than many of our leaders. Yes I know many reporters try to get alternate quotes to what leader A or expert B said. That's an improvement, but still not enough. If leader A happens to be the maximum leader of your country, it is often hard to get anyone, much less a person of comparable status, so say something different than what the maximum leader just said. It's your job to seek the truth, as best you can. If any leader's or expert's statement doesn't sound right to you, it is your duty to work all the harder to contact others with different interpretations of the situation, than the one the leader or expert gave, or to research yourself what the facts are, and state what you have found. Simply quoting leaders and experts is hack reporting. Think.

Too much deference.

There is way too much **deference** to leaders and experts everywhere in the world. We must pay attention to them, because they determine, way out of proportion to their knowledge and intelligence, where our societies go. Somehow we must evaluate their proposals intelligently, rather than just accept them. Ideally, reporters should be among the first to get rid of their **obey authority** memes. Such reporters may find it difficult to get jobs in some media organizations. But nowadays they can become bloggers and be their own persons, **autonomous** human beings, **autonomous** investigative reporters.

PORTRAIT: Rest in Peace 45.16.

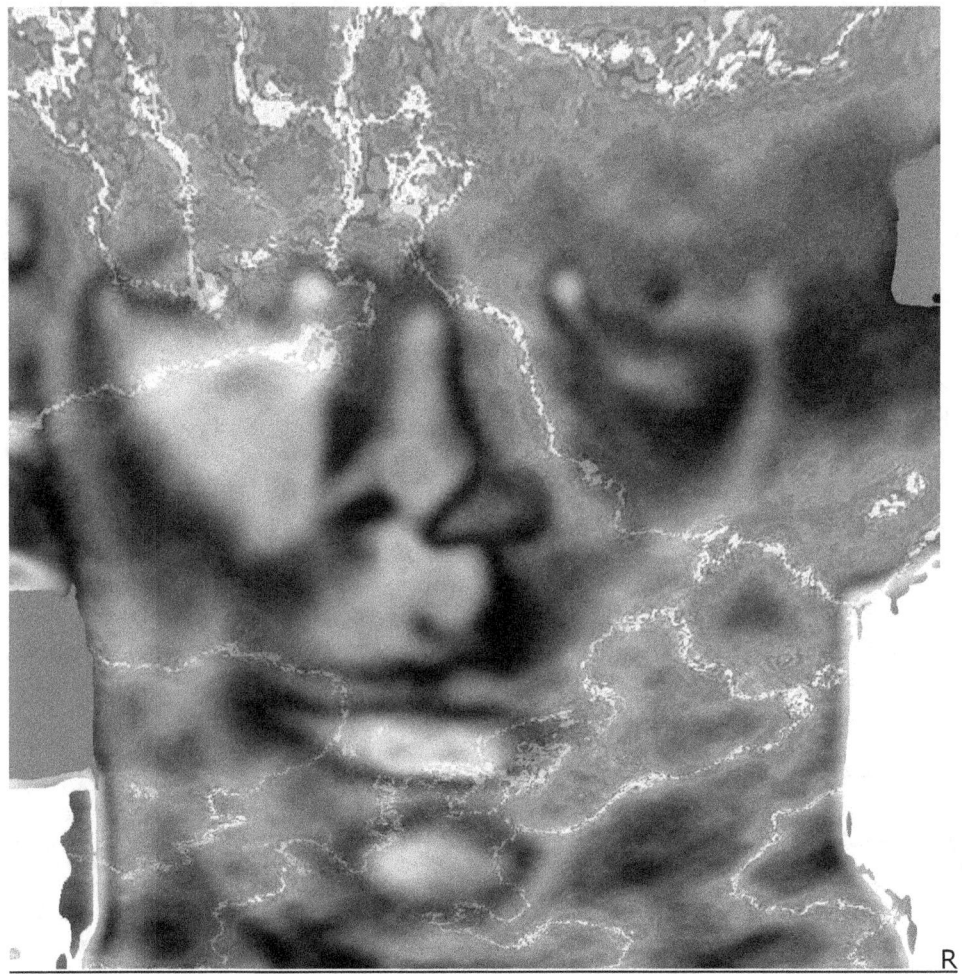

Reporters and the fear meme.

Fear laden memes that are **spread** through the media, whether deliberately or not, can lead to war. **Fear** of job loss, can keep reporters and editors in line. **Fear** of leaders with excessive **power,** can keep other leaders and experts in line. We live now in a world where war is common. Reporters can be **fired**. Others who **deviate** from the **party line,** can **suffer** bad consequences in an **authoritarian,** hierarchical society. Correctly evaluating any situation, requires realistically evaluating any **fear** associated with it. But the **fear** of job loss, and the related **fears** of bad consequences, from not conforming to the leaders' memes, are real in almost every country. The right of **freedom of speech,** is only legal, not actual.

Mass media can easily bypass meme filters.

Many aspects of the mass media make it difficult for our meme filters. Through radio, TV, movies, and videos, **fear** laden ideas, and images, can be thrown at us in rapid succession. We get sound **bites,** and **snippets,** of **death** and **destruction**. There is little time to **suppress fear** and **think**. Notice that this is **inherent** in how these mass media work. Quick cuts, music, and other methods are aimed at **modulating** emotions directly. Commercials every few minutes in TV programs, as we have noted, are **interruptions** to **thought**. We can read at a pace we determine. Of course writing can present memes in **fear** laden **snippets** too, but we have much more control, than when we listen to radio, watch TV, movies, or videos.

Leaders stir up fears in the population.

Leaders who want to use a foreign **threat** to consolidate **power,** use the mass media to **spread** the foreign **threat** memes. This is the way many leaders maintain their **power**. Politicians in democracies also use war memes to get themselves reelected. The idea is to stir up **fears** in the population, and suggest that the politician is the best person to overcome the **danger**. Their opponents are accused of being **soft** on whatever. See also the **machismo** meme. They also maintain that it would be foolish to change leaders during a war or dangerous situation. A real war **danger** in such tactics, an **unintended consequence**, is that it may stir up hostile responses, in the countries described as **threats**. This can lead to an **escalation spiral** to war.

Mass media are often mind pollution.

So the mass media are **crucial**. Although they can **spread** bad, (for us), memes, they can also **spread** good, (for us), ones. The mass media are a monster meme **mashup,** because all memes want to get into the mass media, and all kinds of memes do get in. The mass media can be mind **pollution,** because they can easily fill millions of minds with **disconnected**, **incoherent**, **unrealistic**, and **contradictory** memes.

Our sources of information and the memes we absorb define our reality.

Our **reality** is defined by the information we have about it. The basic information we have about our bodies, and immediate surroundings, comes to us directly through our senses. The basic job of our brain is to regulate our bodies. The brain gets huge amounts of information about every part of our bodies continuously. It also continuously gets huge amounts of information about our immediate surroundings. [Damasio, 2003]. We get information about the people we interact directly with, also mostly through our senses. We get information about our wider culture through communications media. Communications media have greatly increased their capacity over time. In rough order of appearance the important communications media are: human messengers; story telling, narratives, oral traditions; writing that could be transported; the telegraph; the telephone; sound recordings; radio; movies; broadcast TV; cable TV; the internet; satellite TV. So our **reality** beyond our **immediate experience,** comes to us **through** communications **media,** via memes. Mass media allow **one,** or a very **few,** people to send the same memes, or copies of the same memes, to millions, and thousands of millions of people, at the same time. The mass media can be used by the **few** to **control** the many, because it defines the major part, or all of their **reality**.

Media define reality.

For most people, the mass media are their **sole source** for information about the larger world outside themselves, and their relation to that larger world. A person could travel all over the world, and interact personally, with many other people from all the world's cultures. Very few people do this. The mass media tell people what their **place** is in the world. And for most people it tells them they are on the **bottom**. It tells them they are not **worth** much. It tends to make people **dependent** on the media. Why should media have memes that make people **dependent** on them? Well, for the reasons given above, the **success** memes want to get, and keep, **large** audiences. So from these memes' point of view, the more people's **time,** and **attention,** can be monopolized by the mass media, the better. The more people **accept,** through their behavior, that a particular medium is the **sole source** of information, memes, truth, the better for that medium. Until very recently, for most people, all the information they got about the world, beyond the limited set of people they personally interacted with, came through the mass media. And the same was true for most everyone that they personally interacted with. People got their memes from the mass media, directly or indirectly, via a small number of steps, through the people they personally interacted with.

Mass media in decline.

Now the mass media is **changing** historically very quickly. It may be in serious **decline**. Printed newspapers and magazines will soon be **extinct**. Major broadcast TV networks are in **decline**. Cable TV channels have **small,** fragmented audiences. **More and more** news and information about the external world, comes to people **through** the Internet. The number of independent sources on the Internet is much greater than the 500 cable and satellite TV channels. How will this **change** the **reality** the media define? It will surely **change** what people consider the truth to be, and how they should behave. The number of independent sources of memes is **increasing,** and the audience size for each source is **decreasing**. When there were only a **few** sources there could be **large coherent** audiences. A large number of independent sources could mean a greater **diversity** of available memes. With many sources available how do people sample sources? Do they access many or only a few? Will we get many people **exposed** to large sets of **diverse** memes? Or will we get a large number of small audiences, each with not many memes in the audience members, and with a great variation of memes across the audiences? Will the media divide a population into a **small** number of groups with **coherent** and **consistent** memes within each group but **divergent** memes across groups? Or will there be a large number of small groups? These are all good research questions. It will be interesting to see what happens.

The mass media diminish people.

At the present time, through advertising and programming, the mass media tell people the **purpose** of their existence is to **buy** things. They teach that it is good to **have** things, that the **more,** and **bigger,** and **better,** and **more** expensive, things one has, the **better**. Therefore the **more** money you have, the **better**. So the **richer** you are, the **better**. So the **rich** are **better** than the rest of us, most of us. So here the mass media establish a **hierarchy** defined by personal **wealth**. Since **fame** and **success** are correlated with **wealth**, both **fame** and **success** define a very similar **hierarchy**. In these worldviews, each of these **hierarchies** put most of us on the **bottom**. We spend a lot of our time contemplating our relative **inferior** position. We are reminded of it daily, many times a day, when we see all the **tempting** ads, for things we don't have **enough** money to buy. So we are constantly **reminded,** that we are not **as good as** others. So what's so bad about that? Clearly it's the natural order of things that some people are **stronger, smarter, kinder, richer, better** in some way, than others.

Mass media push the you're no good meme.

To have the meme, **I'm not as good as other people,** limits a person. Let's shorten the description and slightly intensify this meme by calling it the **you're no good** meme. A person with this meme will believe, that there are many things she cannot do. So it's not worth **trying** to do any of those things on that long list. As a child, why should I bother to pay attention to my parents, when I'm never going to amount to anything anyway? Why pay attention in school? Why work hard? Why work? Why obey laws? Why do anything? May as well be totally passive. Shit happens. Vegetate.

Media also push the you can do it meme.

But don't the media also push the **you can do it too** meme? What about all the sports on TV? Somebody always wins. What about all the glorifying of movie stars? Doesn't that promote the idea, the meme, that one can **succeed**, the **success** meme? After all, it shows another human being **succeeding**, who shares with you many of his memes. Doesn't this promote the **you can do it too** meme? It would seem that the so called reality shows, which claim to show ordinary people in realistic competitions, especially do this. The sitcoms glorify family life, as the family meme has evolved over time. The westerns were definitely glorifying myths of the power and competence of an idealized national character. Clearly the media do promote the **you can do it too** meme, because we can, and do, identify with, share memes with, the winners.

Mass media never all one thing.

The media **push** all kinds of memes. This is not surprising. Their memetic incentives are to **push** any memes that can capture and **hold** large audiences, and to **push** memes they are directly **paid to push,** in ads, and programming, that promotes consumerism. And from a meme system balance point of view, a relentless pushing of the **you're no good** meme, with nothing to counter it, might create a totally passive, do nothing, population that wouldn't work, and we would all starve. So we should not expect to see the media as all this, or all that. **Incoherence** and **contradiction** among memes, make both ads, and programming, **more effective** in **pushing** memes into audience minds. **Incoherence** and **contradictions** stir up **emotions,** and cause **confusion**. This makes it easier for memes to be accepted into unsuspecting minds. **Incoherence** and **contradiction** can **reinforce** a person's belief that she is **ignorant**. To keep someone **down, confused, demoralized, passive**, and **obedient**, what could be better than telling them **they are no good,** and at the same time, **they ought to be a winner**? The media present forever churning, and evolving, imaginary sub-cultures, each following its own meme logic. An important question is how could the media memes be organized so as to decrease the **you're no good** memes and give people the confidence to become **autonomous** and **productive** human beings?

Mass media meme filters.

Since the mass media define **reality** for most of the population, and since the mass media are owned or controlled by a **few** people at the upper levels of the **wealth** and **power hierarchies**, and since these **few** people operate the meme filters which determine which memes get access to the mass media, which memes get multiplied to the mass of the population, these **few** people define **reality** for the mass of the population. The **few** control the **many**. The meme filters employed by the **few** may not be conscious. The **few** may not even be aware of what they are doing. A few of the **few** may be aware, but who knows. It doesn't matter whether they are aware or not. In some cases the meme filters are quite explicit. Consider the various censorship boards for movies and TV in the past set up by various religious groups. These were explicit and recognized for what they were doing by everybody. Today there are still formal rules about certain words that may not be used in the media. But more important than any explicit or formal meme filters, are the **informal, semi conscious** rules, (meme filters), that writers, producers, owners apply to themselves usually without any explicit governmental, stockholder, or other outside influence. These apply to the entertainment, news, non-fictional programs, and ads, all the parts of the mass media. These **semi conscious self censorship** meme filters seem to be just there. Nobody necessarily consciously put them there.

One of the reasons they are **hidden** from the **awareness** of those using, and having them, is that we have, (in the United States and some other countries), a meme which everybody claims to honor and use, called **freedom of speech**. To admit we were **self censoring** would provide cognitive dissonance with the **freedom of speech** meme, so one way to avoid the dissonance is to not be aware we are **self censoring**.

How the few control the many.

Another way to say this is that the writers, producers, owners, whoever makes decisions about media content, about which memes can go through the mass media, these people, naturally, are operating according to their own personal memes. If at some particular point in time they all, or most of them, hold to the meme that, say, war with country B is **justified**, memes contradictory to that will not get through the mass media, or very few of them will. The general principle is that any meme that gets through the mass media must first pass through the meme filters of the **few** decision makers, and be **consonant** with their established memes. This is how the **few** define the **reality** of the **many**. This is how the memes of the **few** are multiplied to the **many**. This is how the **few** control the **many**. Most of these **few** may not be aware of what they are doing, but nevertheless, they are **defining reality** for, and **controlling,** most of the population.

Organizational structural meme dynamics.

The above is not new. But expressing it in terms of memetics makes it clearer how it works, and shines light on how **inherent** organizational structural meme dynamics, reinforce and perpetuate, the processes.

Controlling the population can be a war meme.

As with the **fame** meme, putting everyone in a **hierarchy** better allows leaders to lead people to war. See also the **obey authority** meme discussed previously.

The internet.

The internet provides a megaphone to every person almost like the original radio and TV broadcasters had. The difference is there was a limited number of broadcasters. The human population had few choices of whom to listen to. Now there are potentially billions of internet broadcasters. So the problem may become whom to listen to, whom to read. In the age of the old broadcasters the audiences were **passive**. They could not **talk back**. Since the internet gives everyone a megaphone, everyone can **talk back**. Even more, everyone can megaphone back. Will they? The human population will have to undo their learned **passivity**. Maybe enough of them will, if they can see that their **passive** acceptance of mass media memes, has been contributing mightily to our cultures' malfunctions, in particular wars. If people overcome their **passivity,** then they will **act,** they will **seek** information. So this answers the question of whom to listen to. They won't read just one or a few people's blogs. They will search, and be able to get as many facts and opinions as they want. This rejection of **passivity** will take time. Some people won't make the switch. As in some big meme changes in the past, the **passivity** meme may survive until its last host dies. Will this happen? What will happen to the existing mass media? We will have to wait to see.

PORTRAIT: Rest in Peace 23M.

Chapter 9: More on memes.

What are memes?

OK, so what are memes really? Let's look at the definition we gave in Chapter 1.

A unit of cultural information, such as a cultural practice or idea, that is transmitted verbally or by repeated action from one mind to another.

A meme is cultural information. So what is information? Here's one definition from the Merriam Webster online dictionary.

the attribute inherent in and communicated by one of two or more alternative sequences or arrangements of something (as nucleotides in DNA or binary digits in a computer program) that produce specific effects

What is information?

Information is an arrangement, or pattern, of matter (or energy), that is used to do something. If the arrangement or pattern is one way, one thing is done; if the arrangement or pattern is another way, then something different is done. Think of our digital computers. Data are stored in various locations in memory. Data is information. At each location there is some matter that can either have an electrical charge, or not have an electrical charge. If it has an electrical charge, that means one thing. If it does not have an electrical charge, that means another thing. For computers our usual interpretation would be that if it's not charged, that represents the number 0; if it is charged, that represents the number 1. And of course, the computer does different things, depending on whether it finds that particular location to be charged or not.

Information must satisfy two conditions.

There are two critical parts to this definition of information. Both parts are necessary. The first part is there must be some matter, or energy, some stuff, that can be in two, or more, distinguishable arrangements or patterns. The second part of the definition, is that something must be able to distinguish, among the possible arrangements or patterns, and do different things, depending on which particular arrangement or pattern is there.

Digital computers use information.

In the case of our everyday digital computers, we can think of the information stored in it, as strings of zeros and ones of any length. For example: 010010110, and so on. But remember, it's only information if something, or someone, uses it, or could use it. Computers do different things, depending on the information, the programs and data, in them.

Humans use information.

Animals and human beings receive information from their environments. Here's a real simple example. If when you are walking, a snake is lying across the path in front of you, you will probably react by stopping walking. If no snake is lying across your path, you will probably keep walking. Notice we have satisfied the two required parts of the definition of information. We have in this case two possible arrangements of matter. The two possibilities are: 1) There is no snake in your path; 2) There is a snake in your path. And the second part of the definition is satisfied also, since you are the something, or someone, who does one thing if the snake is there, you stop walking, and you do another thing, you keep walking, if no snake is there.

Lots of information.

Similarly we receive many kinds of information through all our senses. We receive information from our own bodies: Am I hungry or not; Am I warm or cold; Do I feel a pain somewhere? We receive information about the world outside our bodies, including information from other people. And we give out information to other people, and animals, by our behavior, how our bodies move, our facial expressions, smells, speech, and touch. So here we are: Memes, we receive them, and we send them out to others. There is nothing mysterious about either information or memes. They are as real as French culture, the number 23, money in the bank, and your smile.

A closer look at memes.

If you want to now, go back to Chapter 5, and review our discussion there about memes. I will expand on some of the ideas presented there. The concept of memes is very powerful. Much can be explained by viewing our world cultures as a vast system of interacting memes. The greatest insights can come if we focus on meme dynamics, how memes spread from person to person, how a single meme can spread from one person to huge numbers of people, and how memes can change over time, or as they spread from one person to another. It will help us to understand this big picture, if we understand in more detail, how individual memes behave and interact.

Let's not be too specific.

The definition of meme said a meme was a unit of culture. What's a unit? It's stuff that stays together, at least for some time. So a meme is some information that, more or less, stays together, at least for a while. This may sound vague, and bother some people. But don't let it bother you. This is an important, and valuable, part of the concept of meme. If for some purposes, we want to be more specific, we can do that. But for now, we should let this concept of meme, be as inclusive as possible. A meme is a unit of cultural information. Memes are chunks of information, that can be in people's brains, be copied, be modified, be sent to other brains, be stored in things people make, (human artifacts), go anywhere, and do anything information can do. So in talking about a meme, we can look at a part of it, and call that a meme. We can look at several memes that seem to go around together, and call that a meme too. We can group memes to suit our purposes. For example words are associated with memes. Sentences are associated with memes. But not every meme is associated with a word or a sentence. A collection of sentences that makes up a story, is associated with a meme, the meme for that story. Memes can have small amounts of information or very large amounts.

<u>Can the same meme be in two different brains at the same time?</u>

Let's look at a specific meme, in one person's brain. In my brain, some how, some way, there is information associated with the word *car*. That information is **my particular meme for car**. We ordinarily use the word *car,* to refer to some specific object, or objects, in driveways, garages, on roads, etc. If I speak of a **car** meme, I am using the word *car,* to refer to the information existing somewhere, about a car, or cars. In my brain, I have information about cars. That is **my car meme**. In your brain, you almost surely have information about cars. That is **your car meme**. Our two **car** memes are not the same. You may be a car mechanic, while I am not, or vice versa. No two people have the same experiences, memories, and knowledge, about cars. No way, never! So how can we ever talk about the same meme being in two people's brains? We can't, if we mean same, to be identical information, in both brains. But we can, and will, speak of the **car** meme, (and other memes), being in my brain, and in your brain, and in the brains of many people, and in books, and movies, and in any particular car. A particular car has a lot of information about cars. Just as we can say the car has contributed to global warming, we can say the **car** meme is in many brains. When we say the car has contributed to global warming, we mean cars in general, all cars, the collection of all cars, has contributed to global warming. When we say the **car** meme can be in many brains at the same time we mean that particular instances of **car** memes are in those brains. If someone says "*The lion is the king of the beasts.*", they are not talking about a particular lion. They are talking about lions as a collection, a category. Similarly for *the car* and *the car* **meme**.

<u>How can we communicate about cars if we each have different car memes?</u>

Many people have **car** memes in their brains. A person's **car** meme consists of all information in her brain about cars. That would of course, include information about particular cars, such as the particular car, or cars, owned by her now, cars previously owned or driven, memories of cars, operating principles of cars, car models, prices, and on and on. All this information is part of her **car** meme. We can say this is her information about cars in general, in contrast to information about a particular car. Let's look at a snippet of conversation. Suppose you and I are planning a road trip together. Let's say we each have cars, and we each have some information about the other's car. So I have a **car** meme in my brain. A part of that meme is a smaller meme **for my particular car.** And I have another part of my general **car** meme in my brain **for your particular car**. Similarly, you have a meme in your brain, **for your car,** and you have another meme in your brain, **for my**

car. Let's say the conversation is going along, and at some point it contains the following three comments:

I say:	*Let's take my car.*
You say:	*I'd rather not.*
I say:	OK. *We can take yours.*

What do these three statements mean? Well of course they could mean many things. There is a context for real conversations, what was said before, what we know about each other, what we each know about where we are planning to go, and on and on. Assume that my car is more fuel efficient than yours, and I know this, and I want to save money on gas. So I say: *let's take my car*. You however, want to bring along a lot of stuff, and you know my car's trunk is too small for all the stuff you want to bring. So you say: *I'd rather not*. The information in **my meme for my car,** that led to my saying: *let's take my car,* was my car's fuel efficiency. The information in **your meme for my car,** that led you to say: *I'd rather not,* was the small size of my car's trunk. For the sake of this discussion, we could even assume, that I have never given a thought to the size of my car's trunk, and you have no information about my car's relative fuel efficiency. So what has happened here, in the few seconds in this conversation snippet? The information in **my meme for my car**, its relative fuel efficiency, that caused me to say: *let's take my car,* is not known to you, that is, it was not, and is not, in **your meme for my car**. And the information in **your meme for my car**, its small trunk size, which caused you to say: *I'd rather not*, is not known to me, that is, it was not, and is not, in **my meme for my car**. So we cannot say, that when two people are talking about the same thing, (my car in this example), they use only information they both share. So it is false to seek the solution, to the "problem" of different people having different memes for the same thing, by saying they use only their shared common information. It's not a problem. People communicate very well, even though they have different memes for the same things. Actually it's an advantage. Two people with different information communicating, is better than one person alone, because the two together have more information to work with, than either would by themselves. Communication is cooperation. Cooperation has benefits. And of course, in real life, what really makes a conversation interesting, is when the two or more people in the conversation have different memes for the same things that they are all interested in. If two people had identical memes, there might not be much they could say to each other, that they each didn't already know.

"We need artful conversation. Cooperation is its operative principle, enthusiasm its divine breath, and its power to raise spirits is supernatural. It can make us not only less socially stupid, but also significantly brainier." --- [Blyth, 2009, page 17].

PORTRAIT: Rest in Peace 10.1.

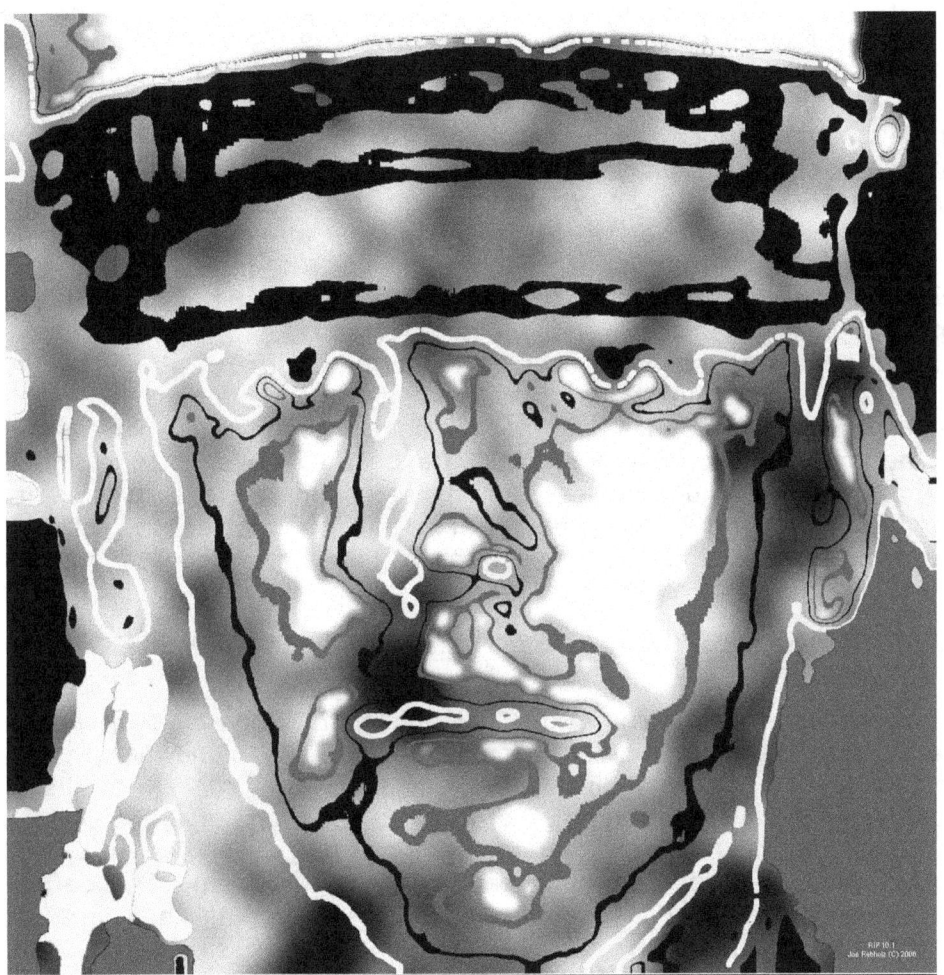

Big memes enter brains gradually, over time.

We speak of memes traveling from one person to another. We speak as if this can happen quickly. How long does it take for a person to get a meme that person does not presently have? Consider the **car** meme. The **car** meme in my brain right now, didn't get in there all at once. No way. There's way too much information in my **car** meme. My **car** meme, and anyone else's, was built up gradually, over a long period of time. From the time I was a baby, and first saw a car, or rode in a car, up to the present time, information about cars, has been entering my brain, and being stored there. Information about ourselves, the physical world, and other people, is coming into our brains all the time. Some of this information is stored there, and added to, or associated with, memes we already have. Or, in some cases new information starts a new meme. There are many connections or associations among memes. It doesn't make sense to have a meme not connected to anything else. Some memes may be more or less static. Maybe they never change. Other memes may be more or less continuously updated over a lifetime. Connections among memes, may be fixed, or changeable, too. Actually, the connections among memes, may be considered as memes themselves, or parts of larger memes.

When you hear or read a single word, only a tiny amount of information enters your brain.

When you hear a spoken word, what happens? Suppose you hear the word *car*. There is always a context. You are somewhere doing something. You are not likely to hear the word *car* all by itself. Somebody is saying something to you. So the word is probably in a sentence, perhaps like in the snippet of conversation we discussed above. First, no way, no how, can a whole big **meme for car** be transmitted to you, or in any way, get into your brain, when you just hear the tiny spoken word *car*. The only thing that goes into your brain, through your ears, is a sound pattern for the spoken word *car*. You already have a **meme for car** in your brain, that was built up over your lifetime, from all your experiences with cars, and all the other information you absorbed from school, books, movies, and so on. What happens when you hear the word *car,* is that this sound pattern directs your brain to access, or do something with, some of the information in your already existing **car** meme. What your brain actually does will depend on the context, on all the other information your brain has been dealing with, before you heard the word *car*. It will depend on what you were doing, thinking, etc. Of course, if you heard the word *car* in a sentence, spoken by someone explaining to you something about cars that you did not already know, then perhaps you will be adding new information to your **car** meme.

Words containing little information connect to big memes with lots of information.

When you hear the word *car,* or read the printed word *car,* some information is being received by you, namely the word *car*. When you hear the word *car,* a particular sequence of sounds goes into your ears, and is converted into some pattern of activities in the neurons of your brain. When you read the printed word *car*, a pattern of light and darkness goes into your eyes, and is converted into some pattern of activities in the light sensitive cells of your eyes, and that pattern is converted into other patterns, which your brain further works on. In either case, the only information coming in, has to do with the word *car*, and is not information directly about the things people ride around in. A **car** meme is already in your brain. The information is already there. Only information in the word *car* is coming in, just the three letters: *c, a,* and *r*, in that order, as you read the word. If I type the word *automobile*, and you read the word *automobile*, then different information is coming into your brain. In this case the letters: *a, u, t, o, m, o, b, i, l,* and *e*, in that order. There is a little common information in the two words *car* and *automobile*. They each contain one letter *a*, but that's it. But either word, when it gets into your brain, leads to pretty much the same information, namely your **car** meme. Actually part of your **car** meme will have information for the word *car,* and your **car** meme will also have information for the word *automobile*. Or at least somehow, your brain connects the patterns that came into your brain when you heard, or read, the words *car,* or *automobile,* to your **car** meme. As I said before, we can say the connections to, or from memes, are part of the meme if we want to. Sometime early in our lives, an association, some actual neural connection, will have been made between our baby **meme for car,** and the word *car,* when, one or more times, somebody said the word *car,* at the same time that we got into a car, or saw a car. In this way, or some way like this, the small amount of information which you receive when you hear or read the word *car,* is connected to the much larger amount of information already in your brain, which is your **car** meme.

Memes and information are less familiar than cars and people.

This may seem like a long winded explanation, but we are talking about things, memes and information inside brains, which are different from everyday things we usually talk about like cars and people. And I want to help all of you understand these things, as much as I reasonably can, even at the risk of overdoing it for some of you.

Memes and emotions.

"As we noted earlier, every experience in our lives is accompanied by some degree of emotion and this is especially obvious in relation to important social and personal problems." --- [Damasio, 2003, page 146].

Memes and emotions are connected. Emotions are connected to feelings. Feelings are fear, anger, disgust, hatred, sorrow, joy, happiness, awe, etc. The kind of feeling, and the strength of the feeling connected to a meme, is a measure of the meme's importance, or goodness, or badness, for us. Feelings are necessary for thinking. Thinking involves making decisions. What shall I have for lunch? Should I marry this man? People whose brains have been damaged in certain ways that disrupt their feelings, cannot make appropriate decisions.

"... In a number of studies published over the past two decades, our research team and others have shown that when previously normal individuals sustain damage to brain regions necessary for the development of certain classes of emotions and feelings, their ability to govern their lives in society is extremely disturbed. Their ability to make appropriate decisions is compromised in situations in which the outcomes are uncertain, such as making a financial investment or entering an important relationship. ..." --- [Damasio, 2003, page 140].

So in normal people, emotions and feelings are physically connected in their brains to their actions, behaviors, and decisions, to their memes. When a typical person, a citizen of some country, is repeatedly exposed to war memes through newspapers, radio, TV, or however, those memes in that person's brain connect to various feelings. If these war memes have been organized in a campaign to gain support for a specific war, the memes and their associated feelings are being orchestrated into a train of thought, thinking and feeling, leading the citizen to an unavoidable conclusion that the war is necessary. Notice that this process is, in no way, any kind of cold, dispassionate logic. In relation to human thought, dispassionate logic is a contradiction. The intensity of the feeling of fear in the citizen, real fear for her own safety, for her own life, and the lives of her family and friends, is built up gradually, over months, or maybe years. One of the most beautiful campaigns, from the war meme point of view, began in September, 2002, and reached its peak, with the awe and fear inspiring cleverly compounded metaphor: *Maybe the smoking gun will come in the form of a mushroom cloud!* Meanwhile, no feelings are built up about the horrors of war that will accrue to others, the soldiers, and ordinary people, who surely will suffer, and die, in the war. And even if such feelings were built up, they could never be strong enough to truly represent the horrors of war. Our brains and memes evolved to help us survive when humans lived in small groups. Our feelings and memes may work more or less well for small groups. But our feelings and memes cannot compute the grief and suffering, much less all the damage done to our societies and culture, damage done to all of us, by all the death and destruction of war. So our memes and feelings can't get war right. They just can't. This is fundamental. Our current brains and memes, have not evolved enough, to fit our present world of billions of people, divided into several hundred nations, religions, and assorted ideologies. That's why we must take control of our memetic evolution. We can start now with our war memes.

Stalin's law.

As we noted above, the processes by which memes and feelings interact in a brain, to make decisions, only work well in limited circumstances. They may have been satisfactory for the conditions existing when they evolved, humans living in small groups. In the past, empathy, the ability to feel what other people feel, and these brain processes involving memes and feelings, worked well to keep small human groups working together, cooperating. These processes don't work well enough for present day conditions, where the sizes of groups we must make decisions about are millions, and hundreds of millions, of people. The feelings and memes, interacting by themselves, can't do the job that needs to be done. We noted this before with the famous statement of Josef Stalin: *"One death is a tragedy; one million deaths is only a statistic"*. You can sit down next to someone, who has recently experienced the death of a loved one, and you can experience some of the very same feelings that person feels. You cannot sit down next to one million such people, and experience one million times as much grief, as you felt when you sat down next to that one person. The feelings processes, however they work in our brains, cannot do that. Our brains and memes have not evolved enough to be able to do that. But you do experience, intensely, and directly, your own fear of some enemy, once your fear has been worked up by the war memes.

The universal reason effect.

There is another way we humans get wars wrong. In the past our best thinkers, our scientists and philosophers, thought that all humans were endowed with what they called universal reason. The idea was, that every normal adult human, had a capacity for reason, which was totally separate from our feelings and emotions, and that this universal reason was exactly the same for everyone. We now know that is wrong. [Lakoff, 2008]. Those old ideas still have negative effects, in that most people today, still think that proper thought, proper reasoning, should have nothing to do with our emotions and feelings. So in analyses of complex situations, emotions and feelings tend to be left out. Of course political scientists, and others who try to understand war, know very well that people suffer in wars. But many of the theories, that have been constructed over the years about war, tend to be abstract, and mathematical, assuming forces and interests of nations, that have nothing to do with real people, or with people's suffering, nothing to do with feelings. Grief and suffering do not count. In these theories, nations are abstract entities, with abstract interests, and abstract powers, which are quantified with numbers, and related with simple, even linear, mathematical formulas. These theories are claimed to be rational. But they don't work very well either. [Bennett & Stam, 2004].

So what to do?

If our memes and the brain's feelings processes can't get war right, what can we do? Well we are humans, who have evolved other tools, other memes. These tools are words and numbers. Even though these language and number memes operate at a higher level than the basic feelings processes, they are based on the basic level and still use it. We use these higher level tools to get around the limitations of the basic level feelings processes. Some of us do. Despite the fact, that there is no such thing as a universal reason, that every normal adult human has equally with everyone else, there is something, there is some ability that we humans have, that we call thinking or reasoning. George Lakoff and Rafael E. Nunez call it real reason.

"Real reasoning includes phenomena like graded categories, various kinds of prototypes (typical, ideal, nightmare, salient examples, social stereotypes), radial categories, frames, metaphors, and so on. Symbolic

logic, no matter how sophisticated its present form, is nowhere near characterizing real everyday human reason." --- [Lakoff & Nunez, 2000, page 139].

The reasoning that we do, and can do, depends on the memes and feelings we have.

Just as no two humans have identical **car** memes, no two humans have identical reasoning abilities. Reasoning is not some kind of infallible process that is the same in everybody. The reasoning that we do, and can do, depends on the memes and feelings we have. And these depend on all our past experiences, all our education, all the things we have learned, all the things we know, or think we know. We use real reason to think about war, to decide for, or against, war. It's all we have. For some people, at least some of the time, real reason amounts to going with their gut, deciding on the basis of their intuition, their hunches, guesses, or looking only at the worst case scenario. Some people may think they have a good theory of war, or international relations, and they attempt to apply their theory. Some people try to live by conscious moral principles such as the fifth commandment: *Thou shall not kill.* Some may evaluate war with the four transcendent values: Goodness, Beauty, Justice, and Truth. For some people, real reason degenerates to the simplest most primitive decider: the feeling of fear. Most people let other people decide for them. Many people are mental slaves to others.

So there's work to do.

Alright, we must kick the depression of that last paragraph. It will be work, but we must seek and spread the best truth we can find. We know some of the mechanisms that lead to war, and we can change, or eliminate them in ourselves, and in our cultures. People can learn when to rely on gut feelings, hunches, and intuitions, and when it is dangerous to rely on them. Scholars and scientists can learn when to rely on mathematical models, and when it is dangerous to rely on them. Bennett and Stam's 2004 book, *The Behavioral Origins of War,* is not negative. It is progress. It's good news. Now we know some things that don't work. So is Lakoff et al's demolition of universal reason. The universal reason meme doesn't work. So it must go. Get over it. The truth, that's us. That's what we humans do. We seek and spread the truth. As best we can find it, and verify that it works for all of us. Goodness, beauty, and justice too. That's us.

The connections among memes and emotions are damaged in some people.

The above discussion about how our presently evolved brains and memes are incapable of correctly evaluating wars assumed healthy, undamaged brains. Antonio Damasio, in his book *Looking for Spinoza,* [Damasio, 2003], discusses brain damage to parts of the brain that are necessary for the proper functioning of feelings and emotions.

"The findings and interpretations regarding the adult frontal lobe patients became especially compelling in light of the recent description of young adults, barely in their twenties, who sustained comparable frontal lobe

damage early in life rather than adulthood. My colleagues Steven Anderson and Hanna Damasio are finding that those patients are, in many ways, similar to those who sustain lesions as adults. Just as in the adult cases, they do not exhibit sympathy, embarrassment, or guilt, ..." --- [Damasio, 2003, page 152].

"We are not suggesting that every adolescent with similar behavior has undiagnosed brain damage. It is likely, however, that many people with comparable behavior that is not due to the same cause have a malfunction of the brain system that had sustained damage in our patients. The malfunction may be due to a defect in the operation of neural circuits at microscopic level. Such a defect may have a variety of causes, from abnormal chemical signaling on a genetic basis to social and educational factors." --- [Damasio, 2003, page 154].

George Lakoff, in his book, *The Political Mind,* [Lakoff, 2008], describes a 2007 study of moral decision making, which compared *"moral decision making of a purely calculative nature"*, to moral decisions which involved *"direct one-on-one physical interaction where empathy was aroused"*. The study showed that *"for normal people, empathy interfered with any abstract moral calculus, either overriding it or raising serious moral qualms."*

"The locus of empathic decision making, the study revealed, is the ventromedial prefrontal cortex. People who have had brain injuries or strokes in that region, however, showed no such qualms. They treated the one-on-one direct contact cases just like the utilitarian moral calculus cases, even when it involved suffocating a baby. Empathy is normal and it takes a special education (such as basic training in the army), a special heartlessness, or a brain injury to disengage it." --- [Lakoff, 2008, page 102].

So, not only is the normal operation of the brain, in connection with our feelings and memes, inadequate for evaluating wars, but many different kinds of brain damage to the relevant brain systems, might well make things worse. Lest you may think that all this talk of memes, brains, and feelings, is rather abstract and far removed from decisions about war, let me abstract and emphasize a phrase from the Damasio, page 152, quote above:

"...they do not exhibit sympathy, embarrassment, or guilt, ..."

These are social emotions and feelings. They are very relevant to our interactions with other people, past, present, and future. They are extremely relevant to the decisions we make concerning our future courses of action toward other people. They are absolutely relevant to any decision to start a war. A person who cannot, or does not, feel sympathy, embarrassment, or guilt, or who has diminished capacity in these matters, is even less likely than a normal person to make a correct decision about war.

The mental defects relevant here may have a variety of causes. Damasio only alluded to one very important cause, when he spoke of a *"defect in the operation of neural circuits at microscopic level"*. An important cause of damage to small areas of the brain is mini-strokes. These are strokes, blockage or bursting of blood vessels in the brain, which are so small that individually they frequently go unnoticed. If enough of them occur over a period of time they can cause noticeable deficiencies and dementias. They are more frequent in people with high blood pressure and vascular disease. The occurrence of these diseases increases with age. People who have had strokes are more likely to have mini-strokes. Also people who have had heart bypass surgery may have strokes and mini-strokes. I wonder how many wars have been caused by old, overweight, and out of shape, leaders with high blood pressure and vascular disease, wars that would not have occurred, if their brains had not been damaged. Actually I can think of one recent possibility rather easily. Former VP Dick Cheney, a brain behind the Iraq war and torture, has had multiple heart bypass operations and his statements and actions seem to indicate a lack of sympathy, embarrassment, and guilt. This of course is speculation. In any case we need more information, about both the mental, and physical, health of all politicians and leaders. We should have brain scans, thorough psychological evaluations, and release of all medical, and academic, records of all politicians and leaders. For a serious science based yet entertaining and exciting presentation of the interdependence of feelings and thinking in decision making read the book *How We Decide,* by Jonah Lehrer. [Lehrer, 2009].

Meme evolution, some details.

Memes are information that is processed in human brains and human artifacts. How is this done? What is possible and what is not possible? In the broadest sense meme evolution is about the development of human culture. The evolution of human culture is not going to be explained any time soon in terms of the mechanics of information processing. Just as the study of the human brain is approached from many directions, psychology, neuroscience, linguistics, and artificial intelligence, we can study human culture from various perspectives. The brain is studied from the bottom up, by studying the operation of individual neurons, as well as from the top down, through psychology, linguistics, and artificial intelligence. We can study culture from the bottom up, by studying memes and individual human behavior, as well as from the top down, through history, sociology, anthropology, and political science. Looking at memes and how they interact in one human brain, how they interact between and among brains and human artifacts, is to approach culture in one way, from the bottom up.

A person's basic set of memes.

How do memes get into human brains in the first place? A person's basic set of memes, come into that person's brain mostly during childhood, by interaction with parents, and others, and through childhood and adolescence. Through the rest of a person's life, new memes are acquired, through further education, and through all the person's interactions with other people, the physical world, and all the things of our culture. Remember, big memes are built up over time. A person's **car** meme is more or less continually being modified. This also applies to almost all big memes, a few of which we have analyzed in Chapter 6.

Big memes are acquired gradually over time.

Bits and pieces of big memes are being added or subtracted throughout life. These bits and pieces of course are also memes, small memes, we might say. This process of getting more information throughout life, acquiring small memes throughout life, and integrating the new information with what is already there, is part of the process of meme evolution in an individual human brain.

Any information.

A meme can contain any kind of information. That is a meme can contain information about anything. This includes information about the person's body and brain, information about the physical world, information about other people, and information about memes. This includes information about ideas and concepts of any kind, from concrete to the most abstract. These are all information, and are memes, and parts of memes, in human brains.

Feelings and emotions are memes and are connected to other memes.

As we discussed above, probably almost all memes in a human brain are connected to feelings. Surely almost all memes we talk and think about, the memes we can be conscious of, and many that we are not conscious of, are connected to feelings. Feelings arise from emotions, which are patterns of muscle activity. Fear may be expressed through a tensing of muscles, a particular facial expression, and maybe a scream. Happiness may be expressed with a smile, a particular pattern of tensing and relaxation of facial muscles. And so on for other emotions. A pattern of muscle activity is information in a brain, or is preceded by information, that specified that muscle activity. Feelings and emotions are information. So feelings and emotions are memes themselves, and parts of other memes.

Unknown feeling and emotion processes.

Feelings and emotions are surely connected in complex ways to all big memes. Some feelings and emotions are connected to the small memes, that may be coming into our brains daily, which we integrate with the big memes we already have. The ways in which the new information coming in, is integrated with existing memes, depends on some currently unknown feeling and emotion processes, operating between the incoming meme, and the already existing memes in the brain. These processes likely depend on the damaged brain areas Damasio and associates investigated. [Damasio, 2003].

The big four: Goodness, Beauty, Justice, and Truth.

We have many big memes of many various kinds. Maybe among the biggest are what [Balkin, 1998], called transcendental. These are Goodness, Beauty, Justice, and Truth. He called these values. Are there feelings for these? Yes there are. For example, there have been a few works of art that have struck me. What was that strike? What happened in me when one of those few works hit me? It was a kind of awe. In each case I saw a kind of unity, a perfection, beauty. Like it could not possibly be improved, that if even one dot, or one line, were taken away, or added, or one bit of color changed, that the work would be lessened, maybe ruined. And in at least one case, I felt as if I were able to perceive instantly, and completely, every line, every color, every form, every dot, all together as an integrated whole, and as above, that nothing should, or could, be changed. Other times it was the truth, as well as the simple, or complex, beauty of the work which struck me. The true absolute horror, injustice, and inhumanity, of war and torture, in one case. The finality of species extinction in another. Did I experience feelings and emotions? I sure did. Certainly strong feelings, of many kinds, are associated with each of these transcendental memes.

Transcendent values use complex and strong connections to feelings.

All normal humans have memes for these four transcendent values, and in normal people, these memes have complex, and strong, connections to feelings and emotions. Strong feelings and emotions are integral to these memes. The **Goodness** meme is strongly connected to our bodies, and individual bodily actions and needs: food, bodily comfort, pleasure, pain, dangers in our immediate environment. **Justice, fairness**, is important in social interactions. It evaluates or measures cooperation, detects cheaters to the social contract. What's **Beauty** good for? What does the **Beauty** meme do? Well I just described one thing above: It can make us feel really **good**. It tells us we have just found something really **special**, something we should **treasure**, something **valuable**, something we can **learn** from, something that can **change** us for the **better**. And the **Truth** meme? It tells how well our memes fit the world. It's a measure of our memes. It's an evaluation of our memes. All four of these transcendent memes are used by us to evaluate things, or classes of things, in our world. **Goodness** started by evaluating physical things like food, for the continued physical existence of our bodies. **Justice** evaluates cooperation between and among humans. **Beauty** probably started as an evaluation of the quality of, the health and fitness of, potential mates. And the **Truth** meme is an evaluation of memes directly. Note that each of these memes is or was binary … 0,1 … Yes, No. Something is either **good** or **bad** for you. A meme or set of memes is either **true** or **false**. A person is either **beautiful** or not. An action or behavior of a person is either **fair** or not. We mostly notice when some action is **not fair**. As we come to understand the world in more detail, in its greater complexity, we replace these binary models by more graduated measures. And of course the domains of application of these memes have expanded over time. Some people still cling to the binary forms, at least in their explicit statements. But their unconscious brains are way ahead of them. These memes are graduated in almost all brains. But we don't know how this departure from binaryness is implemented in the brain. It would be a mistake to assume there is a linear scale. It would also be a mistake to assume the valuations are one dimensional. Since each of these transcendental memes has multiple feelings associated with it, the values are already multidimensional.

Feelings help new memes fit.

So when a new small meme comes into a brain, its information content, and the existing content of the brain, somehow lead it to, or associate it with, one or more already existing memes, and some decisions are made, as to which existing memes it might fit with. As with my example of the perfect painting above, clearly at the moment I was experiencing it, my brain at that instant, would not tolerate even the slightest change to the meme for that painting in my brain. So some memes in some brains can be closed to change, nothing is to be added, or taken away. But generally, probably, the new small meme gets evaluated by the brain, according to what it would do, to the various feelings, presently part of one or more big existing memes. Would it make the big meme more true? If the big meme represents a bowl of oatmeal in front of me, and the little meme is sugar, will the little meme make the big meme taste better? Or will the little meme be bad for my health? As the discussion of the car trip shows, information, other memes, from who knows where elsewhere in the brain, can affect the decision. They all come with feelings. How hungry am I? How much do I want sugar? What are my feelings about my health? What do I think one spoonful of sugar in a bowl of oatmeal would do for my health? It's all feelings here it seems. Is there any logic? Feelings are stored information, evaluations of things, evaluations our brains and bodies have made, based on our past experience. Most of these evaluations are unconscious. But we have no clear ideas, of exactly how all these feelings are put together, in the hypothesized feelings processes, mentioned above. So any logic at work here, does not seem to be like formal logic taught in schools. But since the feelings that are part of our memes, were derived from past experiences, and since the evolution of our bodies, brains, and memes, have gotten us to the present time, it could be, and some people would say, it must be, that the feelings processes used by our memes, brains, and bodies, existing in the world, have some kind of rationality.

Metaphors are real.

From a higher level of brain functioning, language, we do have some ideas of how many memes are related, connected, and associated with one another. In work done over the past several decades, linguists and neuroscientists have shown that metaphors, once thought to be mere unnecessary, roundabout, ways of speaking, are not that at all, but rather, metaphors are fundamental to the ways our thoughts, concepts, and memes, are actually structured in human brains. A metaphor is a mapping of one domain of thought into another domain of thought. A metaphor uses some of the parts of the old domain, and some of the relations, and some of the feelings, of the old domain, to construct the meme for the new domain. And there are physical, neuronal, connections, back and forth, between the domains. These physical connections are the mapping. Each domain is a meme, or set of memes, or a schema, or framework for memes. There is good evidence that these domains, schemas, frameworks, and mappings, exist as neuronal structures in the brain. That is, all of these things --- domains, schemas, frameworks, mappings, and memes --- actually exist as physical structures in brains. They are embodied. There is no need to assume, as many philosophers and scientists did in the past, that there are ideas, or any other kind of mental objects, existing independently of brains. Every new metaphor is a new meme. So immediately we see one way, maybe the major way, or even the only way, new memes have evolved from existing memes! The reality of metaphor, the embodiment of metaphor, is a huge discovery. [Lakoff, 2008], [Lakoff & Johnson, 1980], [Lakoff & Johnson, 1999], [Feldman, 2008]. Anyone interested in eliminating war, or in understanding and promoting social progress, of any kind, should read and understand these books. In particular the book *Philosophy in the Flesh,* [Lakoff & Johnson, 1999], blows away centuries, millennia, of philosophical fog.

Reuse already existing structure.

There may be other ways new memes may arise besides through the invention or construction of new metaphors, and there are many memes besides those related to language. But even those memes not related to language could be expected to use the same types of copying, or reuse with modification, of existing neuronal structures, that the language metaphors use. The reuse of already existing structure is just what evolution does all the time. It's natural and efficient. Programmers do it too. Instead of writing the same or similar code over and over again, they write subroutines, or modules, once.

How are memes stored in brains?

"... Current evidence suggests there is <u>no erasing</u> in the adult brain….long term memory of facts, skills, or situations is captured by structural changes in the connections between neurons. There is no process for selectively reversing these changes. This is why it is so hard to alter your behavior patterns or to change the beliefs of others. The only known neural mechanisms for changing behavior involve inhibiting a pathway or bypassing it with a more active alternative." --- [Feldman, 2008, page 38, emphasis in original].

We do not know in detail how memes are stored in brains. It is known that when animals learn, changes occur in the synapses between neurons. Synapses are the small spaces between neurons where they almost touch one another. When a neuron fires, chemicals called neurotransmitters are released into the synapse. Some of these chemicals move across the synapse and are absorbed by the other neuron. It is known that, as an animal learns something, the neurons involved change the amount of neurotransmitter chemical, that is released by the firing neuron, and absorbed by the receiving neuron. The bottom line is that as a person learns, physical and chemical changes occur in neurons in the brain. The information that is a meme is stored, or represented, or registered, by these physical and chemical changes, and/or by the changed patterns of firing of neurons, that the physical and chemical changes bring about. The following references give more details: [Lakoff, 2008], [Lakoff & Johnson, 1980], [Lakoff & Johnson, 1999], [Feldman, 2008]. See especially Feldman's book *From Molecule to Metaphor.*

Meme filtering.

"Human beings are not simply an inert environment in which memes compete and breed. Our minds select and reject, combine and reconfigure the memes we are exposed to. We do this both consciously and unconsciously, both deliberately and as a side effect of everyday life. We are active participants in the growth and spread of cultural software, even if we do not have full control over the terms of its evolution." --- [Balkin, 1998, page 293].

Brains and bodies selectively absorb information. At every instant vast amounts of information surround us. First of all we are limited by the sense organs we have. Dogs can hear higher pitched sounds than people can. Bees and other insects perceive ultraviolet light that humans cannot. Human sense organs, bodies, and brains have evolved so that certain information can come in and other information cannot. Even with this limitation, there is still way too much information that could come in for us to handle. Not all that information is relevant to our survival, success, happiness, etc. So we are always rejecting huge amounts of information that we might absorb. We look at some things and not others. Our eyes are always moving, looking at only a small fraction of what they might look at. At the meme level, we categorize sources of memes. We don't listen to some political commentators. We watch certain TV channels and not others. In the discussion above of meme evolution, we described how our feelings and values that are parts of our memes, determine whether and how new information, new small memes, are accepted or rejected. The feelings processes are critical for accepting or rejecting memes. The feelings processes filter new memes.

Meme filtering may require little or a lot of time.

I want to clarify something that might have caused some confusion. In our discussions of memes, big memes, in the previous chapters, I often talked as if meme filtering was pretty much an instantaneous process. All perception processes, all brain processes, take time. Sometimes meme filtering can be quick … taking a fraction of a second to a few minutes. But the meme filtering process might go on for an indefinitely long period of time. Next let's look at two real world examples that might take a long time.

Filtering a **new hat meme.**

Let's look at how a person might get a new meme. A person can get a new meme, a meme the person does not already have, from outside, from the physical environment, from other people, from the vast culture we are all immersed in. Any new meme has to pass through the organism's meme filters. Otherwise it is not accepted, it will not be incorporated into the set of memes already there in the person's brain. As we discussed above, a new meme must fit. It must have been evaluated to be of some actual, or potential, benefit to the person accepting it. What does it mean to say a new meme is evaluated to be of some actual or potential benefit to the person? The person has goals, purposes, missions, interests, loves, curiosities. These are memes the person already has. The person evaluates the new meme, if it is to be accepted, as having some chance of being useful for attaining these purposes, etc. This evaluation process will involve the feelings processes discussed in the section on meme evolution. The person does not know for sure whether the new meme will help in the attainment of some purpose. So how does the person find out? The person may try out the meme provisionally. The person might perform one or more experiments with the provisionally new meme. For example a person goes into a clothing store and considers purchasing a new hat. Let's say a specific hat is being considered. Let's say the person's goal or purpose here is to be more attractive, to look good. In our cultures, the clothes we wear send all kinds of messages, memes, to other people. Most of these we are not conscious of. The person will be making a guess, as to whether this particular new hat, will serve this purpose, will be considering the price of this hat, the money available, and make a yes/no decision. Maybe the person tries on the hat in the store and looks in a mirror. The hat might be rejected then and there. Let's say the person buys the hat. So the **new hat meme** has been tentatively accepted. But it's not completely accepted yet. The **new hat meme** has to prove itself first. It must be tested to see if it has the desired effect. It must be worn in public, among people who will verify, whether the new hat, has actually made the purchaser more attractive. If after one or more tests, the new hat purchaser has received sufficient positive feedback, the hat will be worn, this **new hat meme** has been firmly accepted, and at least for some time, the new hat will be worn often. If on the other hand, not enough positive feedback was obtained, the new hat will be put in a closet, never to be worn again; the **new hat meme** will have been rejected.

Filtering a **new math meme.**

Let's say a mathematician comes across a new meme, a meme she has never had or considered before. It may have come to her from the outside, maybe from something she read, or maybe from a friend. Or maybe it came from inside herself, from her thinking about some problems she is currently working on. Maybe one, or several, memes she already had mutated. A mutation might occur if she remembered some meme incorrectly. More likely, she put together some of her existing math memes, which are metaphors, in a clever new way. Or in whatever other ways memes are able to transform themselves in a human's brain, she generated, maybe unconsciously, a totally new meme. To her it might seem as if a totally new idea just popped into her mind. Then what does she do? She behaves very much like the new hat purchaser. When she first considers the **new math meme**, she guesstimates whether it may be useful for one or more problems she is working on. She may abandon the meme immediately, if she decides the new meme has absolutely no relevance to the things she is working on, to the things she loves. But let's say, it's not so clear cut, she's not so sure this **new math meme** won't help her. Then she will consider it. She will begin to examine, perhaps very methodically, all the different aspects of the things she is working on, that she thinks the **new meme** might help with. If at some point it does help, if it yields something new, something which itself she estimates will help her further, or if this new thing is just beautiful, or interesting, or somehow gives her pleasure in and of itself, she will keep, and cherish, this **new math meme**. It will be completely accepted, and incorporated with her other math memes. On the other hand, if after long and careful consideration, she comes up with no new interesting or beautiful results, the mathematician may give up on **this math meme** and abandon it. That means she stops thinking about it. We could say she puts it out of her mind. What she thought might lead to something wonderful did not. It's very much like a lost love. It is a lost love. She is sad. But then she goes on, looking for more new memes to help with what she loves. How long does a mathematician keep trying to make a potential new meme work, fit, fit in? It depends on the complexity of the meme, the complexity of the problems being worked on, the abilities of the mathematician, her personality, and probably many things we do not presently understand. It's a very personal decision. Remember: all memes, especially memes that are important to a person, are complexly intertwined with that person's feelings and emotions. So the feelings processes are surely involved here. The typical person sees math as all logic. It is not. It is vast, often beautiful, hierarchical structures built up from basic bodily metaphors. [Lakoff & Nunez, 2000]. Gut feelings, hunches, visualizations, guesses, beauty, truth and logic, all contribute. Even the logic part works on the basis of feelings. At every step of a logical argument, a mathematician checks a feeling. Consciously or not, she is asking herself: Is this correct? The answer that the brain gives back is a feeling. See the book *On Being Certain,* by Robert A. Burton, M.D. [Burton, 2008]. So mathematical reasoning, even mathematical logic, is based on feelings. The supposed absolute pinnacle of cold dispassionate thinking, mathematical logic, is based on human feelings!

Depends on the person's reality.

Notice that in these meme filtering examples, the acceptance or rejection of the new meme depends on the person's reality, the person's existing memes, and the person's physical, as well as social environment. It is a trial and error process, a testing and evaluative process.

Having a meme versus using a meme.

When a meme is rejected, especially after a long evaluation or testing process, the meme almost surely still exists in the person's brain, but it is not used by the person. If the new hat has been rejected the hat may continue to exist even for years in the person's closet, and the hat meme will still exist for some time in the person's brain as a memory. Similarly the mathematician's meme will remain in her mind for the rest of her life if she spent a lot of effort evaluating it. It's just that she will not be using it in her mathematics research. If it was indeed a lost love, we can bet she will think about it again, every now and then. The point here is, that often when we speak of having a meme, what we really mean is using it in life. We have many memes we do not regularly use if ever. For example we don't usually use the negations of memes we use often. We are often aware of opinions and values we disagree with. That is we have these memes, but we don't use them in running our lives.

PORTRAIT: Rest in Peace 4.3M.

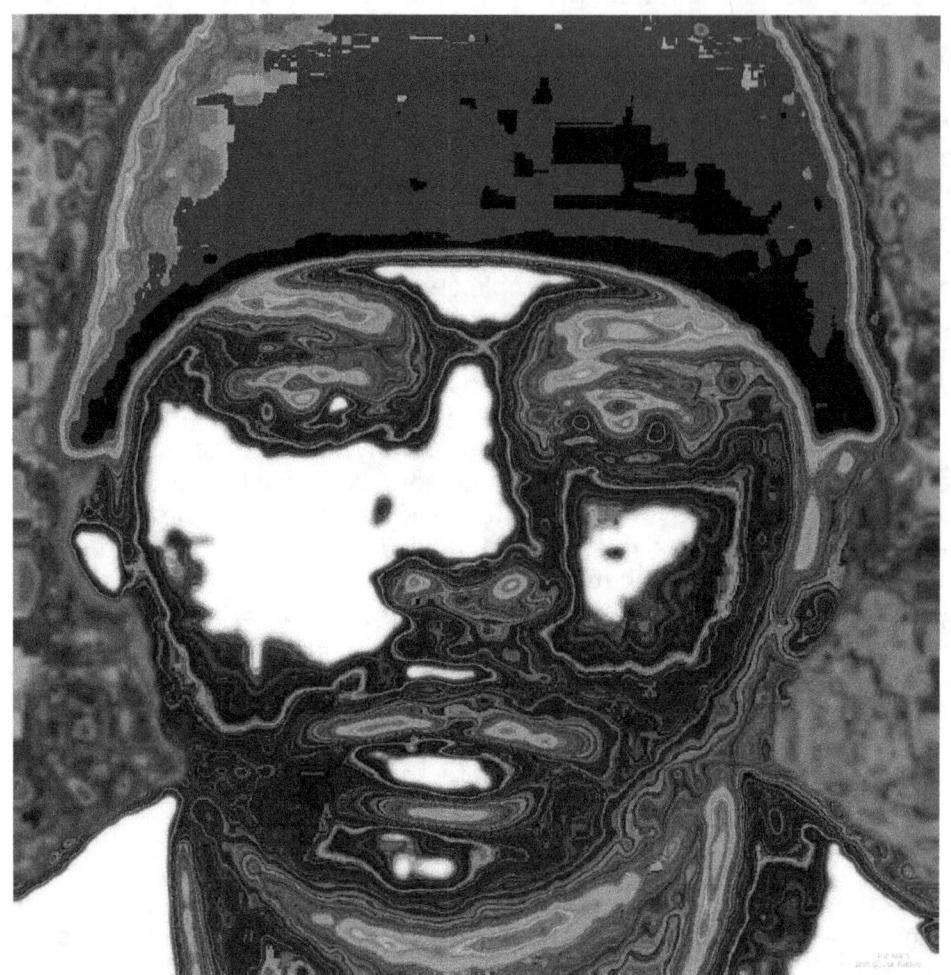

Chapter 10: Meme organisms and memes that promote memetic evolution.

What's a meme organism?

A meme organism is any group of memes interacting and acting as a unit. So for example, each individual human is a meme organism. A pair of identical twins raised together, continuing a close association throughout their lives, is a meme organism. A human couple, who love each other deeply, who are very close, constitute a meme organism. [Hofstadter, 2007]. A group of people working together for some purpose, such as a family, an extended family, a tribe, a committee, a club, a sports team, a symphony orchestra, a company, a partnership, an association, a city, a state, a nation, are all meme organisms, when considered as a set of memes interacting. For our purposes, we take the set of interacting memes to be the union, the totality, of the memes of the individuals, plus any memes circulating throughout any technology, or other artifacts, essential to the operations of the organism.

Are meme organisms real?

A rock is real. The earth is real. People are real. Is a city real? Is money in the bank real? Is a country real? Is Chinese culture real? Is the number 1023 real? Metaphors are real. They are patterns of neuronal connections in people's brains. [Lakoff, 2008]. More neurotransmitters here, less there. Neurons firing or not firing. Information in brains. Larger or smaller synapses, the connections between neurons, more or fewer little bags of chemicals, vesicles. They are all real. Information is real. Memes are real. Meme organisms are real. All real. As real as bricks, ant colonies, bee hives, countries, corporations, species, cars, animals, plants, dirt, sand, air, water, sunshine, and the taste of an apricot.

Self preservation memes.

A meme organism having **self preservation** memes will last longer than one without **self preservation** memes. So over time there should be more meme organisms with **self preservation** memes. There need not be any force to generate **self preservation** memes except the fact that the meme organisms that get them in any way whatsoever, or that get better ones, will tend to outlast other meme organisms. So meme evolution naturally, spontaneously, generates **self preservation** memes for meme organisms. This explains why government bureaus, agencies, many other organizations and ideologies persist long past their usefulness.

Classes of meme organisms.

Every person is a meme organism. So are animals with brains or at least nervous systems. An important class of meme organisms we will talk about consists of groups of people working together. Another class consists of groups of animals working together. There can be higher order classes and meme organisms with parts from different classes. Consider holding companies. A holding company is a corporation consisting of corporations. It can also be considered as mixing categories: A holding company consists of human owners, and employees, as well as the companies it owns. Consider a nation. It can be seen as the collection of all individual people who are citizens of the nation as well as all the various sub collections: states, regions, districts, cities, corporations, clubs, associations, and so on. For our present purposes the most important meme organisms we will be discussing are groups of individual people.

Non human meme organisms.

We mentioned above that animals with nervous systems are meme organisms. Some groups of animals are meme organisms too. Douglass Hofstadter discussed Ant Hillary, an ant colony, as an individual entity. [Hofstadter, 1979]. The ants in an ant colony communicate by using pheromones, (chemicals), produced by the individual ants. When one ant receives, (tastes or smells or otherwise perceives), a pheromone from another ant, that causes the receiving ant to carry out a specific behavior, where different pheromones correspond to different behaviors. [Holldobler & Wilson, 1990]. Pheromones for ants are like words for us. Thus the ants are communicating various behaviors to each other. So the individual ants in Ant Hillary are triggering memes. So Ant Hillary is a meme organism. Other animal groups also constitute meme organisms, such as other colonial insects, and animals that band together and more or less operate as groups, like chimpanzee bands, as well as herds, and schools of fish. There are probably some human created machines we could consider as meme organisms, if they operate more or less autonomously. Most human created machines are designed to closely interact with one or more humans. But for example, a human being driving an automobile, is a human-automobile meme organism, which is definitely a different meme organism, than a single human meme organism walking. We could go further and claim that individual plants are meme organisms since information in the form of chemical signals flows between parts of plants, but this is straying too far from our present purposes.

All meme organisms operate according to the same principles.

The other meme organisms besides individual humans behave like individual human meme organisms in many ways. Meme processing and meme evolution follow the same general principles. But the resulting behavior will depend on the specific memes present, the specific kinds of processing possible, the environment, and the history of the organism. This means some of the science relevant to individual humans, and their interactions, is applicable to other meme organisms, and their interactions. In particular, the science of non-violent communication, developed for interpersonal relations, has been shown to be effective in resolving disputes between and among human groups, from schools and neighborhood organizations, to warring ethnic groups in Africa, to disputes between nations. [Rosenberg, 2005 (a), (b)]. This should work best for meme organisms based on humans such as corporations and nations. But some might work for Ant Hillary as well. And the science could go both ways. It could be said that we already do this. People have explained human behavior in terms of animal behavior often. And of course scientists perform experiments on animals and apply the results to humans.

Is a nation a person?

We often speak of nations as persons: France did such and such. But when someone suggests that we take that identification seriously, we immediately get the response that of course a nation is not a person. We need to examine this a little more. Most wars are between and among nations. A nation considered as a person is a metaphor of course. The common view is that metaphors are unnecessary, that they are just shortcuts that have no connection to the real world. But Lakoff et al convincingly demonstrate that this is not so. Many of our memes consist of metaphors. Our metaphor of a nation as a person is one of our operational models of what a nation is. So the question boils down to this: How complete, how comprehensive, is the mapping from the person meme to the nation meme? Or to be more precise: How comprehensive is the mapping from the person meme organism to the nation meme organism? A nation meme organism doesn't have legs, although the people in a nation do. But both nations and individual people have self preservation memes and goals. Both need material things to survive. Humans need friendship, intimacy, love, respect, interaction with others, creativity, rest, play, and so on. Of these at present it seems nations only need interactions with other nations, and some nations have little interaction with others. It used to be thought by some that nations needed respect from other nations. So the nation as person metaphor works up to a point. Surely almost all metaphors are like this --- there aren't many metaphor mappings that are one to one correspondences. There is another metaphor that a nation is a family [Lakoff, 2008]. Similarly, for the nation as a meme organism there will not be a one-to-one mapping of memes circulating in an individual human onto the memes circulating in a nation. But we can investigate which meme processes operating in individual humans have analogs operating in the meme organism of a nation.

How much of a person is his country?

Some people identify with their nation. They project some of their own human needs and desires onto their nation. Thus for some people their nation must have respect. It should be glorious. It should be great. It should be strong. Maybe it should be loved. Maybe it should be feared. So the person feels respected if he sees his country as being respected. He feels glorious if his country is glorious. He feels strong and tough if his country is strong and feared. How far can this identification go? How far does it go actually, and in how many people? Maybe the nation as person metaphor is going too far here. This identification can occur not only in average citizens but also in leaders. *The state, that's me*, said Louis XIV. I expect this identification goes too far in too many leaders, and whether in leaders or average citizens, wars have resulted from it. The nation as person metaphor needs serious work. People need to learn and use a mapping that does not lead to wars.

Meme filtering for meme organisms.

The same general meme filtering processes are utilized by all meme organisms. Consider the adoption of a new automobile design by a car manufacturing company. Consider the adoption of a new law by a city, state, or nation. Consider the decision to go to war by a nation. In all these cases it's basically trial and error. Meme organisms may try to predict the results of a new meme as best they can, but in the end, a new meme has to be tried out one way or another, and the results observed and evaluated. One problem with nations that decide to go to war is that they are no good at all in evaluating whether the go to war meme helps them attain their goals. And of course often nations do not have clear goals.

The evaluation of new memes by meme organisms.

A meme organism consisting of a group of humans may use different mechanisms to evaluate new memes than individual humans do. For example such a meme organism may use some form of democracy to adopt rules of behavior for its members. Or it may adopt some form of hierarchical structure with leaders giving orders to followers. Or many combinations are possible.

Meme organism goals.

What are meme organism goals? Well, all the goals of individual people, and all the goals of organizations of human beings, all the goals of corporations, governmental subunits, and nations. As we mentioned above all meme organisms have self preservation memes. We can say they want to survive. They also can have goals way beyond survival. They can want to thrive, grow, expand, get money and more money, get power and more power, get more and more knowledge.

Progress?

We must be wary of assuming some kind of inevitable, or built in, progress in the evolution of meme organisms. Inevitable progress was a dangerous and destructive meme assumed to be a logical consequence of Charles Darwin's Natural Selection. Easy popularized memes about *the survival of the fittest* led to racial superiority memes, and this helped support colonialism, and oppression of supposedly inferior races. Biological evolution has no logical consequence of inevitable progress. Biological evolution can degenerate, lose functionality. Surely, memetic evolution can do likewise. Biological evolution and memetic evolution both go wherever their respective processes, interacting with their respective environments, take them. We have no assurance that either evolution will always be good for humans. Both are very complex systems. Complex systems can crash, degenerate, do very strange, and unexpected, things for reasons known and unknown. Arbitrary continuance, or stability, cannot be assumed. At the present time, we can't even design our electrical grids, our financial systems, and our economic systems, to keep them from crashing, so much less should we assume stabilities in the immensely more complex systems of memes. But our scientific understanding of how memes work in the brains, and bodies, of individual people, and how memes work between and among people, is increasing. There are good reasons to believe that we will continue to increase this knowledge. This will allow us to better direct both of these evolutions. We should not expect uniform progress. Remember, the basic process is trial and error.

Some meme organisms can try to improve themselves.

In what sense could a meme organism expect to improve itself through memetic evolution? Well, we humans talk of improving ourselves in various ways. Some people improve their bodies in various ways through exercises, training, diet, and supplements. We improve ourselves by acquiring knowledge. We can improve ourselves and our communities through work. A corporation may seek to improve itself. Corporations reorganize and do other things to improve. A reorganization is a restructuring, a rearrangement of the parts of the organism, a trying out of new memes, or new relationships, of existing memes. A new structure for a meme organism amounts to trying out a new meme. This is similar to the hat purchaser trying out a new hat meme, or the mathematician trying out a new math meme. Any improvement obtained depends on whether the new meme arrangement makes the meme organism better, or more efficient, at attaining its purposes, goals, and interests. Something improves a meme organism if it makes the meme organism better at attaining its purposes, goals, and interests. So within the constraints of their environments, within the constraints of their physical substrates, and within the constraints of the memes they already have, some meme organisms can direct their own evolution. This may sound like a strange loop, [Hofstadter, 1979], but who's afraid of strange loops?

Meme organisms protect and develop their memes.

A meme organism tends to preserve all or most of its memes. This is because its memes are necessary for it to survive and develop. So an effective meme organism can be expected to have memes to protect its memes ... to resist drastic changes from outside. In a broad sense these are self preservation memes. More specifically, for day to day operations, meme filters help preserve existing memes. But a meme organism also needs memes that say acquire new knowledge. Human meme organisms must continuously update their everyday operational body memes, memes about their body, and their memes about their changing environment, as they develop from infancy through adulthood. They also get new memes, and update them regularly, regarding social interactions. A meme organism needs knowledge acquisition memes if it is to be able to adapt and survive in a changing world. There is a step beyond just surviving. A meme organism might have memes which say it is good to develop itself, or that it should develop itself. That is, it might have memes that say it should get more memes, more knowledge, more abilities, beyond the minimum necessary for immediate short term survival. Many or most humans have such memes. This desire for continuous development, for more memes, for more abilities, and for more knowledge, might enhance long term survival. That is one reason to have it. This may explain some of our seemingly useless pursuits like music, art, literature, poetry, and sports. Of course these make us feel good. That's how the memes to seek them work. But we do not need them to survive, to not die physically. These are only distantly connected to adaptation and survival. We seek excellence, and celebrate excellence, in these human communal activities. We might add conversation and any kind of play to this list. It might also explain our love of science. Even though science is justified as being useful, for much of it, especially mathematics, at the time it is done, we don't know what it will be used for, if anything. Some humans slow down these meme acquisition and development processes sooner than others as they get older. Why does this happen? Why does the **develop oneself** meme weaken? Deterioration of bodies and brains may be one reason. But there surely are also cultural reasons. Other meme organisms, besides individual humans, might have the **develop oneself** meme.

The self development meme promotes cooperation between and among meme organisms.

Clearly there are many situations where it is beneficial for each of several meme organisms to cooperate. Cooperation can be beneficial if the cooperating meme organisms have a shared goal, and the goal is sharable. In this case they can work together to promote the **self development** of each. Two meme organisms have more memes than one, and so the two working together, cooperating, have more raw material, memes and knowledge, than either working alone, and thus cooperating, they are more likely, or more quickly, to reach their shared goal. Two people may have the same goal but may be unwilling to share it. Two different men may want to marry the same woman. So we will have competition, not cooperation in this situation.

The self development meme.

The memes in meme organisms, such as humans, are information derived from their environments. The past evolution which led to their present bodies and brains, incorporates huge amounts of information, from the past, into their present body and brain structure. They also have incorporated huge amounts of information from their culture, through their education in their culture. And they derive information from their environment, throughout their lives, through their senses. All their memes, all this information, is used to direct and control their activities in their current environments. In the case of human meme organisms, their current environment includes other meme organisms, other humans, animals, families, corporations, and so on. These other meme organisms dominate the environment of a present day human individual. Meme organisms interact with their environments by sending and receiving memes. How well a meme organism works in its environment, depends on the collection of memes it has, and uses, at any point in time. As the environment changes, the meme organism must update the memes it has, or uses, if it is to continue to function well in the changed environment. In the earliest biological evolution the environment was all physical and chemical --- water, rocks and so on, relatively simple --- but as evolution continued, the environment becomes more complex --- full of all kinds of plants and animals interacting. But the organisms evolving don't have any idea of what's happening. Animals have memes about their bodies and their interactions with their environments. With many animals all memes would seem to be unconscious. Maybe some other animals, like Chimpanzees, have some conscious memes. A chimp might have a meme for herself, and other memes for specific chimps she interacts with. A chimp in her group may or may not have a meme for her group. They do know who is in their group and who is not. In any case we can be sure they don't have a meme for evolution. Only humans have a meme for evolution. It seems only humans have a **self development** meme. Only humans consciously seek to improve their performance through education and training, by seeking new and better training and education, by researching the effects of various foods, vitamins, supplements, and other physical/chemical substances, on their physical and mental performance. And only humans seek to improve their physical and mental performance by physical and mental exercises like meditation, yoga, workouts, and walking. All of these are components of, or instances of, the **self development** meme. And there has been a population explosion in these only recently. So what's going on here? We have a new meme which causes us to actively and consciously **develop** new memes --- a new meme which causes us to accelerate meme evolution. And this accelerated meme evolution goes way beyond what is needed for basic survival. This new meme seems to work mostly at the individual human level, although acquisition of new knowledge is certainly a community activity, and as we discuss elsewhere, much of ritualized sports is communal, team, cooperative activity. There are other memes which may be extensions of, or may be derived from, these **self development** memes, and which are more applicable to communal development, to the acceleration of the memetic evolution of the meme organism called humanity.

To lose oneself in a cause greater than oneself?

What a strange phrase that is: To lose oneself in a cause greater than oneself. Why would someone want to lose herself? She must not be happy with her self. Maybe she feels her life has no meaning. What is it for her life to have meaning? Meaning means to be connected to something else. It is to want something, or to desire something, or to love something. Life has meaning for a person only if that person wants to live, which is to act, to do stuff, to enjoy things, to grow. So if her life has no meaning, then it isn't connected to anything that satisfies her. Personal relationships aren't satisfying enough. Maybe there is no, or not enough, love. Maybe the environment of her life, the people, places, things, ideas, pleasures, surrounding her aren't good enough. Maybe there is little or no goodness, beauty, justice or truth.

Is the meaning of life to love memes?

What are some of the connections people say give their lives meaning? Love of spouse or children. Love of any other person or persons. Love of one's work. Love of humanity. Love of the natural world, perhaps expressed through environmentalism, or study of science. Love of an ideology that promises goodness, beauty, justice, or truth, religious or secular. So there we are: Memes. As the philosopher Dan Dennett has said, to be happy, find a meme and let it take you over. Let it control and direct you. Work for it. Dedicate your life to it. As stated this seems a little scary. This is more than just a connection. It sounds like possession or slavery. But it need not be these. It need not be scary if you understand what is happening. It can be more like love. With love, you are not just connected, or related to, the object, but you actively work to make it thrive, to live, grow, succeed. So Dennett's prescription then becomes: Love a meme. Or maybe several memes, or a set of memes. When you love another person, you are loving some of their memes. Since we can say a person is her memes, and if you know her well, then she and you have many of the same memes, or complementary memes, so you are loving her memes, and your own memes, at the same time. So in all these cases you are loving memes.

A cause greater than oneself.

What kind of thing could it be, to be a cause greater than yourself? What could this be? The cause is a set of memes, perhaps in another person, or persons, or perhaps in an ideology. And of course, if you are loving this set of memes, many of them are already in your mind. So you are loving a set of your own memes, and since loving means wanting to see them grow, increase and prosper, you want to see them grow, increase, and prosper in your own mind, and in the minds of others. If you love the environment, then you want to protect the environment, you want to see it grow, prosper, develop freely, as it would without human interference. You must work with other people in this process. You want the people you love to be happy, to grow, to develop, to the maximum extent possible as human beings, to become all that they can become. (Sadly, the phrase *be all that you can be* is used in army recruiting posters. How sad and sick.) To love another person is not a one way process. The two of you work together, to develop each of you, and both of you together. If you love science, if you work in science, you want to see your scientific theories grow, be made more clear, more comprehensible, be able to explain more phenomena, become more and more beautiful, be accepted by more and more people. And if the love of your life is an ideology, you want to reinforce it, and spread it far and wide. If you are a lawyer, and you love justice and the rule of law, you may work with others to promote these memes, to spread these memes, to see that the constitution and laws of your country are being followed. And if the love of your life is all of humanity, then you work with other people to eliminate war, to eliminate disease, to eliminate hunger, to eliminate poverty, to provide justice, and fairness, and education, and all good things, to every living human being. If your sphere of love extends to all animals on this earth, then you also work to eliminate the suffering of animals. Maybe you no longer eat meat. You may join an organization which spreads memes about how cruelly animals are treated. If you love all life on this planet, or all life in the universe, or indeed the whole universe, then you work to protect these things, you work with others to increase our knowledge of these things --- our memes about, and for, these things. You want to see these things, and the memes for these things, grow and develop in their natural ways --- you want to make sure that we humans don't destroy them, or mess them up. In these ways, the cause is greater than oneself, because the objects of love are outside the self, and you are working with others, while the memes for them are being incorporated into your self. Thus one's self becomes greater and greater too. This is a positive feedback process, ever increasing the memes you love. Memes and minds are hardly ever still. Memes in an unread book may be static; brains sleep for brief periods. But the memes in the cause, and the other memes in the person's mind, and the memes in the minds of others, are forever evolving together, growing together, feeding back on one another, in myriad loops and cycles. It is a system wonderful, awesome, and beautiful to contemplate.

Meme takeover?

What does the above say about memes taking us over? The above might suggest they really are taking us over. But they are us, and we are them. Memes are a way of describing how our brains and bodies work, and interact, with other brains and bodies. They have always been a part of us. Memetic evolution, cultural evolution, the history of the development of more complex culture, all suggest that memes are playing larger and larger roles over time. But *takeover*? That's not the right word. It's like saying our brains are taking us over. It's as if some primate ancestor of ours could miraculously appear among us and seeing us say: *Wow, evolution really took us over*. It's just evolution --- meme evolution, cultural evolution. Evolution is change. So we will change. Some people don't like change. Long term stasis does not seem possible for us. As we scientifically investigate memetic evolution, and understand it more and more, as we have done with our physical environment, it will not be scary. We will be able to direct and control it. People are already doing that, but they are often not aware of what they are doing. The anti-slavery movement did it. The women's liberation movement, still underway, is doing it. So is the environmental movement.

Direct and control memes.

Earlier we talked of memes doing their own thing independent of any benefit to humans, independent of any human concerns. That is just a shortcut way of saying that we must evaluate the memes we are using --- the memes circulating in our culture. If we don't evaluate the memes we are using, then we may be using some that are harmful to us. If we don't pay attention to what memes are doing in, and to, our cultures, then yes, they will seem to be running amok. It's just the scientific method --- theorize and test --- trial and error. Memes running amok is a scary idea. It's scary partly because culture is viewed as being beyond our comprehension, as too big, as too complicated. But we made it. We can change it. We don't have to play dead and pretend nothing can be done. It's up to us to keep memes from running amok. That's what this book is about, at least with respect to war. Obviously we can do the same things in other problematic areas of our culture.

It's only scary if we let it be.

So memes will take us over if we let them. We will let them take us over if we don't study them scientifically, find out what they do, and change them if necessary, so they do what we want. So in this sense, it is scary to think of memes taking us over. In this sense, they have taken us over somewhat --- the war memes have --- because we have let them run wild, without understanding how they work, and without understanding all the harm they cause us.

The greatest invention so far ever made by memes.

And love? What about the **love** meme we discussed above? This must be one of the greatest inventions ever made by memes. Just look how critically it is involved above in all these major methods of meme expansion. But some of you may think that **love** is the wrong word. Too mushy! Too mystical! Too far out! Other words might be: **interest**, **curiosity**, or **passion**. Or maybe **nurturing**. These words could do. Feel free to substitute your favorite if you wish. But I prefer **love**.

Alien memes.

It's interesting how some mostly older people, who have not yet gotten the meme for animal rights, or who have not gotten the memes for protecting our environment, the meme to love our biosphere, how for them, these things, these memes, so dear to many of us, are meaningless. There are some people for whom animal rights organizations and all they stand for make absolutely no sense. For those people these memes truly seem to be alien creatures or viruses that are doing senseless mischief.

Killer love memes.

For many people, the meme to love the universe, seems glorious and beautiful, a meme they value highly. But of course a good meme, from the meme's point of view, would want to be such that humans would want it. To be glorious and beautiful, from a human's point of view, is one way for a meme to make humans want it. So the question is: is this meme, and are these other memes, good for humans? Clearly some of the ideology memes, at least the extreme versions of some of them, cause much grief to humanity. Ideologies sometimes cause wars. Excessive love of your ideology memes, enough to kill for them, is too much love. So we must control our memes, keep them on a leash. It seems simple and sometimes it is: Any meme that causes people to kill one another is a bad meme from the human point of view. This is not surprising. What needs explanation is why we continue to allow such memes to run free. Viruses kill people, bacteria kill people, tigers kill people. We try to avoid these killers, or control them. So why don't we control the killer memes? The answer is that not enough of humanity appreciates that some memes kill people. Yes, the killer memes are scary, but the others aren't. There are other memes that are bad for people besides those which kill us. There are many memes of course which can injure us, make us unhappy, memes that diminish us in various ways. These also need to be recognized and controlled.

Control your memes.

Is the meme **to lose oneself in a cause greater than oneself** a war meme? The answer is clearly yes if the cause is a war, or a cause that leads to war. Probably it leads to war if the cause is any killer meme. So control your memes. Be careful which memes you let take over you. But find one, or some, which are good for you, and good for the world too.

The love meme promotes meme evolution.

As discussed above, the **love** meme must be one of the greatest inventions ever made by memes. Greatest from the meme point of view. Why? Because the **love** meme is a great **generator,** and spreader, of **memes**. Suppose you meet an interesting person, someone who seems to have some interest similar to yours, or who seems may have knowledge about something you are interested in. What do you do? First thing is, you two talk. Each of you immediately wants to increase your knowledge about the other. You want information about the other. You want to know their memes. You want to add their memes to your memes, or at least some of them. Suppose two people **love** each other. They see each other often, or maybe they live together. All the time they are together they are exchanging memes. The closer they are, the longer they are together, the more they are exchanging their memes. People really close can complete each other's sentences and be correct almost 100% of the time, their memes overlap so much. Suppose you **love** some activity, say stamp collecting, or baseball, or mathematics, or art, or music. What do you do? You seek that activity. You do that activity. You study and buy stamps, you play baseball again and again, and you get better and better at it. Maybe when you get older you watch baseball games played by others, at ballparks, on TV, and read about the baseball teams and players. If you love mathematics, you study mathematics; you learn until you can make your own contributions to mathematics. The same goes for any science. If you **love** some art, you do all you can to learn about it. You seek the best teachers. You observe all the art you can. You may make art. You keep learning more and doing more. In all these activities involving **love**, you are seeking and acquiring new memes. And you are **giving** and **spreading** memes to others. So the **love** meme is one great meme **grower**, meme **spreader**, meme **evolver**! **Love** makes us interact with one another, and with the world. Interact = spread, grow, evolve memes! So the **love** meme is a great meme invention, great for memes.

The love meme grows.

We see the **love** meme expanding its domain of influence, its area of application from primitive times up to the present. In primitive times humans only cared for their immediate relatives in the small bands they roamed around in. Look at human history, and the history of culture. As people learned farming and domestication of animals, they could live in larger groups, all of whose members were more or less interdependent. When cities arose the number of interdependent people in the group could become even bigger. Interdependence means communication, means that the people were exchanging memes. The number of people that mattered to them in some way increased. To say that all the people in some ancient city loved one another in anything like our modern sense, would probably be wrong. But as more and more people became interdependent, as they mattered to one another, even if in just small ways, this was the beginnings of **love**, at least in the sense that they probably cared for the other people enough to work with them. Language groups, ethnic groups, religious groups, nation states, all provided larger domains for the **love** meme to operate in. Historians of culture can provide a much more detailed exposition than I can. But even without every detail, I think it's obvious there has been an evolution of the **love** meme, from a very primitive state, and limited domain, to ever larger domains, from specific application to other humans, to application to material things and ever more abstract things, to memes.

Love memes have partitioned humanity.

For many centuries now, we have seen the **love** meme for other humans, being extended to our nation, but no farther; to all our co religionists, but no farther; to those who speak our language, but no farther; to our own race, but no farther. The abolitionists extended the domain of the **love** meme to the slaves. Those who fought for women's rights, and for women's liberation, extended the domain of the **love** meme to women. But any look at our present world, shows that the domain of the **love** meme, has not expanded uniformly across the planet. Above we talked of **love** of all humanity, **love** of animals, **love** of the environment, **love** of the biosphere, the earth, all life, and the whole universe. But for most people of the earth, the domain of **love** stops at their nation's border, or at the edge of their religious group. A few wise men in the past were inhabited by various expansive versions of the **love** meme and attempted to spread those memes: The Buddha, Jesus, and other prophets. But, even after thousands of years, many of those claiming to follow the teachings of these wise men still don't get it.

The Internet is a great love meme.

The **love** meme, in its specific instantiation as the **love the world** meme, has evolved into the great **science** meme complex. In the vast domain of **science** memes, some have evolved into the computer memes, and the **Internet** memes. The **Internet** is a great **love** meme because it greatly facilitates the preservation and transmission of memes. With it memes can zip at near the speed of light, between almost any two people on the planet. It's becoming a vast repository of all the world's knowledge, information, memes, soon available to every human on the planet. It will help all of our **love** memes. It will store and protect them and allow us to **grow** them. It is causing memes to **grow**, **evolve** and **proliferate**. It is most definitely a **love** meme.

The love meme can be bad for people.

Are the **love** memes good for people? As above in the discussion of the **lose yourself in a cause greater than yourself** meme, if a **love** meme gets so strong that it makes its host kill, then it's obviously bad for people. Or if a **love** meme damages people in some other way, then it's again bad for people, by definition. I imagine that we can think of situations where a **love** meme that is not on the surface bad for people might turn out to be bad for people anyway. Some memes derived from the **science** memes are very dangerous, very bad for individual people as well as for humanity, for example the **hydrogen bomb**.

PORTRAIT: Rest in Peace 113.2.

<u>And the greatest of these is the love meme.</u>

So the **love** meme is an expansion of the **self development** meme. The **self development** meme puts the emphasis on meme evolution in an individual whereas the **love** meme emphasizes meme evolution in cooperation with others, in communities, in meme organisms consisting of groups of humans, in all of humanity, and beyond humanity.

<u>Two more memes that promote meme evolution.</u>

The **free speech** meme is a great meme invention, great for memes and people too. This meme is good for memes because if people have it they will let other people express their wildest memes. The **liberty** meme is also a great meme for memes, because it lets people express themselves by their behavior with minimal restraints. The **liberty** meme goes beyond the **free speech** meme. Both these memes tend to spread themselves.

<u>Free speech.</u>

What a meme invention! Think of it. This meme says let everybody express their memes, whatever they may be. No restrictions! As the number of people who adopt this meme increases the more likely it, and all other memes in these people's brains, will be transmitted between and among them. More memes will be available to more and more people. These memes will mix it up in people's brains. They will combine, and mutate, and metaphorize, and in other yet unknown ways, new memes will evolve from the already existing memes. This meme pushes the meme evolution accelerator to the floor and keeps it there. The larger the human population having this meme becomes, the more it will spread, or leak, into human populations not having this meme. Technological communications media will help this meme spread to the whole human population. The latest technological communications medium, the internet, which allows any person on the planet to become a kind of broadcaster, will also accelerate the spread of the **free speech** meme and all memes.

<u>Can anything stop the **free speech** meme?</u>

The above might suggest that meme evolution will go on forever if we just let loose the **free speech** and **liberty** memes. Humans will get smarter and wiser and more creative, onward and upward, forever. But there can be no guarantees. The above acceleration effect of the **free speech** meme, assumed that people will like the **free speech** meme, that they will easily let it in, that their meme filters won't block it. Is this a valid assumption? People could be programmed to see the **free speech** meme as **evil**. Their meme filters just would not let it in. This could occur in rigid ideologies, those with a strong version of the **one and only true way** meme. If an ideology holds that it has the truth, the whole truth, and nothing but the truth, then it has no need for **free speech**. **Free speech** will be dangerous, and insofar as any speech deviates from the ideology's truth, it will be suppressed. But memes leak. No meme filters work 100% all the time. No ideology can totally isolate its members from outside memes. Since **free speech** promotes meme evolution, a group with the **free speech** meme will evolve better memes, over time, than any rigid ideology.

The **liberty** meme promotes memetic evolution.

Liberty means freedom of behavior, which includes **speech**. But behavior is expression of memes. Behavior is one way memes may be transmitted from one meme organism to another, assuming the meme organisms may observe one another. So clearly limitations on **liberty** limit memetic evolution of meme organisms in two ways: 1) by limiting transmission of memes from one organism to another, and 2) by limiting the expression of new memes by a meme organism, the meme organism may have diminished desire to generate the new meme for the new behavior.

Limits to **liberty.**

Even Libertarians espouse limits to human **liberty**. Clint Eastwood's characterization of Libertarianism as *Everybody leaves everybody else alone*, implies certain restraints on **liberty**. People shouldn't assault or kill one another; more generally people shouldn't harm one another. Now the big question for human societies is exactly what constitutes harm. Many disputes and controversies about the limits of **freedom**, and the specifics of which laws to have and enforce, derive from various opinions as to what constitutes harm by one person towards another. There are more complex questions about what non human meme organisms such as corporations should be allowed to do. These are clearly very important subjects, which I do not propose to examine in detail here. For our purposes, the point is that meme organisms --- such as nations --- have some kinds of internal and/or external memes that control and limit the behavior of their components. For example: "***Thou shall not kill.***" So when we speak of the **liberty** meme as being good for memetic evolution, we mean **liberty** with some limits.

Democracy and the force of memetic evolution.

For city, state, and national meme organisms, true **democracy** with **free speech**, maximal **liberty** --- with minimal constraints necessary for **civility** --- and encouragement of **civic involvement** --- **interest** in, or **love** of, the **civic** meme organism --- should be the best form of government. A **democratic** meme organism will evolve faster, will be able to try out more new memes, such as more variations on what constitutes harm between humans, and variations on rules for the behavior of corporations. This follows immediately from having **freedom of speech** and maximal **liberty** and **civic** participation. This way, memes generated by anybody, have a chance to circulate, and be considered by everybody, and since there is **interest** in **civic** participation, people will pay attention to new suggested memes, to be adopted as new laws, and tried out for a while. The collection of citizens, the meme organism that is the city, state, or nation, can see if the new law, meme, works, or not. They can check if it seems to be an improvement or not, and act accordingly, by keeping the new law-meme, or getting rid of it, and trying something else. The contrast with a tyranny, or dictatorship, or oligarchy, is that these evaluations of new memes --- laws, or rather, dictates of the dictator or oligarchy --- are only evaluated by him, or the limited number of persons in the oligarchy. The new memes may even be only generated by him or them too. So we have in the one case, memes generated and evaluated by one or a few people, versus memes generated and evaluated by thousands, hundreds of thousands, or millions, of actively meme generating human meme organisms. Clearly, over the long run, true **democracies** with complete **freedom of speech** and **thought**, with maximal **liberty**, and with sufficient **civic interest**, will out compete, out perform, any form of government that limits **speech,** or **thought,** or **behavior,** or **civic participation**. True **democracy** has the force of memetic evolution on its side.

A long way to go.

So there is a natural meme force in favor of **free speech, liberty**, and complete **democracy**. Any group having these three memes will have greater meme evolution than a comparable group without them. Their knowledge of themselves and the world will be greater. They will adapt better to themselves and the world over time. Ideologies, tyrannies, oligarchies, and so on, are naturally **self limiting,** in that they hold back memetic evolution. They will be left behind and fade away. The degree to which these three memes are operative matters. Sadly, today, _in all countries_, there are way too many totally unnecessary restrictions on **free speech** and **liberty**. These restrictions are both overt and covert. Many so called democracies today are disguised tyrannies or oligarchies.

Are democracies efficient?

But what about the messiness of **democracy**? Might not the **democratic** process waste a lot of time and effort? The answers to this depend on the technologies for implementing the **democratic** process, as well as the distribution of knowledge throughout the population, and the **democratic** structure. **Democracy** doesn't have to mean every question is voted on by everyone in the population. The structure of a **democracy** should never be assumed to be fixed. **Democratic** structures are memes, and should be carefully evolved **democratically**. And the memetic development, the education, of every individual in a **democracy**, should be maximally promoted. The more memes in every individual, the greater the education of every individual, the more memes circulating among the people in a **democracy**, the better and faster the **democracy** will evolve. This of course has been recognized for more than two centuries. But, education occurs best, in a healthy mind, in a healthy body, in a healthy community. So an optimal democracy, would have an economic system, that made sure every person had all of life's basic necessities, such as adequate clean and healthful water, food, clothing, shelter, health care, and as much education as they wanted. But sadly many so called **democracies** are making no progress in promoting education for all their citizens.

Empirical evidence that democracies are better.

There is some evidence that **democracies** are less warlike than other forms of government. [Cashman & Robinson, 2007].

Other memes that are good/bad for meme evolution.

We have discussed some. **Censorship** and **secrecy** inhibit meme evolution. **Free speech, liberty, democracy,** the **love** memes, (including **science** and the **internet**), promote meme evolution. In general, **rigid ideologies**, that is **ideologies** which have strong **self preservation** and **spread me** and **one and only true way** memes and are fundamentally based on unverified, or unverifiable, memes, inhibit meme evolution. Could there be **ideologies** which promote meme evolution? Are **free speech, liberty**, and **democracy** ideologies? Is **science**? **Free speech** and **liberty** are relatively simple memes. **Democracy** and **science** are more complicated, more like what we think of as **ideologies,** in that they each consist of a rather larger set, of interacting sub memes. Do **democracy** and **science** try to keep contrary memes out? Yes they do. **Democracy** opposes **tyranny. Science** consists of memes which are empirically verifiable, or which can be derived logically from empirically verifiable memes. **Science** filters out memes which do not meet these conditions.

Unverified or unverifiable memes.

Memes are information. Humans use memes to construct their models of reality. The process of verification is the method we use to test if a meme corresponds to reality. So an unverified meme should not be accepted into our model of reality. It might be accepted provisionally, if we estimate, or hope, it may become verified. If a meme is unverifiable in principle, there is no place for it in our models of reality. It may be used for logical exercises, play, fantasy, etc., but not as reality. So the problematic ideologies are those based on unverified, or especially unverifiable memes. These will tend to inhibit meme evolution. This assumes that memes based on, and containing verified memes, have a memetic evolutionary advantage --- that verified memes are better than unverified, or unverifiable memes --- that verified memes will last longer, proliferate more, have more descendents than unverified, or especially unverifiable, memes. In other words, this assumes that truth matters.

Some memes inhibiting or promoting meme evolution.

Inhibiting: **secrecy, censorship, tyranny, authoritarianism, ignorance, propaganda, excessive conformity**.

Promoting: **Curiosity**, the **self development** meme, all the **love** memes, **science, art, sports, games, play, fantasy, creativity, free speech, liberty, democracy, books,** (and all other **storage** of memes in human **artifacts**), the **Internet,** (and all other technologies which enhance the **circulation** of memes), **cell phones, education, socialization, logic, artificial intelligence**. In general all memes which promote the **storage** and **preservation** of memes in humans and human **artifacts**; all memes which promote the **circulation** of memes in and among humans and human **artifacts**; all memes which promote the **empirical, logical, playful, artful, fantastical, creative combinations** and **recombinations, abstractions** and **consolidations** of memes in humans and human artifacts.

Cooperation among meme organisms.

In our current cultures, competition seems to be overused. At least it is overrated. Much more cooperation occurs than people realize or allow themselves to realize. An individual human isolated from all contact, from all communication, with other humans, for a long enough period of time, ceases to be human. Solitary confinement, without any communication with other people, is a form of torture. It makes people insane. To be fully human, we need to interact with other people. We exist as humans only in communities. Our biological evolution has occurred in communities. Our memetic evolution can only have occurred in communities. All our main memes, our big memes, all our conscious memes, and most of our unconscious memes, all memes that go between people, are about interacting with other people in groups of people. That's how the memes evolved. They evolved to enhance the survival, development, and success of the group and thereby promote the survival, development and success of the individual. Living and working together in communities is cooperation. We are cooperation. Without cooperation we would all die in a short period of time, in a month or two.

Conditions of scarcity can be replaced by conditions of plenty.

If resources are scarce there can be conflicts between individuals. In situations of plenty there need not be conflicts for resources. Knowledge and art --- memes --- can be shared with unlimited numbers of other people after some fair compensation is made to their creators. Physical things can be scarce. Our societies and cultures could be organized so that the basic physical needs of all humans were met. Information --- memes --- can be reproduced arbitrarily at near zero cost. As the things desired by meme organisms shift away from physical things to the non-physical, to memes, to information, conditions of scarcity can be replaced by conditions of plenty. Then cooperation will be able to flourish even more than it does now.

Conflict and competition are not the same.

Conflict is fighting. Competition only rarely involves fighting.

Sports: competition is cooperation.

Formalized competition as it occurs in sports is a form of cooperation. In team sports each team as a unit, as a meme organism, works by the members of the team cooperating, at least most of the time. The competition between two teams is ritualized. It follows rules. The two teams and their members follow the rules of the game. And what is the purpose of this cooperative competition, this whole enterprise we call sports? It is to develop, promote, evaluate, and celebrate human excellence. But not only individual human excellence. In team sports the purpose is also to develop, promote, evaluate, and celebrate communal, team, meme organism excellence --- excellence that occurs as a result of cooperation toward a goal. In formal sports the active human participants develop themselves through exercise, training, and practice. The sports are promoted to and celebrated by human observers. The brain mechanisms that allow us to enjoy watching sports are exactly the same as those which allow us to feel what other people feel. We know what other people feel by watching them move. This is true when we are watching them run, jump, throw or when we see them smile, frown, cry, or tense their body and face muscles in fear. It's empathy. It's mirror neurons. It's the brain using the same circuitry, when we see something being done, as when we actually do it ourselves. [Iacoboni, 2008]. And most everybody thinks sports are all about competition! Competition is only one part of it. Competition is a tool, used by the larger human community, to evaluate the individual and group human excellence, that sports develops and promotes. Sports is a big meme saying: Look at us! See what we can do! We're special! We're great! Of course sports also celebrate individual human excellence. But the main message of sports is not: Look at me! See what I can do! No, the message is: Look at us! Just ask yourself why do we, almost all of us, feel so good, when we see some excellent individual athlete break some old record, or execute some beautiful play? It's not about the individual. It's empathy. It's about us. All our big sports are communal. Very communal. Make a list of all sports which have no human audience besides the active participants. It won't be very long. No, even when we celebrate an individual athlete, we are celebrating ourselves, we are celebrating humanness. This celebration of human excellence, in sports, in music, in literature, in visual art, in science, and in every human domain proves that we can, and do, love humanity. Even wars are stopped, temporarily, for a world class soccer game.

Cooperation is much more important than competition.

It is commonly thought that there is an opposition between competition and cooperation, that the only way to get ahead is to be competitive in as much of life as possible. There is little knowledge of, and little appreciation of, the indispensable role, that cooperation plays in our present societies and cultures. It's everywhere, all around us, necessary for our continued existence, yet most people do not see it. In terms of real effects, competition is insignificant, compared to cooperation. This is what I meant when I said competition is overrated. This over emphasis of competition, relative to cooperation, probably comes from misunderstandings of biological evolution, or inappropriate metaphorical mappings, from biological evolution to human societies. Or maybe it comes from classical capitalism. The later, in its mix of cooperation within meme organisms, corporations, and competition among them, according to agreed upon rules, is analogous to team sports discussed above. The competition only operates within a context of cooperation. The competition is constrained by agreed upon rules. And lack of cooperation within a corporation is inefficient. The analogy is deficient since the purpose of capitalism is much more than developing, promoting, and celebrating excellent corporations. But capitalism is too big a subject to pursue further here.

Modularity and evolution.

Both evolution and human engineers produce modular designs. That means more complex things, are made up from simpler, more or less self contained parts, each of which performs one, or a few separate functions. Human and animal brains and bodies, are made up of various modules. For example, there are structures devoted to seeing, others for hearing, others for coordinating muscles, and so on. An automobile has an engine, a steering system, a braking system, a suspension system, and so on. There are many explanations for the benefits of modular design. One explanation is that modular systems are easier to modify. Thus a modular body design for animals would be easier for evolution to work with. It has been argued, that even the four and one half billion years of earth's existence, would not have been enough time to evolve humans, if the design had not been modular. [Blum, 2004]. So human brains and bodies had to be modular. Evolution necessarily makes modular systems. A necessary consequence of modularity is communication between modules, and cooperation among all the modules that make up a system, if the system is to be efficient. Suppose a system had a module that had no communication with any other module in the system. Such a module may as well not be there, because it does nothing, except possibly take up space, and maybe other resources. And to be efficient, the modules need to cooperate. If two different modules are trying to do opposite things at the same time, the system is inefficient. If the engine of a car is trying to increase the speed of the car, while at the same time, the brakes are on, that is inefficient. Similarly the modules in an animal brain/body will have evolved to cooperate. Our memes are modules. They are units of cultural information, chunks of information that go around together for some time. Their communication is their interaction with one another, and other parts of the body, as we have been discussing. Since our cultural memes have evolved, and are evolving, in groups of people, and groups of people are clearly modular, a group of people will have a tendency to evolve toward efficiency and cooperation.

Meme evolution --- the bigger picture.

Meme evolution could theoretically go on in a single isolated healthy adult human. Such a person would have to be in a nice stable environment --- lots of nutritious food available easily from nature, with little or no work required to get it, no deadly or harmful viruses, bacteria, no dangerous animals, a warm, stable, pleasant, climate not interrupted by storms. Such an evolution wouldn't go too far. Even in a pleasant environment, a person totally isolated from all human contact and communication, might go insane before too long. Even if he didn't go insane, he will die sooner or later. The memetic evolution will then be over. But this is a deceptive thought experiment. Why? Well, where did this isolated human start from. Presumably he came from our current human culture. He was raised by parents, educated as a child, adolescent, and an adult in our present culture. So he already starts out with a nice big chunk of our culture's memes. He didn't just get them all by himself in some kind of struggle for survival since birth. So there really is little point in focusing on the memetic evolution that could occur in an isolated human.

You cannot understand one without understanding the other.

The brain and body is a unit. You cannot understand one without understanding the other. Similarly the individual and her community is a unit. You cannot understand one without understanding the other. My high school had inscribed above the stage of its auditorium the motto: *Mens sana in corpore sano.* This is translated from Latin as: *A healthy mind in a healthy body.* In understanding people, it makes no more sense to focus on individual behavior, to the exclusion of the behavior of the community, than for someone to say: I only care about my mind; I don't need to be concerned about my physical body.

So how and why did groups of humans evolve mimetically?

The very idea of memes, at the least the kinds of memes we have been discussing, memes that go between people, memes that constitute a culture, requires more than one person, requires a group of interacting people. So the very concept of human memetic evolution requires that we must look at groups of individual humans. The forces of evolution have gradually shifted, from individual survival and well being, to the survival and well being of the group. Our primate ancestors could see each other's behaviors. The mirror neuron connection, between the observed behavior of others, and our own behavior, gives a nice physiological explanation, of how biological evolution, could bring about increasing observation, and **imitation,** of other people's behavior. Person 2 sees person 1's behavior, and does the same thing, **imitates** person 1. So there we are --- a meme traveling from one individual to another. So when one individual discovered something useful, something that might promote her survival, such as finding a new, or more nutritious, food, a second individual could imitate the behavior --- get the meme for it --- and thus promote the survival of himself. In this way, new beneficial behaviors, would spread to the whole group. Immediately there is a biological, genetic evolutionary force, acting on individuals in the group, to have good, and better, and/or more, mirror neuron structures in their brains: Individuals deficient in **imitation,** will be less likely to adopt the new behaviors, and thus have a decreased chance for survival. On average, they will have fewer children than those with the better mirror neuron structures. Then, assuming the better mirror neuron structures depend on genetic differences, over time, those with better mirror neuron systems will predominate. Biological evolution provided mechanisms in some animals which made **imitation** possible. The **imitation** meme was discovered and started meme evolution. So meme evolution is off and running, and already influencing, or directing biological, genetic evolution. And, as they say, the rest is history. Let's look at a few snippets of this history.

The birth of the spread me meme.

So far the process described above is passive. Individual 2 sees individual 1 doing something beneficial and then **imitates** the beneficial behavior. The interesting activity is in individual 2. Now let's add the next step in group memetic evolution --- the **spread me** meme. If individual 1, the discovering individual, has a desire, urge, or force, to convey her discovery to individual 2, we've added some more force to memetic evolution in that group. Beneficial discoveries can spread to the rest of the group more completely, or faster. How would individual 1 get an urge to push her beneficial discoveries to others in the group? Well maybe she gets a pat on the back, or a smile. After all, she just made a discovery which is useful, valuable, or otherwise beneficial, to the other members of the group. So in the future when she makes another beneficial discovery, she is likely to call other members' attention to it, so she can enjoy their expressed appreciation. Maybe the next time she finds another new good food, she offers him a bite. It probably was a long time after the invention of the **imitation** meme before the **spread me** meme was started. Consider the behavior of herds of animals and schools of fish. It would seem that they have the **imitation** meme but not the **spread me** meme. They have the **cooperation** meme too, at least in the sense that they are coordinating their behavior.

OK, what's next?

Then spoken language is evolved:

"... the mystery of the origin of human language is not likely to be solved any time soon. But it is not a profound mystery. Everyone agrees that expressive language conveys very significant evolutionary advantages on groups that can use it. Biological evolution moves too slowly to explain the rise of language (and modern civilization) in just some thousands of years, but cultural evolution is easily fast enough. In a general way, it must be true that the genesis of language was neither a biological event nor individual learning, but a social phenomenon. The biological precursors, whether specific to language or more general, were almost certainly evolving well before the rapid rise of language...." --- [Feldman, 2008, page 328, emphasis added].

Language of course is a huge meme evolver. As language becomes more and more important for group survival or prosperity, it becomes essential for more and more areas of life. So it will be harder for an individual who knows one language to be assimilated into a group having another language. Groups may expand until they bump into another group with a different language. Thus as discussed previously, language can partition humanity.

Group meme evolution can deterioriate.

As long as a group can easily get the resources for the members of the group to survive, various cooperation memes, like the spread me meme, can flourish and evolve further. But if the population gets too big, or the environment changes, so that there is not enough food for all the members of the group, cooperation can break down. New discoveries might not be shared. There might be fighting over food and other resources.

During scarcity negative memes can evolve that persist into good times.

There have been attempts to construct meme sets to damp down discord and promote cooperation during periods of scarcity. The meme set surrounding the ten commandments is an example. But in times of severe physical scarcity of necessities, these don't seem to work very well. But they might work somewhat. Physical self preservation memes may lead to discord and fighting for the scarce necessities. Those who win such fights, get first choice for the available food, or other scarce resources. The losers get the scraps, if there are any. This can be the beginning of a dominance hierarchy. So during times of scarcity, a group's memes can evolve toward dominance hierarchies. Since those at the higher positions of the hierarchy get the best, or first choice at, the necessities of life, they have a great stake in maintaining the hierarchy. So it is not a big step for them to turn the group's memes into a rigid ideology, which ends up being used to promote the interests of the few, at the expense of the many. The leaders get enough to eat while the peasants starve.

<u>In times of plenty, group meme evolution can accelerate.</u>

However in times of plenty, when everyone in the group can easily get enough to eat, the whole group may have time left over after gathering their necessities. They would then have what we call leisure time. What do they do with their extra time? Maybe they procreate more. They may have feasts, dancing, singing, and storytelling. Maybe they play games, sports. The extra procreation can lead to exponential population increases, which end the period of plenty. While the period of plenty lasts, the self development meme, discussed above, can flourish. Then the group is generating new memes just for the fun of it --- sports, art, music, dancing, making up and telling stories, having good times with family and friends, at feasts, and through casual conversation. Although to the group members, it may seem that they are engaging in these activities just for the fun of it, or more likely in earlier times, they don't think about why they do these things, the new memes they are generating, can have various short term, and long term uses. Sports and dancing with music condition bodies and brains. Coordinated behavior, such as dancing and singing, rely heavily on the mirror neuron systems, and likely develop and reinforce these systems. These behaviors may develop abilities valuable in hunting. Not only that, but much more important for meme evolution in the group, all of these activities are developing, and reinforcing, cooperation among the group members. What does making up and telling stories do? Well, we have our first histories, cosmologies, explanations for our existence. We're making our first theories. And what is casual conversation doing? The memes are playing, being creative. And a serious conversation is similar, except it may have a specific purpose or goal. A two person conversation is like a game of tennis or ping pong. The two people are tossing memes to each other and each responding to the memes they receive. They find out, learn, not necessarily consciously, that two people communicating, cooperating, can be more effective than either alone, because the two of them together have more memes to work with. The memes of each person in a conversation are working on, and modifying themselves, and being modified by the memes of the other people in the conversation. The group's memes are evolving.

Some conditions speed up memetic evolution, others may slow or reverse it.

So memetic evolution of a group of humans accelerates, under conditions where all the members of the group, have all the necessities required for survival, under conditions of plenty, when they have time left over, after providing their necessities. During conditions of scarcity of necessities, discord, conflict, fighting may occur; cooperation may be forgotten, and individuals may hoard resources for themselves. Then memetic evolution slows down and maybe goes backward.

Memes to regulate individual behavior for the survival of the group.

Since meme evolution occurs only in the context of a group, successful groups evolve memes to preserve the group, memes to push the group members to work together, to cooperate, and memes to suppress inter member discord and fighting, since fighting can kill or injure members, and most members are valuable resources for the group. Memes in general need not be conscious and group preservation memes need not be conscious either. But in some cases they are conscious as the examples of the ten commandments and laws in general show.

Intra group dynamics vs. inter group dynamics.

So far in this discussion of meme organisms, the focus has mostly been on group self preservation memes in connection with the group's internal dynamics. But when human groups started to bump into one another, the environment in which group memes evolve changes. A group's environment now contains other groups. A similar thing happened in biological evolution, when the populations of organisms became large enough, that the environment in which they evolved, now contained other organisms. So now, we can talk about our human groups, as meme organisms, that must evolve in an environment which includes other similar, but different, meme organisms. This is an environment where wars are now possible, war being an analog of fighting between two individual humans. So now we have the same problem, up one level, that a group of individual humans had. Namely how do you evolve memes promoting cooperation between and among groups of humans. Well, what memes have been discovered in groups of individual humans? We mentioned above: the imitation meme, the spread me meme, the self development meme, and the love meme. What would be the analogues for nations, religions, ideologies, or other groups? 1) Let other nations, groups imitate you. So you would have to let them see, know what you are doing so they could imitate beneficial behavior. Nix secrecy. 2) The spread me meme would suggest that a nation that has found something beneficial would actively give that information, those memes to other nations. 3) The self development meme would say play together, exercise together, converse, communicate, have formalized competition, experiment together, evaluate the results together. 4) The love meme would say first seek to understand, then help them to grow, develop, and prosper both as groups and as regards each individual person, as communities; and ask them to respond similarly, to help us to grow, develop, live long and prosper, so that we and they, all of us, can take pride and joy at what our cooperation will accomplish. Maybe that old bumper sticker from the Vietnam era applies here: *Make love, not war.* But we all have a lot of work to do if we want the humanity meme organism to live long and prosper.

Why are there forces for meme evolution?

Why have groups of humans acquired memes that promote meme evolution? One answer is to say, that it is just part of the process of evolution, matter and energy, physics and chemistry, doing their thing, the universe computing itself. [Lloyd, 2006]. For most people this explanation is probably too compact. So let's try a less compact explanation. Something has to enable every step of evolution. There had to be brain and body physiology that allowed imitation and cooperation. There had to be some feedback to get the spread me meme started. A new thing has to bring some benefit for it to survive. And a particular new thing can arise only in the right circumstances. In other words if you are going to have evolution something has to make it happen. A new thing, a new meme, must have the right preconditions and some benefit --- or something --- that causes it to be kept. First meme evolution built directly on genetic evolution. Now it builds on previous meme evolution. So the evolution that's occurred up to a particular time supports and allows further evolution. But from a human's point of view, what's the force to actually take the next step? What promotes it? What pushes it? It's the fact that what we've got so far is never good enough. What we've got so far is our model, or models, of the world. The memes we have are the information we use to continue existing in our physical and social worlds. This is all we've got. Our memes are our models of the world, and these models are forever incomplete. All our evolution, all our history, all our experience, have taught us, absolutely reinforced in us, that our models, our memes are incomplete. Why is this? Because shit keeps happening no matter what we try. Shit keeps happening! Famine, floods, hurricanes, wars, economic collapse, and on and on. Unintended consequences, surprises, random events! So we haven't gotten it right yet, and we never will. We need better models. We need better memes. We know this at some level of consciousness or unconsciousness. We also know we can make better models, better memes. And at some point our ancestors knew these things too.

Individual and Community.

Let's review what we have been exploring in connection with the relationship between individuals and their communities. We have seen that a person totally isolated from all contact with other humans ceases to be human. And a community is a group of interacting, communicating, cooperating individual humans. So neither an individual human, nor a community of humans, can be understood without the other. This is a problem to be addressed, since many discussions and theories of human interactions, have been constructed with emphasis almost totally on one or the other. Primacy has been put on the individual. Primacy has been put on the community. And there are problems with all such either/or approaches, not surprisingly, since as I just noted, neither can be understood without the other.

PORTRAIT: Rest in Peace 7.1 R.

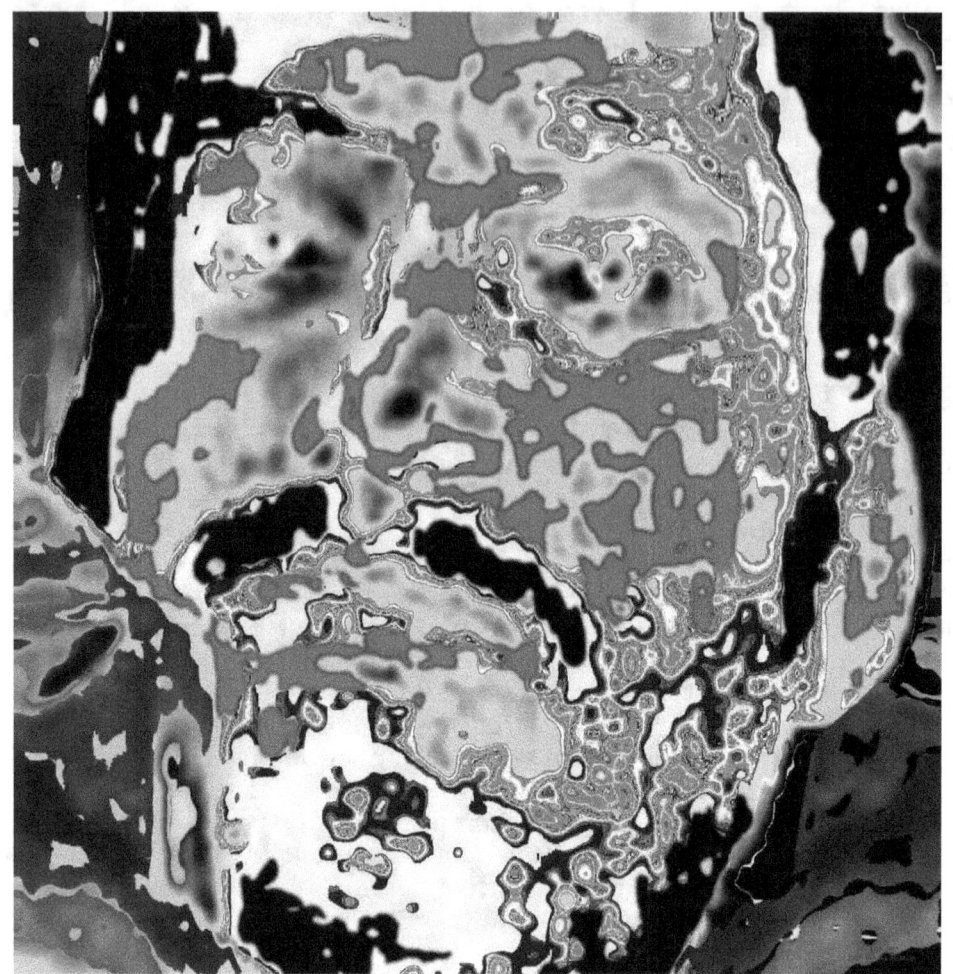

<u>Nurture.</u>

Individual humans are nurtured into their culture through their upbringing by their parents. The memes of their culture, or group, are passed on to them, planted in them, first by their parents, and later as they grow up, by their schooling and their interactions with other people and artifacts of their group.

<u>Memetic evolution in groups of humans.</u>

Memetic evolution only occurs in groups of humans, with few exceptions, that are not important, at least as far as the memetic evolution that has occurred up to this time. Yes, an individual human, brought up by his group, may come up with a new meme, some useful idea no one had come up with before, but he is building on the memes he has at that instant, the memes he has received from his group. If that new meme is not communicated to others in his group, it dies with him. That's not much evolution. So it does not make sense to speak of memetic evolution in individual humans except in the limited sense just mentioned. Human artifacts embody memes, and may generate new memes: writing, the abacus, and the computer, help preserve and generate new memes. But if any such new memes are to amount to anything, they must, at least for now, pass back into individual humans. So memetic evolution occurred in the past, and is occurring now, in groups of humans. For our purposes it is fair to say that memetic evolution only occurs in groups of humans.

<u>No memes = vegetable.</u>

An individual human without the memes of his group, would die in infancy, or become a helpless vegetable. It wouldn't even be as good as a vegetable, since such a sad creature could only be kept alive, through intravenous feeding, like in advanced stages of Alzheimer's disease. This disease shows just what happens as your memes go away one by one. An individual must be infused with the memes of some community, otherwise we don't have a human. So we cannot explain a community only in terms of individuals.

<u>Individuals matter to communities.</u>

Can we explain an individual human only in terms of communities? Can we put communities first? Could we have communities where individuals didn't matter? Even if we could, I don't think we would want that. Communities arose through genetic and memetic evolution, because individuals in communities, communicating, cooperating, working together, could find more and better food, protect one another, live longer, and have more children than individuals with lesser tendencies to associate with others. If this were not so, then communities as we know them would not exist. Individuals would predominate, like in animals where the males only associate with others of their kind, when it's time to mate, and mothers only associate with their young, until they are grown enough to leave. The memetic evolution which has brought us to this point would not have occurred. So communities arose because they provide a survival advantage for the individual members of the group. So the survival and well being of the individuals in a group, at least on the whole, had to matter to the group. If the group didn't have good enough memes, so that a large enough percentage of the individuals survived to produce children, and bring them up with the group's memes, then the group would not survive. So successful groups must nurture individuals but not necessarily all individuals all the time. Some nomadic groups supposedly abandoned old members who could no longer keep up with the group. It is reasonable to think that in general the more successful groups would nurture and support as many of their members as available resources like food and their physical environment would allow. Bottom line: Successful communities cannot ignore individual survival and well being.

Communities need individuals.

Communities need healthy, productive, communicating, contributing, individuals. Part of the continuity of a community is the passing on of the memes to future generations. This includes the memes each generation starts with as well as any new memes discovered in that generation. A more productive, efficient, successful, community will not waste human resources. Such a community will try to assure that all its members have sufficient necessities, and resources, so that they are healthy, and strong, physically, and mentally, since the larger the number of individuals who can contribute to the further memetic evolution of the group, the better, the more efficient, productive, and successful the group becomes. Sooner or later there will be education for all. As much education as each individual can happily handle, so that discovery of new memes, can make the production of necessities most efficient, in terms of time required, and use of resources. And leisure time for all, so that meme evolution can go wherever it wants. So, also, we cannot explain an individual in terms of communities alone, as if individuals were secondary or did not matter, since communities are based on, and need communicating, interacting, cooperating, and productive individuals.

It's one thing.

This shows we must stop trying to put primary emphasis on only one of the two: individual or community. It is not one or the other. It is both. It's not *or*. It's *and*. But this is not enough. We need to go further. It's not two things: individual and community. It's one thing. To even think of it as two things is wrong because two implies separateness. And we have just seen that individual and community are not separate. Not only that, but they simply can not be separated conceptually. It is absurd to try to separate them. When you try to separate them, when you try to understand one without the other, you cannot understand either one.

Community.

The next step would be to make up a name for this new unity. For some people the word community already has this unitary meaning, so maybe we don't need a new word. But most emphatically, new word or not, we do need this unitary meaning.

The unity of community is real.

But how can we just decide that something that we used to think of as two things is now properly one thing? Can we do this? Of course we can. It's just a new meme. It's a better meme than what it replaces. It better corresponds to reality. It's a better understanding of reality to see individual and community as a unit than to try to understand them as two separate things. Indeed, as I said above, it's impossible to understand them separately.

A real meme organism.

The above gives weight to the idea of a community as a meme organism. This meme organism is a thing, a unity, that has parts, totally interdependent parts that, in this case, are very near and dear to us, namely, us! Individuals and their community will succeed or fail together. They will survive or die together. We are our community. Our community is us. This unity, this togetherness will increase as memetic evolution continues.

Less mischief.

For some people the above may be obvious. But much mischief has been done in philosophy, morality, politics, and economics, by failing to see the above unity. Much harm has been done to real people. Many people don't appreciate the magnitude and importance of the interdependences of the parts, the individuals, in human meme organisms, local communities, nations, and now all of humanity. They focus on the individuals. They talk of maximizing the interests of, the well being of individuals, as if this had nothing or little to do with the efficient and effective operation of communities, or as if simply having each individual maximize his own individual interest automatically produces an optimal community, or as if there were no community in which an individual operates. In the extreme the community is taken for granted. It is not seen. Other people, focusing on the community, apparently can't see the importance of individual well being. They act as if some one particular organizational form of a community is automatically optimal for individuals, in all circumstances, now and forever, as if the particular organizational form is more important than, or takes precedence over, the well being of individuals. They act as if such an organization could be efficient, and effective, while not attending to the well being of individuals. In the extreme, individuals are taken for granted. They are not important. They are secondary. All of these views, all of these meme sets, which attempt to separate individual and community are wrong. All are unrealistic. All end up helping some individuals, and neglecting, and harming, others. Resources are wasted on some and denied to others. Those denied necessities, such as sufficient food, shelter, health, and education, are themselves wasted human resources. If they had these resources they would not only lead better, happier, self developing lives, but they would also contribute greatly to the well being of the whole community, to the well being of everybody. So these binary systems are inefficient. They hold back memetic, and thus human, evolution. We must come to understand, and accept, the reality of unitary humanity.

All of humanity must become one community, of maximally diverse and free individuals, in arbitrary maximally diverse and free sub-communities. We are all in this, our tiny blue dot, our planet earth, together. We've got to work something out to stop the wars and killing. Wars and killing are bad, ugly, unjust, wrong, wasteful, and inefficient for the meme organism, the community we must become, that we call humanity.

We will be proud to be human.

A human individual cannot remain human isolated from communication with other humans. A baby, abandoned at birth to an orphanage, where it is nurtured only enough to keep it alive, cannot become a full human being. Humans must grow and develop in, and with the help of a family, and a larger community of other humans. We are social creatures. The memes we have been talking about in this book only make sense in terms of an interacting human community. Memetic evolution only occurs in communities. An individual can survive and grow only if he or she is in a community that survives and grows. The only evolution that matters right now is the memetic evolution of communities of people. We have looked at some memes which have promoted memetic evolution. The imitation meme maybe started it all. Then the spread me meme helps groups of humans by causing an individual who has discovered something useful to spread the information to the rest of the group. This not only helps the individual but also the whole group. The self development meme causes individuals to seek new memes even though they may have no obvious use for immediate survival. This helps the group as well as the individual. The love meme extends the self development meme to the development of other people, other groups of people, and beyond. So for a very long time now, at least thousands, and probably tens of thousands of years, the survival, development, happiness, well-being, of any individual human, has been inextricably intertwined with the survival, development, and well-being of the community that individual belongs to. To attempt to separate conceptually an individual human from her community is absurd. It is impossible for one to exist without the other. The memes in an individual are the result of the memetic evolution of her group. Today a person's group is all of humanity, the meme organism we call humanity. So the humanity meme organism needs memes to make all its parts cooperate, so that it, and all its parts, and all individual human beings, may survive, develop, prosper, so that it may become a community of nations, and all kinds of other groups, and individuals, and so that someday, we, all of us, all of humanity, may be able to say proudly: Look at us! See what we can do! Aren't we great!

By now you know how we can start this process.

Chapter 11: My Vision.

People will understand.

The ideas in this book will spread, over time, to a significant majority of the population in every country of the world. These majorities will realize that wars are never worth their costs in human lives, in human injuries, physical and mental, in the destruction of material things, houses, buildings, bridges, factories, infrastructures, and in the damage and destruction of cultural institutions, civility, respect for laws, rules of commerce, art, science, the beauty and pleasures of life. They will realize these things, because the level, and quality, of their education, and development, will have changed. They will know the destructive power of war memes. And they will eliminate them just as we eliminate destructive pollutants from our environment.

Settled science.

Our social scientists will have researched, all the various ways, that war memes lead to war. They will have researched exactly which memes are dangerous, and how they are dangerous, how they reinforce one another, how they spread unintentionally. They will have researched, how good memes can counteract, and replace, the destructive war memes. It will be settled science, as to which memes must be eliminated, or their expression limited to benign areas, such as games. It will be settled science, how people can guard against unwanted memes. It will be settled science, how people can make inventories of, maybe a hundred, of their most controlling memes. Perhaps this will be done with the help of social science practitioners, sociotherapists, meme doctors, who will be analogous to our psychotherapists, and psychiatrists. Maybe it will be done through the ways children are educated. The social sciences will have flowered like they never have before. There will have been a renaissance in the social sciences.

Meme brain coding.

Cognitive science will have experimentally researched brains from top to bottom, and from the bottom up, meeting in the middle. High level concepts like memes, words, sentences, metaphors, stories, theories, hunches, feelings, and emotions, will be explained in terms of intermediate concepts. The physical/chemical operations of individual neurons will be completely understood, as will the operations of all cell types. Small networks of actual, operating neurons, will be investigated, and simulated, and it will be completely understood, how they store information, and how they process information. It will be understood how smaller networks are combined, or connected, to accomplish more complex processing. The operations of brains and nervous systems will be completely understood, first in principle, and then in more and more detail. Meme storage, and use, will be understood in terms of the behavior of cells, perhaps using new concepts working at intermediate levels.

Every educated person will understand that wars are never worth their costs.

Economists will have nailed down definitively the costs of wars, whether measured in physical things, deaths, and injuries, or psychological and cultural losses. Every historical war of the 20th century, will have been analyzed backwards and forwards, from top to bottom, and there will be no doubt about the results. Every educated person in the world, will understand, and accept as scientific truth, that wars are never worth their costs.

Multiple techniques to avoid conflicts.

Psychologists and sociologists will have researched experimentally, exactly all the various techniques and methods, that allow people, groups, organizations, and nations, to head off potential conflicts before they occur. The majorities in each nation, will understand multiple techniques to avoid conflicts, and arrive at acceptable solutions to differences of opinion, or different desires. It will be second nature to use these methods in daily life among individuals, groups and nations. We will never even get close to war. Everyone will know, deep in their souls, that war is never an option. Wars will seem as much an absurd, primitive, past activity, as gladiators and dualists fighting to the death, now seem to us.

For every war a complete case history.

Historians will dig up the facts that the economists will need. Historians will also dig up the facts that psychologists, and memeticists, will need to analyze the specific memetic evolution, that brought about each and every war of the 20th century. They will trace every major war meme, from its first occurrence before a given war, through the conclusion of the war. They will examine every mass media, day by day, for the occurrences of words and memes. This will be easy since all newspapers, magazines, books, movies, videos, recordings of TV broadcasts, etc., will have been stored on the internet. They will examine everything that reveals the expression of memes. They will count frequencies of occurrence, evolution of meaning, acceptance and promulgation by elites, leaders, and every strata of society. These will be correlated to decisions made by political and military leaders. This is an obvious extrapolation of what Philip Smith did in his excellent book *Why War?* [Smith, 2005]. So for every war, we shall have a complete case history of how it came about. They may even be able to pinpoint, for each war, the point of no return, the day after which war was inevitable. What an eerie thought! To imagine, that there might have been a specific day, before WW I started, when something might have happened, or not happened, that would have prevented that war, and after that day had passed, nothing could have prevented it! Realistically, they probably will not be able to nail it down to a specific day, but maybe month, or surely, a year. They will have done the same for WW II, the Korean war, and the Vietnam war. PhD graduate students will do the same for little wars. What an exciting opportunity for historians and the other social scientists.

Artists of every kind.

Novelists, poets, and artists of every kind, will have made their contributions. They will see ahead. They will depict the horrors of a future world ravaged by wars: nuclear wars, biological wars, global warming wars, internet wars. They will be ahead of everyone else as they always are. They will extol the beauty of the goal, and the joy, and excitement, of this noble journey to eliminate war. Cultural anthropologists will have been busy modulating all these scientific studies for every culture and nation on earth. Political scientists will be updating their theories based on the results that are coming in from all the other social sciences.

This meme complex will spread.

My vision is that the meme complex of this book will spread, first from individual to individual, in the current anti-war movement. Then it will spread to academics, educators, and other intellectuals Then to the general public. It may not spread to political leaders, at least in democracies, until a large enough majority of the voting population, has adopted these memes, because in democracies, the successful politicians, must reflect the predominant memes embedded in the population. Maybe in some countries an enlightened tyrant, or dictator, may adopt these memes, before a majority of his or her people do. It is not necessary now, nor is it possible, to see exactly how this meme complex will spread. But by its very nature, essential to the whole idea, this meme complex, or its evolved descendants, or something similar, must spread to a large number, probably a majority, in almost every country of the world. Otherwise this program won't work. But the people who do read this book, will understand this, and will have an incentive to spread these ideas. Thus there is a relatively strong spread me meme in this meme complex. It will get stronger in time. If there are many countries that still have war memes, then there will still be war. So one of the memes in this complex is the idea that even though a country may have a majority who no longer believe war is effective, they must still allow for the possibility they might have to fight a war, since not all countries believe as they do. But even as these ideas spread in a given country, the citizens are more likely to be more sensitive as to what leads to war, and they will work to avoid war. This in itself, will reduce the number, and duration, of wars, but not yet eliminate them. So as the number of countries, with a majority holding these memes, approaches some tipping point, suddenly there will be no more war. We probably will not recognize this point until some time after the fact.

This meme complex will spread because it is self spreading.

This meme complex will spread because it is based on empirically verifiable science. The memes of this book are better models of reality. As people see this they will of course adopt these better models, in their individual and communal lives, and they will thus be more successful in their individual and communal lives, and other people will see their success, and wonder why, and come to discover these memes, and then also adopt them. So, in so far as the memes of this book are better models of our reality, at this point in time, compared to their rival memes, the memes of this book have a survival advantage, and will be self spreading. Truth, even if approximate, is an advantage for a meme. If these or similar memes are adopted widely, the world will be a better place, it will be more beautiful, and it will be more just. These will also help the meme complex of this book spread. People will see that this program can succeed, and that it will succeed faster, if they help spread it. Given the objective absurdity of war, these, or similar ideas, will be accepted. This, or some similar meme complex, will spread, through space and time, to enough of humanity, so that there will be no more war.

Chapter 12: Take Action Now.

OK, I hope you are convinced this program can work. If you are not convinced please reconsider. Maybe go back and read this book again. Or read some of the books listed in the References section. All the ideas in this book are based on the ideas of others, especially the expert authors listed in the References section. This subject, the elimination of war, is critically important for all of humanity, for all of us, for our families, and friends, and all the people we know and love. If you have found errors or flaws in my arguments, please try to fix them and publish the results, if that is possible. Individually we are each a single finite human being. We are not perfect. Perfection is the enemy of the good. We're all on this infinitesimal blue dot, our planet earth, together. There may be nothing like us anywhere else in the universe. It just does not make sense to keep having war after war after war. We together, surely now, have the knowledge and skills to change. At the very least we can begin the process. If I've got it wrong, please, let's not give up. There are more than six billion of us amazing and beautiful humans on our small blue dot. Surely some of us can work seriously to eliminate war. Some of us six billion can devote the remainders of our lives to this effort. War is so ugly. Do the research. Encourage the research. Push for the research. We can do this. I think we are close. There are some forces in the world, powerful forces, that may be pushing, without anyone much realizing it, to eliminate war. Globalization may be one. I know there are problems with globalization, and these need to be fixed. But it's a force that makes us all much more interdependent. Also it may help us see past our suspicions and fears. The Internet is another powerful force. It is making all the knowledge of all the people of the planet available in an instant to every other person. It too is helping us see beyond our differences, suspicions, and fears. Most important of all, our knowledge of our own biology, psychology, and cultures, is growing rapidly, and this will allow us, individually and collectively, to better direct our behaviors. The environmental movement, and global warming in particular, require all the people of the planet to work together. Maybe the love meme, as it grows and spreads, all by itself, will eliminate war. These all seem to be pointing in the right direction. But there are serious dangers. The nuclear weapons still exist. Many countries are unstable. Many countries are headed by tyrants. Some leaders are ignorant fools. Globalization brings possibilities of global screwups. We may be close to succeeding in eliminating war, but we might still destroy ourselves.

So we don't have time to waste. Take action now. If you don't think you understand this program enough, please read the book again. And read the excellent books listed in the references section. Clean up your own war memes first. Then be forever vigilant about accepting any new ones. Join an anti-war group. Or join several. Donate money if you can afford to. Or found your own anti-war organization. The anti-war movement will need many diverse organizations to succeed. We need some organization to look out for new war memes and counter them. We need organizations to promote, direct, or guide research. We need organizations to disseminate and popularize research results. We need organizations to promote the ideas in this book and rework the ideas where it is wrong. We need organizations to monitor politicians, and leaders, and scream bloody murder, when they push war memes. We need to become as powerful and pervasive as the environmental movement is now.

It's time to act. We are not doomed to repeat bloody war over and over and over to the end of time. We are smarter than that. We, all of us, on our beautiful blue planet, can eliminate war forever. We can do this. Let's do it.

Project as Performance Art.

I hereby declare, at 12:08 PM, November 20, 2007, that this project is a work of art. Not the book but the project: The process of minds disinfecting themselves of their war memes, one mind at a time, and spreading the process to other minds, is the work of art. This artwork will be completed, when this process has been spread to enough minds on planet earth, so that there are no more wars. I hereby create the concept, define the art, and start the process. I invite everyone to participate in the creation of this artwork. The people who adopt the process and spread it are the co-artists, the co-creators. When it is completed, we will have a lavish reception for all the artists, and we will invite all the rest of humanity. Then this will be the most valuable work of art ever created so far. It will be cared for, preserved, and cherished, far into the future.

PORTRAIT: Rest in Peace 29M.1.

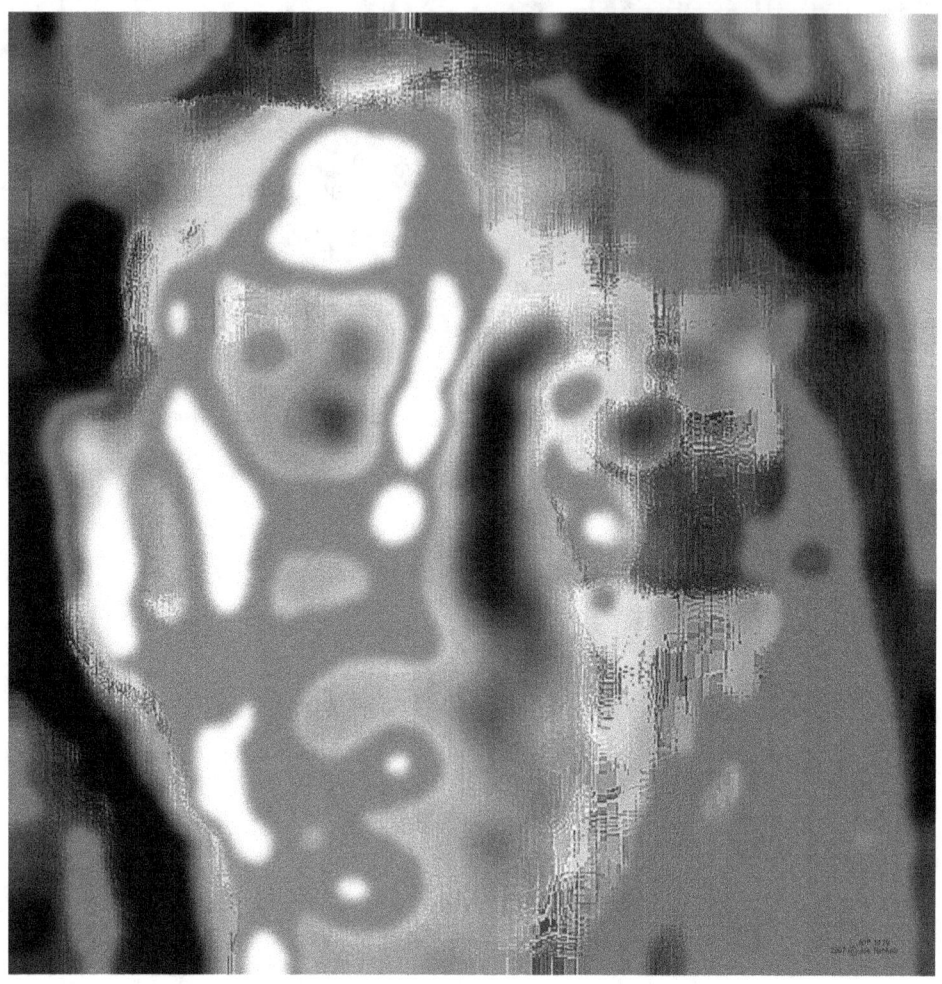

Acknowledgements.

I thank all those who have contributed to this book. I will only be able to list some of them. I thank my parents, because of course without them, this book would not exist. I thank my brothers and sisters, my children, and all the other members of my families, past and present. This book might not exist without them, and it surely would have been different, if I had not known them. I thank all my teachers at primary school, two high schools, and two colleges. In all I estimate that I had at least one hundred flesh and blood professional teachers, who taught me in person, day after day. This book would not exist without them. I thank all my teachers' teachers, and all their teachers. I thank all my friends, lovers, acquaintances, and associates, past and present. I thank my co-workers in all the companies and organizations where I have worked. I thank the management, and owners, of those organizations for making my employment, and continued development with them possible. I thank all the authors of all the books, articles in journals, magazines, and newspapers, I have ever read. And the workers, managers, owners, of the organizations which published them. I thank all the creators, producers, workers, etc., of all the TV shows, movies, videos, radio programs, phonographs, tapes, CDs, DVDs I have ever watched or listened to. I give special thanks to all the composers whose music has given me great strength and joy: 1) Bach; 2) Beethoven, Bruckner, Haydn, Schubert, Reger; 3) Sibelius, Tchaikovsky, Prokofiev, Philip Glass, Martinu, Messiaen, Henry Cowell, Brahms, Rheinberger, Shostakovich, Wagner, Rossini, Verdi, Moondog, Mozart, Harold Shapero, Jeff Panther, Puccini, Debussy, Bartok, Poulenc, Saint-Saens, Jean River, Vierne, Vaughn-Williams, Stamitz, Cannabich, Vanhal; 4) Schumann, Mendelsohn, Hovhaness, Ives, Nielsen, Schulhoff, Alexander Mosolov, Leonardo Balada, Stravinsky, Antheil; 5) Liszt, Berlioz, etc. I should also mention all the conductors, soloists, orchestra members, managers, support staff, distributors of CDs, makers of CD players, amplifiers, speakers, through which the memes of these composers got into me. I thank all the car companies and the workers in them who made all the cars I have used, owned, and loved. I thank all the previous owners, and all the mechanics who worked on these cars, for taking enough care of them, so that they were still useful to me. I need also to thank all the gas station attendants, all the oil companies, all the people whose land the oil was pumped from, all the people who built the roads I drove on, the government and all the people in the government, who designed the roads, maintain the roads, the police, who get dangerous drivers off the roads, all the legislators and municipal governments, which pass and enforce appropriate laws, so that traveling by car is reasonably safe and enjoyable. I could go on and on. I haven't mentioned all the people who built the houses and apartments I and my families have lived in, nor the clothes I have worn, nor the food I have eaten and enjoyed, nor the water I drink, nor electricity, the telephone, the internet.

Now count up all the people I have mentioned. How many are there? Surely one thousand is way too small. Maybe one million is a better number. Now consider this. Just as these million or so people have supported me, have given memes to me, and made it possible for me to survive to this time, and write this book, each of them, could make a similar list of one million or so people, who's support allowed them, to do what they did for me. And so on. So the memes in this book, came from, and through, and with the help of, millions, or billions, of people. I can't name them all but I acknowledge them all.

The closest, most important, and direct contributors of memes to this book are all the authors listed in the References. I thank them.

My friends here in the community of Tucson, Arizona have given me various other memes without which this book would not have been written. I especially thank the members of the artist groups I have been a part of: Raices Taller Art Gallery and Workshop, Central Arts Collective, and Dinnerware Artspace. They have tolerated me, encouraged me, cared about me, taught me much, and given me strength and courage I never dreamed I would have. I name just a few who's art, examples, encouragement, and collaboration, most helped in my journey to this book: Simon Donovan, John Salgado, Michael Cajero, David Ray, and David Aguirre. I thank David Ray, Judy Ray, and Simon Donovan, for their comments on an early draft of this book.

References.

Angel, Norman 1912. The Great Illusion – A Study of the Relation of Military Power to National Advantage. London: William Heinemann.

Annis, Michael; Palacek, Mike; Trettien, Whitney editors 2007. Cost of Freedom. Berthoud, CO: Howling Dog Press.

Aunger, Robert 2002. The Electric Meme. New York: The Free Press.

Bennett, D. Scott & Stam, Allan C. 2004. The Behavioral Origins of War. Ann Arbor: The University of Michigan Press.

Balkin, J. M. 1998. Cultural Software A Theory of Ideology. New Haven: Yale University Press.

Baum, Eric B. 2004. What Is Thought? Cambridge: MIT Press.

Blackmore, Susan 1999. The Meme Machine. Oxford: University Press.

Blyth, Catherine 2009, The Art of Conversation. London: Gotham Books.

Brodie, Richard 1996. Virus of the Mind. Seattle: Integral Press.

Brownmiller, Susan 1999. In Our Time. New York: Random House

Burton, Robert A. 2008. On Being Certain. New York: St. Martin's Press.

Carson, Rachael 1962. Silent Spring.

Cashman, Greg, and Robinson, Leonard C. 2007. An Introduction to the Causes of War. London: Bowman & Littlefield Publishers, Inc.

Davis, David Brion 2006. Inhuman Bondage. Oxford, New York: Oxford University Press.

Dawkins, Richard 1976. The Selfish Gene. Oxford: Oxford University Press.

Damasio, Antonio 2003. Looking for Spinoza, Joy, Sorrow, and the Feeling Brain. Orlando: Harcourt, Inc.

Dennett, Daniel C. 1989. The Intentional Stance. Cambridge: The MIT Press.

Dennett, Daniel C. 1991. Consciousness Explained. Boston, Toronto, London: Little Brown and Company.

Dennett, Daniel C. 1995. Darwin's Dangerous Idea. New York: Simon & Schuster.

Evans, Martin; Lunn, Ken editors 1997. War and Memory in the Twentieth Century. Oxford, New York: Berg.

Feldman, Jerome A. 2006. From Molecule to Metaphor. Cambridge: The MIT Press.

Firestone, Shulamith 1970. The Dialectic of Sex. New York: William Morrow and Company, Inc.

Flexner, Eleanor & Fitzpatrick, Ellen 1959. Century of Struggle. Cambridge: Belknap Press.

Friedan, Betty 1963. The Feminine Mystique. New York: Norton.

Frith, Chris 2007. Making Up the Mind. Blackwell Publishing.

Gilbert, Martin 2001. A History of the Twentieth Century. New York: HarperCollins.

Godel, Kurt 1962. On Formally Undecidable Propositions. New York: Basic Books.

Gornick, Vivian 2005. The Solitude of Self. New York: Farrar, Straus, and Giroux.

Gornick, Vivian 1978. Essays in Feminism. New York: Harper and Row.

Hedges, Chris 2002. War is a Force that gives us Meaning. New York: Public Affairs.

Hellmann, John 1986. American Myth and the Legacy of Vietnam. New York: Columbia University Press.

Herr, Michael 1978. Dispatches. New York: Alfred A. Knopf.

Hofstadter, Douglas R. 1979. Godel, Escher, Bach: an Eternal Golden Braid. New York: Basic Books.

Hofstadter, Douglas R. 2007. I am a Strange Loop. New York: Basic Books.

Holldobler, Bert and Wilson, Edward O. 1990. The Ants. Cambridge: Belknap Press.

Iacoboni, Marco. 2008. Mirroring People. New York: Farrar, Straus, and Giraux.

Lakoff, George 2008. The Political Mind. New York: Viking.

Lakoff, George 2002. Moral Politics. Chicago and London: The University of Chicago Press.

Lakoff, George and Johnson, Mark 1980. Metaphors We Live By. Chicago: The University of Chicago Press.

Lakoff, George and Johnson, Mark 1999. Philosophy in the Flesh. New York: Basic Books.

Lakoff, George and Nunez, Rafael E. 2000. Where Mathematics Comes From. New York: Basic Books.

Lehrer, Jonah 2009. How We Decide. Boston, New York: Houghton Mifflin Harcourt.

Lloyd, Seth 2006. Programming the Universe. New York: Alfred A. Knopf.

Lynch, Aaron 1996. Thought Contagion. New York: Basic Books.

Millett, Kate 1970. Sexual Politics. Garden City: Doubleday & Company, Inc.

Newell, Allen 1990. Unified Theories of Cognition. Cambridge: Harvard University Press.

Rosenberg, Marshall B. 2005 (a). Non Violent Communication. Encinitas, CA: Puddle Dancer Press

Rosenberg, Marshall B. 2005 (b). Speak Peace in a World of Conflict. Encinitas, CA: Puddle Dancer Press

Sargant, William 1957. Battle for the Mind. Wm. Heinemann Ltd.

Seldon, Mark & So, Alvin Y. editors 2004. War & State Terrorism. London: Bowman and Littlefield.

Smith, Philip 2005. Why War? Chicago: The University of Chicago Press.

Stiglitz, Joseph E. and Bilmes, Linda J. 2008. The Three Trillion Dollar War, The True Cost of the Iraq Conflict. New York: W. W. Norton & Company.

Suskind, Ron 2008. The Way of the World. New York: Harper Collins.

Westen, Drew 2008. The Political Brain. New York: Public Affairs.

White, Matthew 2003. "Source List and Detailed Death Tolls for the Twentieth Century Hemoclysm" in Historical Atlas of the Twentieth Century. http://users.erols.com/mwhite28/20centry.htm

Wink, Walter 1998. The Powers That Be. New York: Random House.